D0077312

ACKNOWLEDGMENTS

FIRST OF ALL, I WOULD LIKE TO THANK WAYNE MILLER, WHO GUIDED ME
through the exhibition and answered countless questions regarding Edward Steichen's grand undertaking. Wayne was patient and generous, all the while remaining
true to the original intent of the project that Steichen and he undertook in the 1950s.
Grace Mayer, the curator of the Steichen Archives at the Museum of Modern Art, has
been very gracious to me over the years. She maintains the Captain's legacy at the
museum and is a remarkable woman. Reece Mason gave me good insights into her
husband Jerry's role in publishing *The Family of Man* book. Martin Manning of the
United States Information Agency archives turned my attention to the American National Exhibition in Moscow (1959)—a very good subject, as I found out. David
Nye, Professor of American Studies at the University of Odense, Denmark, gave me
the opportunity to present portions of this study to European colleagues at a specialized seminar at the Netherlands Institute for Advanced Study in the Humanities and
Social Sciences. His NIAS colleague, Professor Mick Gidley of the University of Exeter,
offered me the same possibility in England. The three of us went prospecting through
the photography archives in Haarlem, thus producing the valuable Dutch example.
John Raeburn and Peter B. Hales read and thoroughly critiqued chapters of this book.

My thanks go to the University of Wyoming for giving me research and travel
support over the past ten years. This project was first aired at a meeting of the Pacific
Northwest American Studies Association in Portland, Oregon, in 1982. Since then the
Great Lakes, Mid-America, and California American Studies Association regional
chapters have listened to parts of the developing text. Audiences in Luxembourg, England, Turkey, France, Sweden, and the Netherlands have given me valuable international perspectives on this subject.

Finally, my thanks go to Edward Steichen, who did not hesitate to think big.

Eric J. Sandeen
Laramie, Wyoming
July 1994

PICTURING AN EXHIBITION

PICTURING AN

University of New Mexico Press   *Albuquerque*

ERIC J.
SANDEEN

EXHIBITION

*The
Family
of Man
and 1950s
America*

Library of Congress Cataloging-in-Publication Data
Sandeen, Eric J., Picturing an exhibition : the family of man
and 1950s America / Eric J. Sandeen. — 1st ed. p.   cm.
Includes bibliographical references and index.
Contents: Introduction — Constructing a world of photography — Picturing the exhibition —The family of man on
the move — The family of man in Moscow — Edward
Steichen, Robert Frank, and American modernism.
ISBN 0-8263-1558-5
1. Photography—Exhibitions. 2. Steichen, Edward,
1879–1973—Exhibitions. 3. United States—Social life and
customs—1945–1970—Pictorial works—Exhibitions.
I. Title.
TR6.A1S26 1995   779'.2'0747471—dc20
94-3205 CIP

Designed by Linda Mae Tratechaud

CONTENTS

Acknowledgments
vii

Introduction
1

chapter one
Constructing a World of Photography
11

chapter two
Picturing the Exhibition
39

chapter three
The Family of Man on the Move
95

chapter four
The Family of Man in Moscow
125

chapter five
Edward Steichen, Robert Frank, and American Modernism
155

Notes
201

Bibliography
213

Index
223

To my family

INTRODUCTION

IN 1954 EDWARD STEICHEN SAT TO BE INTERVIEWED BY WAYNE MILLER FOR the television series *Wisdom*. This conversation, filmed while the two men were assembling the pictures for *The Family of Man*, serves as a prologue to both the exhibition and to this examination of it, for Steichen's view of the world, of humankind, and of the function of photography lies at the center of the enterprise. The remarkable biography of Edward Steichen established his stature. Beginning in 1900 he traveled between New York and France, studying the modernist movements and masters in Paris and bringing their work to the Little Galleries of the Photo-Secession, the gallery at 291 Fifth Avenue that he and Alfred Stieglitz established in 1902 as the focus of the Photo-Secession movement and the place where avant-garde European art was displayed. Later he sent to Alfred Stieglitz the works of art by Picasso, Brancusi, Matisse, and Cézanne that appeared in the famous Armory Show of 1913. During this time, he rejected painting and took up photography, schooling himself in the possibilities of the frame by making over a thousand photographs of a cup and saucer. During World War I he pioneered aerial photography with the Army Signal Corps. Upon his return to the States he achieved popular fame as a photographer of celebrities, charging as much as $1,000 for a sitting. In the 1940s he served the wartime effort by heading up a navy photographic unit in the Pacific and mounting two important war-related shows at the Museum of Modern Art. After 1945, as the head of the museum's Photography Department, he had fostered the development of young photographers, delivered more than twenty shows to the museum, and gradually turned his attention to a large-scale project that would center on the unity of the human family. When he and Miller sat before cameras, *The Family of Man* was being formed, and, at the age of seventy-five, Steichen could claim to be the best-qualified person to construct this world of photographs.

Four themes in this conversation can guide us through the story of this monumental exhibition. First, Steichen's message was given special force by his experience in two world wars. During the Second World War, when he had returned to service in his mid-sixties, he had become determined to photograph the actuality of war. "If we could really photograph war as it was, if war could be photographed in all its monstrous actuality . . . that would be a great deterrent for war."[1] Characteristically, this did not mean entering the meat grinder of the battlefield and tightening the

1

frame on human misery and death. For Steichen's unit in the Pacific, the assignment was to focus on the individual sailors, "photographing them in everything they did." A generalized statement about the inhumanity of war had to look beyond the particularities of the preparation for battle on the aircraft carrier *Lexington* and gain its articulateness through the portrayal of enduring human emotions. "The ships and planes, they would be obsolete before long, but men never get obsolete, and war doesn't seem to want to get obsolete."[2]

Second, Steichen made a distinction between a positive and a negative approach to delivering a message through photographs. His three war exhibitions at the Museum of Modern Art—the two on World War II and a third on Korea—relied on the negative approach of showing what war took away. "People look at the pictures—they say they are wonderful pictures, they are exciting pictures, and occasionally they shed a tear at some tragic thing; and they tell me it was a wonderful job, and then they go out and have some drinks."[3] *The Family of Man* presented a positive approach toward human attributes: "instead of making pretty pictures or technically perfect pictures, we are going out to get life."[4] The lasting imprint on the individual viewer was made on the heart and not the head. To forget the power of the emotions was to surrender human sympathy to the modern world that was created by, and, in turn, dominated, humankind: "On the one side, we overintellectualize everything; on the other, we are overmechanized. We can understand the danger of the atomic bomb, but the danger of our misunderstanding the meaning of life is much more serious."[5]

Third, Steichen had faith in the revelatory power of photographs: if you took pictures of everything that a group of pilots did, for example, you would record history.[6] This was a powerful conviction that guided the assembly of the photographs for *The Family of Man*, as it had helped construct Steichen's frame during the 1920s, the decade during which he produced many great portraits for the Condé Nast publishing firm. The secret of this work was to encourage his famous subjects "to forget themselves for an instant and be themselves."[7] This is a revealing phrase, for here Steichen advocated stripping away celebrity, the constructed personality, to expose the character that lay underneath and trusted that a photograph could capture this inner being that had been discovered.

Finally, Steichen consciously chose to generalize the human condition through *The Family of Man*. The collection was built of a rhetoric of unity, the only structure powerful enough to oppose the perils of the modern period: "the ever-present elements of bigotry, and the snarl of intolerance, the hate and fear that is generated all over the world."[8] To engage these ills at any specific, historical level would be to indulge in a negative approach that would not succeed. Success would come through moving people with a positive message, by reminding them of the web of human associations and emotional ties that would buoy the individual above the hazards of life in the nuclear world.

Often, it seems to me, Steichen has been criticized for being an un-self-conscious romantic and manipulator of photographs. At the beginning, before examining the photographs or the message that Steichen attempted to construct through them, we should acknowledge the purposefulness of his task. In his own words:

From day to day we are brought face to face with the differences in life. Of course, those differences are there. They are differences of race; they are differences of creed; they are differences of nation. But you measure up those differences against the things that we are alike in. That we must make our prevailing theme. We can't overlook the differences, but unless we arrange these pictures so that they stress the alikeness—the similarity—we have lost out. We are not as alike in everything as we are in such direct things as birth and death. But there is also love. That is the same all over the world. That has always been there. This is the one thing that we have really learned the importance of. Unless we have the element of love dominating this entire exhibition—and our lives—we better take it down before we put it up.[9]

The exhibition did get put up and was a smashing success. It premiered at the Museum of Modern Art at a particular moment in the 1950s, when, as *Harper's* editor Russell Lynes said, "the world was briefly tired of warring."[10] It attempted to persuade a middle-class audience that newly technologized, atomic war would bring human annihilation. In order to bring this fundamental point home in the positive way that Steichen assumed to be more effective, he chose emotionally charged pictures. He also created a display of aesthetic sophistication. Minor White, a photographer and critic, recognized both the beauty and the earnest popularity of the exhibit.

Steichen was very conscious of [the exhibition's popular appeal], and he tried to make an exhibition which would perhaps take us away from further wars and show people what they are. It did show that vast numbers of people could be very excited by a photographic exhibition—it was at their level. Not the aesthetic stuff but very straight-forward semi-photojournalistic documentation. Some of it, though, was really magnificent aesthetically.[11]

This book argues that the visual economy that supported *The Family of Man* was established during the Second World War, when scores of photographers confronted a worldwide event and audiences learned to rely on them for views of unfamiliar but important scenes. With the deployment of photographers in foreign lands already practiced in wartime, photographers could depend on *Life* magazine, among others, to keep them traveling during peacetime as well. Their readership, with a curiosity bolstered by affluence and the mantle of world leadership, eagerly followed. The object of Chapter 1 is to answer the question of what the compilers of *The Family of Man* collection, chief among them Wayne Miller, had to consult. Put another way, what were the materials that built this exhibition and how were they valued, both by the exhibition organizers and their potential audience?

The Family of Man is both a familiar and an inadequately understood text. Most of Chapter 2 is devoted to the history of the assembly process and to a close look at the photographs that were selected. The show was a hit—not so much a successful photographic exhibit as a widely publicized and enthusiastically attended event in the popular culture of the day. The view of this chapter remains focused on the exhibition and draws little from *The Family of Man* book, a widely circulated compilation of exhibition photographs that is still in print. Steichen put his effort into the exhibition; this was to be a clear statement of his principles—both about life and about the practice of photography—that used this moment in the public realm to speak of the perils of the atomic world. The book was an exercise in good layout.

The power of the exhibition can be measured through the reception it received at the United States Information Agency, which toured the photographs throughout the world in five different versions for seven years after the closing of the original display at the Museum of Modern Art. We can ascertain the value of the exhibition to that agency only if we survey the history of American cultural diplomacy and information policy after World War II, the main task of Chapter 3. For the new United States Information Agency, unsure about the relationship between information and propaganda, *The Family of Man* offered high prestige and measurable success. As the exhibit traveled away from a domestic audience and the moment of its original display in 1955, it lost the specific historical references that Steichen had directed to his audience. Increasingly, the message of the photographs became one of human sameness and emotional unity. This produced a deeply moving experience for many of the 9 million viewers worldwide and assured an unintimidating success for those who exhibited the photographs.

Chapter 4 situates the exhibition in one specific foreign location, as far as Steichen was concerned the most important stop of the long tour, Moscow in 1959. In the context of the first bilateral exchange of expositions between the United States and the Soviet Union, the photographs appeared in a specific and significant spot. Within the ideology of the American National Exhibition in Moscow, however, it occupied a secondary place, a palliative among exhibits sharply focused on those American consumer goods that would create the greatest longing within the audience at Sokolniki Park. Within these American exhibition grounds Richard Nixon met Nikita Khrushchev in the famous Kitchen Debate, but, despite the location of this well-publicized interchange at the center of American domestic space, the family had a different meaning from that found in the photographs scarcely one hundred yards distant. In this post-ballistic world, the home had become the center of consumption, and the goods amassed there were the arsenal of the cold war.

Steichen's work has been criticized over the past twenty years for its lack of historical consciousness and its trusting assumptions about the legibility of photographs. Chapter 5 sketches how this statement in photographs has been weakened—not silenced, surely, because the collection is still a popular part of our visual world, but stripped of many of the specific references that Steichen placed in this work. Not only has *The Family of Man* been dismissed because of its sentimental humanism, but the art of its construction has been overlooked. Steichen used a modernist aesthetic in assembling the photographs. He addressed a public audience and did not bow to the conventions of museum display. His eagerness to reach a large public also brought out the full potential of photographs to be reproduced in limitless sizes and multiple, indistinguishable copies. In the 1950s we can see the development of an oppositional, highly idiosyncratic modernism, here represented by Robert Frank, and the emergence of a fractured view of what had appeared as a unitary American culture. The upheavals of the 1960s stand as a shorthand for cultural tensions that had subtly appeared since World War II. Steichen's work seems to be on the other side of a cultural divide.

Steichen's audience was the middle class, a people of plenty. David Potter's book by that title appeared at the same time as *The Family of Man* and gives us a view of the importance of abundance in American culture. In three important ways Potter describes the context in which Steichen was self-consciously crafting this serious statement that he intended for the public culture. First, America meant abundance, according to Potter. The proliferation of goods, and the inclination to measure progress by their accumulation, was everywhere.

> [W]e have, per capita, more automobiles, more telephones, more radios, more vacuum cleaners, more electric lights, more bathtubs, more super-markets, more movie palaces and hospitals, than any other nation. Even at mid-century prices we can afford college educations and T-bone steaks for a far higher proportion of our people than receive them anywhere else on the globe.[12]

The prosperity of the postwar years had only made material abundance more obvious. We have taken these benefits for granted, Potter claims, so much so that we have seen through the first cause of American exceptionalism—abundance—to its manifestations. The American frontier, asserted by Frederick Jackson Turner as the source of a unique American character, would not have been the cultural crucible that it was without an abundance of natural resources that beckoned settlers westward.[13] Even such a critical concept as "freedom" cannot be properly defined (or enjoyed) without the easy availability of goods and the prospect of increased leisure during which these items can be enjoyed.

Second, middle-class Americans did not realize how the American political ideology that was promulgated as a part of national foreign policy was enmeshed with the peculiar economic success that the United States enjoyed after World War II. As a world power the United States promoted its own democratic ideology, unaware of how much this cheery capitalism relied on the effortless production and easy consumption of goods. This fundamental fact defined American difference and brought to the new world landscape both opportunity and peril. The advantage of a uniquely global perspective, balanced by the sobering responsibilities of self-anointed world-wide leadership, was offset by the envy that brashly displayed American abundance engendered in other countries.[14] We assumed falsely that democracy could be exported throughout the world because, Potter asserts, we did not see that "economic abundance is conducive to political democracy."[15] The American attitude, that everyone can be dealt into the action of an expanding economy, would come face-to-face with political and economic impediments once one visited other countries. Down on the austere plain of political repression or economic deprivation, this American profligacy could be downright dangerous.

> A democracy . . . setting equality as its goal, must promise opportunity, but the goal of equality becomes a mockery unless there is some means

of attaining it. But in promising opportunity, the democracy is constantly arousing expectations which it lacks the current means to fulfill and is betting on its ability to procure the necessary means by the very act of stimulating people to demand them and go after them.[16]

Finally, like so many American Studies texts of the 1950s, *People of Plenty* sought to introduce definitions of "culture" from the social sciences to the study of American national character. Americans who go out to meet the world had better realize who they are and what cultural qualities they will encounter. The scholar who attempts to study national character should venture into the behavioral sciences to discover what sociology and anthropology can contribute to a view of how different cultures work. For the interdisciplinary scholar the key terms are "personality" and "culture." Potter establishes personality as the building block of national character:

> [N]ational character is not a separate phenomenon in itself but simply one specialized manifestation of group character. Group character in turn is but a composite of individual characters, and individual character is simply a pattern in that complex of human processes and qualities which are designated nowadays by the term "personality." The study of national character, therefore, is properly a branch of the study of group character and of personality.[17]

Culture is "a screen or filter" that brings certain phenomena or qualities of the environment to this personality or blocks some stimuli from reaching it, thereby accounting for a dynamic national character that is reflected in individuals who exhibit its traits differently.[18] This same culture was the audience for Potter's work.

As Russell Jacoby has pointed out in *The Last Intellectuals*, the 1950s was virtually the last decade in which intellectuals felt enfranchised to speak to the public culture. While we can dispute this view of creeping quiescence, there can be no doubt that during this decade elements of civic culture were debated in public. Within the expanding academy, the new field of American Studies developed the perspective of the myth/symbol school of criticism. The vocabulary of American Studies scholars was built from concepts of irony and paradox to form a view of culture that functioned (or foundered) on the different planes of thought and action. Significantly, these writers, of whom Potter was one, were connected to a larger discussion. In much of 1950s commentary we can find the anxiety of affluence that contemporary writers have used as a label for the decade.

In this book I make little attempt to engage the rich literature of public intellectuals writing about American culture. John Kenneth Galbraith, Arthur Schlesinger, and Michael Harrington make brief appearances—as do writers like William Faulkner and Norman Mailer—but the main voice of the times is one that was delivered to many middle-class homes at least once a week. In fact, I believe that scholars have underestimated the ways in which a publication like *Life* magazine dealt with the burdens of affluence. The distinction between the presumed frivolity of the weekly press and academic discourse may well be, in part, a product of the appropriation of seriousness by members of the academy during the 1950s. In a 1948 Round Table discussion of the pursuit of happiness, one of a series sponsored by *Life* to which I will refer in Chapter 1, Erich Fromm undercut the statistics of American success with the following statement, summarized by the moderator:

> He [Fromm] pointed out that there is often a wide gulf between what people think they are and what they really are. We must therefore distinguish between the facts about happiness and opinions about it. There is always considerable pressure on the individual to persuade himself that he is happy, because this is part of the American "pattern." But underneath the surface there may exist conditions of unhappiness, or conditions that cause him to do things that will make him unhappy.[19]

Shortly thereafter, in his important book, *The American Mind*, Henry Steele Commager concluded:

> Although still persuaded that his was the best of all countries, the American of the mid-twentieth century was by no means so sure that his was the best of all times, and after he entered the atomic age he could not rid himself of the fear that his world might end not with a whimper but with a bang. His optimism, which persisted, was instinctive rather than rationalized, and he was no longer prepared to insist that the good fortune which he enjoyed, in a war-stricken world, was the reward of virtue rather than of mere geographical isolation. He knew that if there was indeed any such thing as progress it would continue to be illustrated by America, but he was less confident of the validity of the concept than at any previous time in his history.[20]

This same Round Table series expressed a mistrust of the persuasive power of advertising. The availability of goods was a sign of national greatness, but too much of a desire for things demonstrated self-indulgence. Goods enticed, and marketing skills coupled with more sophisticated use of media could overwhelm an audience with cash in its pockets. This impatience to buy clouded Americans' feelings of happiness, created a demand for housing that could not be satisfied, and inflected film production toward the facile and the merely entertaining. The American urge to buy immediately and the selling of goods through compelling media presentations had to be contained by a moral leadership that distrusted ephemeral pleasures. According to the *Life* Round Table:

> [A]dvertising cannot escape the moral and cultural implications of its deeds, some of which are deplorable. But it was also agreed that advertising cannot be expected to provide cultural leadership. This must be done by editors, educators, the clergy and various individuals and institutions immediately concerned with the enlightenment of the people. If such leadership is provided, however, so that people begin to get a better grasp of the principle that happiness is not to be found in mere pleasure and self-gratification, then advertising can help carry the load.[21]

David Potter expressed similar reservations. He saw advertising as virtually an alternate form of education for the mass, occupying as much attention as what went on in schools. The classroom educated citizens; advertisements taught the culture to consume. A popular magazine, he asserted, is primarily a vehicle for the myriad items displayed in advertising layouts; indeed, during the 1950s advertising space, more than pictures or copy, caused Life to expand in size. The advertisers, in theory, have the power to commission articles that correspond to their own tastes, which, in fact, might be quite high: "In a sense, the advertiser is prepared to buy better authors for the reader than the reader is prepared to buy for himself." However, they also must increase circulation.

> At this point a fixed cycle is virtually inescapable: millions of readers are essential to secure a large revenue from advertising, advertising is essential to enable the magazine to sell at a price that will secure millions of readers—therefore, the content of the magazine must be addressed to the millions. Thus the best writers, those who have proved able to write for the most discriminating readers, are put to work writing for consumers who may not be readers at all.[22]

The media "are concerned not with finding an audience to hear their message but rather with finding a message to hold their audience."[23] The implications for American culture were dismal. The message brought to the masses must not deal with the obscure or the out-of-the-way, since that would lower its appeal. Second, the message "must not deal with any subject at a high level of maturity," because that quality was lacking in the consuming public. Finally, the message could not be "controversial or even unpleasant or distressing" (it is as though Potter wanted to write "thought provoking") because that would cause the reader or viewer to put down the article or switch off the television.[24]

Life magazine gave a psychoanalyst, an academic with European pedigree, a voice in its Round Table. Henry Steele Commager, a history professor at Amherst, published a book, with the appropriate scholarly apparatus, that became a best seller in 1950. Both the magazine and scholar David Potter worried about the appetites that consumption indulged. The barrier between the university and the public was permeable in the 1950s, in terms of subject matter, approach, vocabulary, and personnel. Edward Steichen did not recognize dividing lines between the academic and the popular any more than he conformed to conceptions of high-, middle-, and lowbrow culture in the construction of The Family of Man. Photography was not primarily an art to be savored by a few practitioners; through its immediacy the image could communicate to all viewers. "I am no longer concerned with photography as an art form," he explained. "I believe it is potentially the best medium for explaining man to himself and to his fellow man."[25]

Throughout this book I use Life magazine to represent middle-class opinions and appetites in the 1950s. The magazine's photo essays are a convenient reference point, for Wayne Miller drew many of The Family of Man photographs from the Life archives. More significantly, the "conservative populism" of these articles links the

8

picturing an
exhibition

magazine with the massive photographic projects of the 1930s, with Edward Steichen, and finally, as James Guimond points out, with the United States Information Agency's projections of American images abroad during the 1950s.[26] Miller found *Life* to be more helpful than *Look* in his months of prospecting for photographs. Either could have served as the accompanying voice to the images that Steichen and Miller arranged. Through these weekly publications "readers could indeed believe the camera was a magic eye enabling them to imagine they were seeing and conquering the world."[27] Faced with my own assault on the archives, I decided to let Wayne Miller be my guide.

This was not a capricious selection, for *Life* magazine, with a circulation in the mid-1950s of about 6 million copies, has been used to good effect by scholars seeking to enter the world of the middle class during what Andrew Ross calls "hegemony's moment."[28] Elaine May and Stephanie Coontz used the magazine as a way of weaving the cocoon that enveloped middle-class women during the 1950s.[29] James Guimond surveyed decades of *Life* articles to assemble the generalization that "virtually everyone [in the photo essays] is white, middle-class, and a member of a small nuclear family." In his view, *Life* identified white Americans with "the nation's prosperity, fertility, power, and intellect." Minorities appear in articles devoted to America's problems.[30] Through my own reading of ten years of the magazine, I have come to appreciate the cracks in this hegemonic edifice, the moments in which the magazine was not sure of itself, could not adequately digest contemporary events, changed its mind. These episodes were few, admittedly, and these momentary waverings took place within a circumscribed, middle-class domain. This realm was framed by countless photographs and embellished by the advertisements that gave the magazine more heft during the 1950s.

This book makes no apologies for *The Family of Man*. I strive to explain rather than defend, to give resonance to the voice of an exhibition that, especially over the past two post-Vietnam decades, has been reduced from cultural pronouncement to simple statement. The exhibition is worth retrieving, for it did speak strongly to its audience at a particular time in American cultural life. Perhaps we have become jaded about the power of images, a legacy of the horrific commonplaces of the Vietnam War and our increasing suspicion about the technical manipulation of reality. We see differently now. This is an obvious statement. The culture reconstructs the text. However, much of our view of *The Family of Man* has been projected back onto 1950s experience, and that does violence to the original interaction between photograph and viewer. I try to recover some of that founding power, but only some. The true weight of these photographs can be measured only indirectly at this historical distance, by the countless bits of anecdotal evidence that people were visibly moved by their walk through this world of evocative photographs.

Through my ten years of interaction with this exhibition I have compiled my own anecdotes. One represents for me the historical elision that justifies the reinterpretation of a cultural text. In November 1984 I had my first interview with Wayne Miller, Edward Steichen's chief assistant. I arrived at his house in California to find the installation pictures and floor plan for *The Family of Man* arrayed in his studio. He took me on a mental tour of an exhibition then thirty years in the past. We had gone through about two-thirds of the exhibition and had just passed down the tight baffles of the left-hand wall of the exhibition. He referred in passing to the small room at the end of that series, which contained, he informed me, an explicit reference to the perils of the nuclear age. I had seen only the book version of the exhibition that had, curiously enough, omitted this reference. His information transformed my view of Steichen's enterprise. I prefer to hold until Chapter 2 the full description of this discovery. To reveal now the contents of that room would be to anticipate the narrative climax of a story it took Steichen three years to construct.

This is a quirky book. The main subject is an exhibition that I have never seen but have reconstructed in my mind, with the help of Wayne Miller, who made Steichen's work come alive for me. I have tried to create several contexts in which these photographs might be read as a part of 1950s culture, and, at the same time, I share the misgivings that present-day critics have expressed about the legibility of such texts. I have tried to remain true to what both Steichen and his audience assumed: that a picture could tell a thousand words and that an emotional impact was to be valued and not distrusted.

I thought that I had completed my *Family of Man* project when I published a lengthy article on the exhibition in 1987.[31] Only two years later I found myself in the presence of the one remaining set of *The Family of Man* photographs in Clervaux Castle, Luxembourg. It was a remarkable experience; for the first time, I could, quite literally, measure the dimensions of Steichen's work. The United States government had given the set of photographs to the country of Steichen's birth in 1966, when Luxembourg decorated its native son with the title of Commandeur de l'Ordre de Mérite. The 503 images were already travel-worn by that time. However, in 1989 the Luxembourg government wanted to restore this exact copy of the Museum of Modern Art photographs in honor of the 150th anniversary of their country's nationhood and, coincidentally, of the invention of photography.[32] To be able to lecture on *The Family of Man* in the presence of the images was to witness a reincarnation. It was as close as an academic can get to a mystical experience. After that, this book became an imperative.

And, in fact, the subject of Steichen's labor deserves to be examined again. As I constructed my own text, the phrase "family values" became loaded with the ideological ammunition of the 1992 presidential election. As I sit before my computer screen in the summer of 1994, Yugoslavia is devouring itself in ethnic and religious warfare. To think of humankind as one, in these circumstances, may not be an unhealthy exercise. We cannot deny the weight of historical experience over the past forty years—the world, we have come to realize, needs a lot more than love—but, it seems to me, there is more to cultural life than the particularities of the moment. We cannot believe that one form of family life can be projected onto a world of experience, but there seems to be a special imperative these days for empathy, maybe even for respect.

CONSTRUCTING A WORLD OF PHOTOGRAPHY

ON THE NIGHT OF JULY 19, 1941, MARGARET BOURKE-WHITE STOOD ON an open roof in Moscow, photographing with her large-format camera the first German air raid on the Russian capital. It was, she reported, "one of the most outstanding nights of my life." Although German shells and tracer bullets put her in some jeopardy,

> the opening air raids over Moscow possessed a magnificence that I have never seen matched in any other man-made spectacle. It was as though the German pilots and the Russian antiaircraft gunners had been handed enormous brushes dipped in radium paint and were executing abstract designs with the sky as their vast canvas. [1]

Throughout the next several days Bourke-White used her legendary powers of persuasion to take pictures where few others were allowed to have cameras and to stay above ground in blown-out buildings while civilians were sent to air-raid shelters. She invaded the Kremlin, working her way past attendants to photograph Stalin himself, an impatient subject but as much a personification of the embattled Soviet Union as the panorama of destruction on the street.

Her diligence had been rewarded, for getting to Moscow to bear witness to the beginning of such a massive attack had been no easy matter. She and her husband, Erskine Caldwell, had flown to Hong Kong in April, dragging over six hundred pounds of baggage with them, and had spent two months working their way overland to Moscow. They had fought visa problems, the rigors of Asian transportation systems, and the privations of shortages that surmounted their resourcefulness in order to be near the action. The resulting pictures, published in *Life* magazine, offered Americans a revelation.

> Everything she photographed was essentially unknown to Americans, or at best known only through a Russian propaganda filter. . . . Margaret's pictures demonstrated what photojournalists pray for the chance to prove— that there are not only new ways to see the world but new things to see. In effect, she became America's eyes, seeing for everyone back home life and death in Moscow. [2]

Life, in its turn, highlighted the cool heroism of its photographer even as it distanced itself from the terror of nighttime bombing in a war the United States had not yet entered. The narrative, supplied in New York, added its own syncopation: "The crash of the anti-aircraft guns and their deeper echo were described by Miss Bourke-White as a classical chord in counterpoint to the jazz of the whining planes and the whistling bombs."[3]

Her wartime heroics did not end on the Russian front. On December 22, 1942, her ship was torpedoed off the coast of North Africa, and she was forced to abandon ship. This experience did not daunt her but caused her to switch to a Rollei, a camera producing a smaller, almost square, negative and offering increased mobility during the travails of war.[4] Her account of her own resourcefulness and heroism did not surprise her fellow correspondents, for Bourke-White had cultivated her own image and had become a larger-than-life figure before the outbreak of war. These combat adventures, spread before the public in the weekly press and through books such as *Shooting the Russian War* (1942), did nothing to diminish her stature as a globe-trotting adventurer. The drama of this worldwide event gave her and hundreds of her colleagues weekly opportunities to shape the figure of the photojournalist.

While Bourke-White gained her stature by being cast against gender stereotype, Robert Capa fulfilled the image of the ingenious, imperturbable, and adventurous photojournalist. He, too, began his World War II career by chronicling the devastation of bombing, by photographing in detail the experience of one London family during the blitz. He made the crossing from North Africa to Italy and followed the European campaigns, most notably beginning with D-Day. Capa attacked the war from the west. Although he did not maintain an eastern front as Bourke-White did, he logged thousands of miles following the troops. He photographed for *Collier's*, the British magazine *Illustrated*, and, reluctantly, for *Life*. At the same time, he maintained his ties to Ernest Hemingway, another legendary adventurer, and promoted himself as the greatest war photographer in the world through books and articles.[5] Like Hemingway, Capa had covered the Spanish Civil War during the late 1930s and had produced famous images of that conflict. However, this action on the Iberian Peninsula was a mere prelude to World War II photographically as well as tactically.

The Second World War gave photographers unprecedented mobility. They saw exotic scenes—admittedly under duress—and reported on them to an American public eager for whatever news it could receive. If photographers were tourists they were also witnesses, recording the actions of war. The perils of aggressively adventuring into the world were rewarded with the concerned attention of a mass audience. Capa and Bourke-White gained stature from these encounters. Capa's dictum, "if your pictures aren't good enough, you aren't close enough," became the slogan of the photographer's war, and Bourke-White's calm during the horrific liberation of the concentration camps after V-E Day was well known.

The war effort of *Life* magazine gives some indication of the thoroughness with which battles were documented. The magazine put in the field twenty-one photographers who were designated as part of the pool of photographers following the action of both the army and the navy. *Life* photographers spent more than 13,000 days on assignment during World War II, and permanent foreign bureaus were established to help with the logistics of supply and control that went with a worldwide conflict. Much like Capa, the *Life* photographers had to keep their bags packed. George Rodger, later to break away from *Life* to form the Magnum cooperative, logged more than 75,000 miles in eighteen months covering the action on both fronts.[6]

Carl Mydans recognized the disorienting quality of such enforced travel but also acknowledged the power of these circumstances to create an identifiable persona for the resourceful combat photographer. He always traveled light and protected his livelihood, habits he had learned while a member of the Farm Security Administration photographic team during the 1930s: he would leave anything else behind but cradled his camera like a child and saw to it that exposed film was sent out.[7] Less glamorous, or marketable, were his efforts to reconnoiter the terrain he was to capture on film. Like any good tourist, he attempted to make sense of the landscape that surrounded him. While covering the war in Italy in 1944, not only did he keep a journal of his experiences but he also constructed a cultural landscape, book in hand.

> I had all kinds of little notes, all kinds of clippings, and an Italian travel
> guidebook with me so that when I got into a town I could sit down and
> read the history of the town—see what various conquerors had been
> there before—so that when I looked at things I saw a second dimension.[8]

The more the technology of warfare was applied to this landscape, the more this historicizing exercise became an act of reading a palimpsest. Photographs of Monte Cassino after the Allied bombardment show how conquest could be related to massive historical erasure. The gesture toward the guidebook was an attempt to humanize the upheaval of war, often a painful, ironic collision between the architecture of appreciative texts and the rubble of wartime action. However, allegiances were clear: a just cause and the right of the conqueror allowed the Allies, particularly the Americans, to replace old writing with new. Recording this staking of claims would frame the view of the photographic tourist after the war.

The context for the war was historical and personal, sometimes all too personal. Photographers felt separated from the action by viewing it through the frame of the camera, but in Mydans's case the war engulfed the lens through which he attempted to view it. He and his wife had been trapped in the Philippines at the beginning of the war and had spent many months in Japanese prisons before they were exchanged in 1943. After having pursued the war on both fronts, he witnessed the public ceremony of the Japanese surrender and told in *Life* magazine his experiences as a prisoner in the infamous Santo Tomas internment camp in Manila. To cover the war meant mobility—a 35mm camera and the ability to con a ride on an army transport plane. Behind such inspired tourism lay the conviction that "what I am doing is important . . . I am making an historic record of a period of our times."[9]

W. Eugene Smith covered the war, too, but was thoroughly repulsed by it, as so many of his successors in Korea would be. At the same time he acknowledged how easy it was to succumb to both power and prestige. "*Life* was really the only outfit to work for if you covered a war. They had the greatest freedom, the greatest power, and the best expense accounts."[10] Carl Mydans had used the camera's viewfinder as a shield from the action but had found this protection to be inadequate. Smith composed his pictures for emotional effect, imperiling his sensibilities, not just his safety.

> He intuitively grasped that human events take place within an emotionally charged sphere—a space that is given meaning by the nature of the event. He learned to move *inside* the emotional sphere of an action. By composing his photographs within this space, he, and the viewer, shared the event rather than observed it.[11]

What Smith saw in the Pacific caused him to respond with "hatred and disgust." He retreated to the photographic essays upon which his fame rests—the country doctor or the Spanish village fit better into his frame than did the war.

This was a grizzly war. Only the fortunate casualty was dispatched with the heroic gunshot to the chest.[12] More often soldiers were simply shredded by a war-making technology too strong for dignity, not to mention resistance. While the photographer could be surrounded by the technicolor of carnage, bombardment, and conquest, only selected portions of this reality could penetrate to the black-and-white negatives that were sent home. At the beginning of the war, Allied corpses could not be shown, and even as late as 1944 American casualties were discreetly anonymous. The death of an enemy, particularly a Japanese soldier, was shown in individual, excruciating detail. Indiscretions of explicitness, visual misstatements, and the serendipity of the quick finger on the shutter release were judiciously edited in New York. Every photographer was put in a position of weighing emotion against purpose, news gathering against disgust. These day-to-day emotional collisions were salved by absorption into the larger narrative of a just cause. Despite horrific jolts, photographers stayed in combat zones for months at a time.

Before the war, photojournalism had been of relatively low status even at *Life*, the foremost picture magazine, where writers, not photographers, had control of stories. As Loudon Wainwright states, the public image of the news photographer during the thirties was that of the hardened, intrusive, flash-bulb-popping character of detective movies. The war broadened this impression by giving photographers a culturally important role to play.[13] At the beginning of the war, reporters were billeted with the officers while photographers slept in enlisted man's territory. By the end of the war, photographers could claim equal status. After the war, the world begged to be revisited, both by photographers and, vicariously, by veterans and their families, who had not had the chance to enjoy the ambience of Manila or Rome or Paris the first time around. Finally, there was a broader purpose to wanting to know about the rest of the world, for the United States had emerged from the Second World War as a preeminent power.

John Morris, London-based picture editor for *Life* during World War II, later viewed this exercise of loyalties through the Vietnam experience and saw a glorification of war. He asserted: "The photographer's image was only selectively the true image, for his work, like the war itself, was largely intended to serve a higher purpose."[14] This statement underestimates a sense of purpose that has created a gulf between the Second World War—the last conflict accepted as a just crusade by a majority of Americans, including the photographers—and the Asian adventures of the 1950s and 1960s. As Susan Moeller points out, most World War II photographs focused on conditions surrounding the individual soldier.

> Documenting the soldier in war was an expansion of these photographers' prewar project of documenting the people of the United States. It was a continuing attempt to reaffirm and repossess the democratic ideals of the country. During the succeeding wars, in Korea and Vietnam, the photography of combat came to be an exposure of America's and Americans' limitations; during World War II, the photography of Americans at war was still an affirmation of what was possible.[15]

The frame of the photographer of the 1940s captured individual resolve; chroniclers of later wars would freeze a national conundrum for their viewers.

Ironically, *The Family of Man*, an exhibition advocating peace among humankind, was born of war. Many of the images of *The Family of Man* were created in the foment of the war years, and photographers who participated in the exhibition—among them Margaret Bourke-White, Eugene Smith, David Duncan, Wayne Miller, and Steichen himself—had gone to the front. Production and consumption of photographs were immensely increased by the war experience, and the momentum carried on well into the early years of television, before being smothered by the small screen. The province of the photographer was expanded to the world and was maintained by ample magazine expense accounts and the noblesse oblige of an identifiable professional type who had already proven his or her worth. After having defined the virtues of the home front during respites stateside, photographers could now extend human virtues and document injustices on a larger scale. Many of the photographers of *The Family of Man* already had felt what the organizers and the middle-class audience of the mid-1950s were also to perceive—a reassuring sense of domain, voice, and audience for photographs.

Edward Steichen had insisted on participating in World War II. Already sixty-two at the time of Pearl Harbor, he had to use personal influence to obtain a commission and had to persuade the navy that a photographic crew operating freely among the ships of the Pacific Fleet was a worthwhile enterprise. To help convince the navy of his worthiness, he put together a large show at the Museum of Modern Art, originally entitled *Panorama of Defense* but changed before the opening to *Road to Victory*.[16] Later during the war years a second massive photographic display, visually similar to *The Family of Man*, appeared—*Power in the Pacific*. After retirement he kept the title of Captain and preferred to be addressed by that rank at the Museum of Modern Art.

The story of the selection of Steichen and his crew became legend. Steichen received a call from Washington asking if he would be interested in photographing for the navy. He recalled that "I almost crawled through the telephone wire with eagerness." In order not to appear too anxious he replied that he had an appointment in Washington the next day, and he took an overnight train to meet with Commander

Arthur Doyle and Captain A. W. Radford. Personal persuasion—and a considerable amount of name-dropping—overcame Radford's reservations about Steichen's age, and the project was underway.[17] By an almost mystical process of selection (or election) the crew was assembled: Wayne Miller, Charles Kerlee, Fenno Jacobs, Horace Bristol, Victor Jorgensen, Barrett Gallagher, and John Swope. "Off duty, almost every one of them sooner or later came to me separately and said he understood why he had been chosen for the job, but he couldn't understand why some of the others had been," Steichen commented.

Steichen's story of the unit's formation echoed Wayne Miller's recounting of his own selection. He had entered the navy after Pearl Harbor and was interested in applying his skill as a photographer while in the service. One day in Washington he was showing his photographs to a superior, who said that there was a guy—"Steeken, or something like that"—who was putting together an outfit that he might be interested in applying for. The problem was that he would have to go to New York to show "Steeken" his photographs. In order not to appear too eager, Miller related, "I told him that I just happened to have a wedding to go to that very weekend. That was a lie, but I really wanted this."[18]

He met up with Steichen in the offices of Tom Maloney, the editor of *U.S. Camera*, and had the opportunity to present a portfolio. It was the first time that Miller and Steichen had seen each other. The relationship between the two would deepen and would endure until Steichen's death in 1972. Years later, Miller mustered the courage to ask Steichen why he had been selected for the Photographic Unit. Miller wanted to know what had interested him in the pictures? "There was nothing in your pictures," Steichen replied. "They were terrible. It was your enthusiasm that I liked."[19] Linking the sense of stature of the master's account and the self-deprecation of the apprentice's reminiscences is the familiar pattern of the assembly of a band of comrades.

This anointing with myth may obscure the many ways in which the experiences of Steichen's group in World War II epitomized that of many other photographers. Like so many others, the group was highly mobile; in fact, by mid-war they had open orders entitling them to free passage throughout the Pacific theater.[20] While this put them frequently in harm's way, it also produced dazzling changes of scenery. During the last year of the war, Wayne Miller went around the world courtesy of his camera. In February 1945 he was in the South Pacific. In March he sailed to the Indian Ocean with the USS *Saratoga*, which rendezvoused with the British fleet. He traveled through the Suez Canal and Cairo to Italy, where he went ashore to photograph the homeless children of Naples, and then plunged back into the war action with the invasion of southern France. He had returned to Washington in time to photograph Franklin Roosevelt's funeral on April 12, 1945. In August he was on a troop ship in the Pacific when he heard that the atomic bomb had been dropped, and in September he was at ground zero, surveying the damage at Hiroshima.[21]

Like so many other photographers who lived out of suitcases and duffel bags, Steichen and his crew largely abandoned the clumsy, large-format Speed Graphic cameras they had been issued by the navy and picked up more portable Rolleiflexes and 35mm cameras. The latter were especially prized and were the sought-after object of exchange in Washington, where the photographic unit would barter what they could lay their hands on—sheets of color film—for the cameras the navy would not issue them.[22]

Commercial war photographers were enmeshed in the established production procedures of magazines and news-gathering services. All men and women carrying cameras faced the same challenges to the technology of taking pictures. To their customary problems of deadlines and story lines were added logistical questions that at times were almost insoluble: how to get film out of a combat zone, how to preserve exposed rolls under tropical conditions, how to give editors in New York an idea of context, and, conversely, how to get an idea of what had actually been shot and received. Steichen's crew avoided many of these circumstances and, instead, churned out images according to the working pattern of the Farm Security Administration photographers whom Steichen so admired. He had faith in the eye of each of his crew members and also trusted in their ability to produce.[23] Although there was no shooting script as there was in Roy Stryker's instructions to the Farm Security Administration photographers, the object of this sympathetic gaze was to show the suffering and the bravery of the individual sailor.[24] The benefit for the navy of such sustained attention was obvious.

Steichen had seen war from the air before. In fact, he was a decorated veteran of World War I and had pioneered the use of aerial photographic reconnaissance. These earlier views created utilitarian images that layered bits of information in the geometry of European fields and villages. Now his object was to make the war human. The focus of his camera in the Pacific was seldom on the machinery of war and most often on the men encased in the technology of combat initiated from the air. This intimacy differentiates Steichen's pictures of the Second World War from those produced in the First. Aerial photography emphasized the distance between the photographer and war and the invulnerability of the artist before the aestheticized landscape.[25] Taking pictures of men in aircraft encouraged an investment of emotion in the exchange between photographer and subject. The most famous picture taken of Steichen during this time shows him on the carrier *Lexington*, straining to photograph men in the cockpits of airplanes on the runway.

As it was for so many photographers during the war, the epiphanies and apparitions that captured and haunted this crew were personal, humanizing. Faces, groups, and men at work dominate the photographs more than airplanes and ships. "If a real image of war could be photographed and presented to the world," Steichen wrote, "it might make a contribution toward ending the specter of war."[26] Many other war photographers not only believed this but received their own apotheoses: Capa at D-Day on the Normandy beaches, Bourke-White before the corpses of Bergen Belsen, W. Eugene Smith in the jungles of the South Pacific, Wayne Miller at Hiroshima.

World War II is given scant attention in books devoted to the history of photography. Beaumont Newhall, for example, dismisses these events rather quickly: "the most telling and dramatic photographs of World War II were made by magazine photographers or under their influence. *Life* ran a school for army photographers and sent its own photographers to the front."[27] The compendious *A World History of Photography* devotes fewer than six pages to the war.[28] Not only photographic skill but also relationships between photographer and subject and producer and consumer (not to mention between photographer and suspect terrain) were established during these years. The framing of the world in photographs and the emotional power invested in images common to photographic practice in the late 1940s and early 1950s are as different from the commerce of images today as the Second World War is from Vietnam.

Photographic production during the 1920s and 1930s accustomed American readers to interpreting events through images. As David Nye has shown, large corporations such as General Electric manufactured not only the consumer goods and technological conveniences of twentieth-century life but also the reverential perspectives from which these commodities should be viewed.[29] The massive production of the historical section of the Farm Security Administration justified the social action programs of the New Deal.[30] Maren Stange recently analyzed the connection between the administrative techniques and artistic style of Roy Stryker's Farm Security Administration office and the voluminous photographic archives of Standard Oil.[31] All of these massive projects were assembled into exhaustive repertoires of how the world looked.

A world album also accumulated month by month, and then week by week, through magazines that brought to readers glimpses from beyond their shores. The epitome of this display of curiosity about the world was the *National Geographic* magazine, which promised, through its "Seven Principles" (1915) to bring foreign scenes to its readers with reliable facts, few distractions, and a minimum of disturbing or critical detail. Starting in the mid-1930s a weekly illustrated press, pioneered in the United States by *Life* and *Look*, packaged these views into the familiar shape of photo essays. What remained was a catastrophic, worldwide event that would put the pictures at center stage and give them an important role in digesting events and emotions quickly and helping its audience discern how to act.

In 1936 *Life* magazine announced the purpose of the proposed illustrated publication:

> to see life, to see the world, to eyewitness great events; to watch the
> faces of the poor and the gestures of the proud; to see strange things—
> machines, armies, multitudes, shadows in the jungle and on the moon;
> to see man's work—his paintings, towers, and discoveries; to see things
> a thousand miles away, things hidden behind walls and within rooms,
> things dangerous to come to; the women that men love and many children; to see and take pleasure in seeing; to see and be amazed; to see and
> be instructed.[32]

The vocabulary, both verbal and, by anticipation, visual, was that of the social foment of the 1930s and the photography that accompanied it. The editors could not have foreseen the Second World War and the added power that such extreme times would give to the chronicler of the war and the keeper of home-front stability. Circulation in 1941 was just over 4 million; by war's end more than 5 million people subscribed to Life and, in this time of austerity, each copy was passed on to two other households.[33]

The National Geographic magazine also prospered during the Second World War, as it had during the First.[34] It served a different function than Life. The maps published by the National Geographic Society gave readers a strategic knowledge of theaters of action. As Gilbert Grosvenor, the long-time president of the society, explained in 1942, these maps were "America's biggest stockpile of cartographic information which their Government recognizes as an important war weapon."[35] Franklin Roosevelt and Winston Churchill had personal map cabinets, for which the society received good publicity. The public, too, received its own briefings as campaigns were followed by maps distributed by the magazine. For example, details of combat in one center of American interest, the Pacific theater, were revealed to subscribers through a map featuring "naval bases and table of 861 air distances between strategic points."[36] The files of the magazine contained thousands of photographs of exotic places that had now become of quite practical interest. Over 35,000 pictures of terrain unmarred by camouflage and beaches without fortifications were given to government intelligence agencies.[37] National Geographic brought the world to middle-class audiences in a pragmatic and unproblematic way. Wartime articles were timely and "relentlessly cheerful."[38] The real information was geographical: place names, distances, cartographic knowledge that would provide a rudimentary understanding of what family members were enduring off-camera, over the horizon.

Magazines featuring photo essays, led by Life magazine, explored this new territory and helped readers visualize the perilous events of the day. The photographs were directed toward the middle class, which felt both the static and the kinetic power of the image.[39] Within the frame of the photograph viewers were accustomed to reading a clearly inscribed meaning. Aesthetics supported emotional impact and ideological import. The energy of the image also was intended to move: it sharpened wartime fervor and, coincidentally, continuously whetted the appetite of the subscriber for more images. The commerce of production and consumption was well established by the exigencies of war and produced an economy of extraordinary vigor in the decade following the unconditional surrender of the Axis powers. Thus the appetite for photography—exuberantly fed by an increasing number of photographers who had learned the craft at government invitation—received its fulfillment in the increasing affluence of postwar America. The Family of Man addressed an audience comforted by this luxuriant period of proliferating images in neat packages and enticed by increased curiosity about a world made more understandable by vicarious, visual forays.

After the war photographers relaxed and become super-tourists, conscious of appropriating experiences that were no longer dangerous. Savoring may be a more accurate description of what Leonard McCombe, a British-born Life photographer, felt about one of the fundamental elements of existence.

After going through the bombing of London and its aftermath, and being for many hours in a tiny, steaming hut while Navajo Indians burned the evil spirits out of it for a story for *Life*, I feel I know, or I feel I *feel*, something about the element, fire.[40]

The jump from a metropolis—the beat of the war reporter and, in this case, home as well—to a setting more stereotypically exotic and the province of the anthropologist was characteristic of the photographic tourist and typical of what would appear in *The Family of Man* exhibition.

This ability to see the world brought with it a feeling of mastery, of command. During the war the camera had been a sometimes inadequate shield; now it became a baton, capable of directing reality to conform to the frame. One could see the directorial power of this medium even before VJ Day. Toward the end of the war, for example, Admiral Halsey ordered the Pacific Fleet to steam in abnormally close formation so that Steichen's crew could compose a suitably heroic aerial shot during the aptly named Operation Snapshot.[41] *Life* photographers commented frequently on how the presence of a camera caused subjects to behave as though they were on stage.

The leap from one scene to another was not just aesthetic or, to use an increasingly popular word, cultural, but also spatial. Take the case of Dmitri Kessel, a *Life* photographer whose work later would be chosen for *The Family of Man*. In 1947 he spent two months in Mexico, looking at traces of Mayan civilization. Before he could return to Manhattan from La Guardia airport he received a choice of two assignments from the magazine, one in India and the other in South America. With what seems to be stylized, hard-bitten indifference, he took the latter, even though it would mean being away from the country for over five months, because at least he could spend two weeks in New York before once again packing his bags. Here was a man pointedly busy with travel, so inured to the exotic that the commonplace of home had become a luxury.

In South America he was able to hire native guides for excursions into the mountains and enjoyed the full benefits of the exclusive Jockey Club in Buenos Aires: "Buenos Aires," Kessel reflected, "where in those days a luscious two-pound steak cost only about twenty-five cents and where if you ordered a 'whiskey' you got a four ounce shot of scotch in a glass."[42] Robert Capa, if not Ernest Hemingway, echoed in his words. Kessel commented further on the status of the photographer in the postwar world.

One of the best things about being a *Life* staff photographer was the working conditions. Expense accounts were very liberal. Travel was first-class, whether by ship, plane, or train, and we always stayed in the best hotels. Unless the story had an absolute deadline, we were never hurried when working; for a major essay, it was not unusual to take anywhere from two to five months. We could call on stringers or bureaus for help, and if we needed translators or extra photographic assistants, we hired them. If we needed an aerial, or simply had to go somewhere in a hurry, we chartered a plane or a helicopter. *Life* didn't care, within reason, how long it took to get a story, or how much it cost—as long as you *got* the story.[43]

The confidence with which the photographer approached the world was summarized by Wilson Hicks, the photography editor of *Life*. His paean to photojournalism, *Words and Pictures*, portrayed a photographer who searched out "the socially significant picture."[44] *Life* had become important because it "entered at once the world-wide battle for men's minds." This gave photographers a sense of purpose, so that "if a picture was alive when it left a photographer's hands, because of something he had put into it, it became still more alive for what it was to say as social, political or cultural report and commentary."[45] *Life* photographers were not merely news reporters recording events; they had become disenchanted with surfaces and sought deeper meanings. This confidence was bolstered by a range of experiences—read adventures—that these globetrotters had had in the world[46] and was founded on the belief that photographs would tell the truth if earnestly directed to do so.[47] Among the many practitioners Hicks quoted approvingly was Henri Cartier-Bresson, also a contributor to *The Family of Man*, who intertwined aesthetics and meaning in a single sentence: "To me photography is a recognition, in a fraction of a second, of the signification of an event simultaneously with the recognition, from a chosen position, of a precise, formal organization which brings the event to life."[48]

Loudon Wainwright has summarized the grand economy that *Life* set up with the American middle class:

> Somehow, in a time of increasing affluence and great change from wartime austerity (and an accompanying need for information on traditional stabilizing values), *Life* was playing back to these readers images of their country and of themselves that seemed both authentic and reassuring. One could, figuratively speaking, find himself or herself in the magazine's pages, or recognize one's hopes, or stoke one's indignation, or appease one's need for self-improvement or the need to identify with the great long line of humanity reaching back to the caves. The magazine of the 1950s was a place where millions of people could discover modern American life, be stimulated by it and feel part of it.[49]

The nature of this "somehow" needs to be deciphered, for *Life* saw itself as a great forum in which large issues of national importance were aired. It self-consciously molded public opinion as it catered to the curiosity of its readers about the world and their appetite for consumer goods. Also, the exclusivity of this particular magazine in brokering values to the middle class must be challenged. A competitor, *Look* magazine, sought the same readership, and mass circulation weeklies such as the *Ladies' Home Journal* and *Saturday Evening Post* also thrived. Wainwright portrayed *Life* as an epitome of not only photojournalistic practice but also middle-class culture. While the ability of the magazine to shape its readers may have been overstated, the weight of Henry Luce's corporation could be felt among the producers of these images. It was against this control that photographers rebelled.

Life may have empowered photographers to capture the world, but the machinery controlling image production chafed on many practitioners. Story editors, not photographers, made the assignments and controlled layout. More important, the corporation owned the rights to photographs; what it chose not to use was merely kept on file. The Life family, evoked by Wilson Hicks in Words and Pictures, brought with it a good deal of paternalism. Wayne Miller remembers that if you were considered the fair-haired boy everything went well, but if you were not, your photographs could be rejected arbitrarily.[50] Photographers such as Eugene Smith tried to avoid Life assignments because the handling of their images seemed petty,[51] but the magazine was so prosperous that it was hard to avoid. Smith shot fifty assignments between 1946 and 1952.[52]

During the war years such heavy-handed, tight control had to be endured, if not excused. Photographers could be dislodged from their position as observer and seized by the wartime commerce of patriotism and commodity production. The British photographer George Rodger found his wartime American lecture tour for Life to be a revelation. He had been touted as a 75,000-mile man: in addition to the customary stops in the Pacific and European theaters he had spent time in Africa and even India covering aspects of the war. This globe-trotting made him into a celebrity, whom Life was eager to put before audiences. However, as he discovered, his appearances were carefully monitored by motives of both profit and patriotism.

> I just met people who were likely to buy advertising in Life. When I caught on to this, I was very annoyed. I was reading the accounts of the war in the American papers and I knew very well that the R.A.F. were bombing Germany night after night, and they were hardly mentioned in the American press. The people getting the kudos were the pilots of the Flying Fortresses. At that time, they didn't fly at night and they didn't even go over the borders of Germany. I was mad as hell! Once, in Detroit, I started telling people about it in my lecture, and the man from Life, who was sitting beside me, kept stamping on my foot. I didn't like that. I was asked several questions and I answered them very straight. I said that United States planes hadn't managed to drop a bomb on Germany yet. The man from Life immediately got up and announced that the meeting was over. It turned out that the man questioning me was the president of the Boeing Aircraft Company—and that ended my speaking career.[53]

With the return of an unfettered economy after the war, photographers discovered a seller's market and became restive. Once again, Robert Capa played an important role in defining how photographers would work. The control over image production had always bothered him. In 1947, while waiting for a visa that would allow him to accompany John Steinbeck to Russia, Capa joined David Seymour, Henri Cartier-Bresson, George Rodger, and Bill Vandivert in founding Magnum, an independent picture agency. Photographers were to retain rights to their pictures, and profits were to be distributed among the members. Producers of images were thus liberated from story editors. As Rodger later put it, Magnum was formed "to make our own lives easier so that we could operate, each in his own field."[54] The issue was control, even more than profits.[55] Fortuitously, one followed the other, particularly after 1948, when Magnum sold photographs to the many magazines set up after the infusion of Marshall Plan reconstruction money in Western Europe.[56]

Founded by veterans of World War II, Magnum knew the strategic advantage of deploying itself worldwide. Offices were maintained in Paris as well as in New York. Visual territory was parceled out: "Chim [David Seymour] took Europe, Cartier-Bresson took India and the Far East, Rodger took Africa and the Middle East, and Vandivert took the United States. Capa was to roam at large."[57] Thus, scenes from around the globe began to be marketed to publications, both individually and as coherent stories. Succinctly put by one member, "Magnum was an agency that took big trips."[58] One early series appeared in *Ladies' Home Journal* in 1948 and 1949. Entitled "People Are People the World Over," a series of twelve two-page spreads addressed the curiosity that Americans were assumed to have about the living habits of people in other lands. The series was the idea of Robert Capa;[59] the editor at the *Journal* who bought the project, John Morris, later would become president of Magnum. The series itself was to influence *The Family of Man*, both in its assumptions and in its layout.

The announcement of the series in mid-1948 proclaimed the *Journal*'s intentions. Each month it would display "one important phase of family life." This was to be "nonpolitical reporting"; the approach would be as though the assignment had been given to a magazine on Mars.[60] Each installment would be presented through a circle of photographs surrounding twin globes that would aid the reader in finding Equatorial Africa or Pakistan or Czechoslovakia from month to month.[61] The series revealed its point of view from the start. The family, "still the building block of society," was above politics, history, and ideology. "While the world community waits upon the anxious maneuvers of diplomats, life on the familiar level of hearth and home continues with the constancy of the tides." This bonding with the natural order was made explicit through the selection of only farm families. "Soil—the good earth—is the great common denominator of existence." A social science perspective was inevitable. Coverage and representativeness were made to accommodate the familiar layout and length of the photo essay.

> Here are 88 of the 2,000,000,000 people who inhabit the planet Earth.
> They are 12 families who represent 12 countries, 3 races and 5 religious
> faiths. They speak 11 languages.[62]

The series did not survey family life systematically. Rather, it sampled world variety and presented readers with piquant vignettes. It was motivated by curiosity, not rigor.

The photography for these issues was produced by Magnum staff members and associates, marketing the accessibility of scenes throughout the world to these photographers. The seeming randomness of selection of the twelve sites for this investigation followed the inquisitiveness (and acquisitiveness) of a touristic imagination. The editing of photographs and captions into a synthesized commentary shows the disjointedness that we have already seen in efforts to put together different views from around the world. According to the essay on home life, the Hiatt family spent its evening "sitting by the fire in the English farmhouse. . . . In Pakistan, the villagers set their charpoys (cots). . . . In Germany, the Stieglitzes spend the evening in the parlor. . . . In his African village, Zomba Aluma smokes his evening pipe. . . ."[63]

Over the next year readers followed the families as they ate, played, washed, were educated, slept, and worshiped. As one might expect, tradition played a large role in the lives of these agricultural families, and anthropological discourse quickly emerged from the captions of these pictures of rural life. In the essay on farming, for example, readers learned that in Czechoslovakia "both mother and daughter wear gay peasant blouses"; in Mexico the farmer's "principal crop is corn, basic ingredient for the tortilla"; Japanese farm women "wear kimonos, and the big hats which have been worn since feudal times"; the house of the Chinese family has stood for two centuries and the father "faithfully follows the way of his ancestors." "The Moslem faith," subscribers were told, "forbids eating pork."[64]

The magazine could not retain the dispassion it had advertised. Western values percolated through the series. The American and British families were materially better off. It is clear that their advanced status came from superior technological sophistication. The layout on transportation devotes ten of the twelve pictures to means that would have been considered primitive—the oxcart, pedestrian travel. Only the American and the English families were shown with mechanized means of conveyance, and their pictures were therefore removed from anthropological time and historicized in the Western march of progress. The view was worldwide, but the frame of reference was clear. "Mohamed Usman spends as much time in a trip to the nearest telephone as an airliner takes to go from New York to Cincinnati. There are few filling stations in the desert, few bus lines in the tropics, few landing strips in the steppes."[65]

The benefits of technology were plain, as can be seen from the article on food. Only the American meal—the most familiar to the reader and the least necessary to describe—was given in detail: "pork chops, potatoes and gravy, string beans, bread and butter, rhubarb, cookies, milk and coffee."[66] Rather than being subsistence farmers, readers learned in another installment, American farmers had become "specialized" and bought 50 percent of their food in stores.[67] For many of the other countries there was only meagerness, lack of variety, and hunger. "In Pakistan, the family of Mohamed Usman live no better than their ancestors of a thousand years ago—and can count on dying forty years before the Iowa Pratts. The belt of Asia is eternally tight and each notch means a million lives."[68]

The series made assumptions about technology as an index of progress and about the applicability of this Western idea uniformly around the world.[69] At the same time, the articles showed a belief that people—invariably identified by their family status—reacted the same way to situations that were assumed to be similar. The article on education admits that some cultures do not have the proper respect for schooling. However "Bruce Pratt [U.S.], who is on long division, can easily sympathize with Peter Balogh [Czechoslovakia], who is on multiplication tables, and Bertrand Redouin [France], who has fractions."[70] Here, it is plain that education is associated with Western values. The familiar hierarchy of cultural achievements was linked by a common set of human values triggered by American associations and emotions. The home, in all of its configurations, was stocked with symbols that drew humankind together.

> Home is more than housing. It is a comfortable chair, a favorite thimble, a battered doll, a travel calendar, a black dog scratching himself, a kitchen clock, an unfinished serial story, a framed diploma, a Teddy bear. By such small tokens these twelve families, strangers in a baffling world, are familiar to one another.[71]

Even overtly, the series belied its promise; it was neither nonideological nor nonpolitical. The German family was pointedly shown among the ruins of their country, in which they were now placed in "the American zone." The Nazi period was an embarrassing gap, made more excusable by the information that the couple married in a charming ceremony just before Hitler came to power. The French father was determined that his children would have a good education so that they would "live as free men in a free world."[72] Having taken the point of view of picturing the world community, the series contained a paean to the United Nations, the only agency capable of seeing the same view as the two hemispheres presented every month.

> [N]ational boundaries stand as road blocks on the highroad of good will, and international commerce in ideas is scant. Nevertheless, there is hope that under the large, loose cloak of the United Nations these, our families, may live as neighbors.[73]

This series was undoubtedly designed to satisfy the curiosity of the *Journal's* readers. A companion series, "How America Lives," had appeared in the magazine since 1941 and the "People Are People" installments can be seen as extensions of these stories, which continued to run well into the 1950s. "People Are People the World Over" was also intended to instruct. After the final episode, an address was given so that schools could obtain the twelve installments via film strip.

The lineage from "People Are People the World Over" to *The Family of Man* is clear.[74] In both cases there was an assumed domain for photography and a stable (and admirable) identity for the photographer. Visual rhetoric was supported by anthropological assumptions about how societies function and how a presumably common sentiment could be appropriated from a variety of cultural locations. The influence of the editor in maintaining a Western view of world cohesion was identifiable, albeit unrecognized. However, as we shall see, *The Family of Man* was overtly political in its arrangement of images, and this purposefulness allowed the collection to be subtle. Not only did this reliance on the truth-telling of images liberate the photographs from the didactic captioning of "People Are People," but it circumvented the oversimplifications of a synthetic, written text.

The Magnum-inspired "People Are People" series shows the linkage between the production of images and the emerging postwar order. The pictures were thrown into the commerce of domestic consumption. They were framed by advertisements appealing to appetites that were increasingly indulged and were accompanied by articles that interpreted the culture of affluence. Images also brought the world to the magazine reader without the frenetic context of World War II. More than that, picturing everyday life, both in the United States and abroad, became one more way in which America laid claim to world dominion. The eye of the photographer and the layout of the editor reinforced the deceptively simple ideology of the victors. Finally, these pictures became a part of an American projection abroad that included both marketing and foreign-policy objectives, the two often intertwined. It is important to trace the emergence of this strategic commerce during the first five years of the postwar period, because, later on, The Family of Man would become a part of a complex system of ideological deployment that had little to do with photographs.

It has become commonplace to speak of postwar culture through the metaphor of containment. Women were forced out of the workplace and contained within the hastily constructed confines of suburban houses. Middle-class men were dominated by the well-publicized routine of the corporate world. Children were raised according to Dr. Spock and chastened by the specter of self-indulgent juvenile delinquency. The unmeasured purchasing power of consumers was directed by advertising and driven by the needs of family life. This view of the tightly laced 1950s emphasizes power and control, a paradoxical domination of the middle class by its own economic weight and its impaling desires. The word *containment* emerged in the foreign-policy context of the immediate postwar period, when the terms and territory of the cold war still were being defined. This more fluid and contingent world aroused both American curiosity and disquietude. The negotiation of definitions—and defining silences—between the end of the war and the election of Harry Truman in 1948 was not relegated to the policy makers but was presented to the middle class, through *Life* magazine, for example, as a debate in which all were enfranchised to speak.

Although strategies of containment predate 1946, the legendary utterance of the word is linked with George F. Kennan. What would become a shorthand for pre-ballistic-missile, cold-war strategy was produced with as much drama as history can present. In early 1946 Kennan wrote "The Long Telegram" from his station in Moscow to the State Department in Washington. This secret communication was followed in 1947 by a very public and immediately celebrated article in *Foreign Affairs* by "Mr. X," "The Sources of Soviet Conduct." Kennan was quickly unmasked as "X" and his article was reprised in the July 28 edition of *Life*. In early 1947 he had become the director of the State Department's policy and planning staff; he had not only the celebrity of the "X" article but the position from which to advocate his suggestions.

While there were inconsistencies between the private and public documents, both presented the Soviet Union as less interested in Communist ideology than in the expansion of its sphere of influence. "The political personality of soviet power," Kennan's *Life* article proclaimed, was a product of both "ideology and circumstances."[75] Because of its ideology of socialism, "there can never be on Moscow's side any sincere assumption of a community of aims between the Soviet Union and powers which are regarded as capitalist."[76] Because of its expansionism, Moscow could be counted on constantly to test the resolve of the other world power, the United States. Communist ideology preached the inevitable fall of capitalism, so the Soviets could be counted on to take their time. Territorial ambitions would make the USSR a constant opportunist. Within a web of nations friendly to the Soviet Union, allies of the West, and strategic American enclaves placed abroad, the Russians were to be limited in their ambitions by a "firm but vigilant containment."[77]

Kennan's point of view was quickly adopted by the Truman administration in its deployment of American forces abroad. It also began percolating through to basic strategies used to approach other cultures. According to Kennan, the Russians viewed the world with a peculiar universalism: all nations were susceptible to their influence because all were subject to the ineluctable logic of historical development. Americans should counter this with a particularistic approach. Maintaining and even encouraging cultural differences—even though this was hazardous in a time of developing third-world nationalism—would create an enduring barrier to Soviet expansion.[78] The strategy, both operational and rhetorical, was to portray the USSR as the Other, somehow off the map of the world with which the readers of the "People Are People" series, for instance, should be concerned.

The effect of this strategy was immediately apparent in the actions of the United Nations. Even though the USSR was included as a permanent member of the Security Council, by 1950 it had been thrust—and had maneuvered itself—to the periphery of the organization. The number of Russian vetoes was tallied by the popular press, including *Life* magazine, as an index of the recalcitrance of a regime that refused to engage in civilized discussion. Indeed, the police action of the United Nations in Korea, beginning in the summer of 1950, would not have been possible if the Soviet Union had not walked out of deliberations from which it felt estranged. In the years between the signing of the United Nations charter in San Francisco in 1945 and the completion of the main complex of buildings on the East River in New York City in 1952, the United Nations effectively represented a Western view of a universal community. By displaying the flags of each nation it acknowledged the particular characteristics of each national culture. By using the rhetoric of international goals and principles, it bound the members together with one view of what was admirable and what was unacceptable in all human cultures.

For terrain closer to home there was concern aplenty, as terrible dislocations and virtual dismemberments of previously congenial cultures confronted anyone who visited countries within the Western sphere of influence. In 1944 Carl Mydans had photographed and described Italy after the destruction of Monte Cassino, an ancient seat of learning and monastic discipline. In 1947 Edmund Wilson visited that country and found a sordid economy of prostitution in Rome and the "stink of the killing of Mussolini" in Milan.[79] Islands of civility remained, but this was truly a "Europe without Baedeker," for there was no guide to this new situation. If you looked away from your plate at a café, children would steal your food.

Along with containment came *reconstruction*, an important element of American foreign policy and a useful term when looking at the postwar middle class in the United States. In the face of an ambitious and aggressive adversary, Kennan had warned against "psychological malaise" on the part of the United States and its allies. Particularly in the devastated areas of Europe and Japan, Communist incursions could be expected. The deployment of the European Recovery Administration, the product of the Marshall Plan, would claim at least the western portion of Europe for the United States. David Ellwood has documented how the Americanization of Europe accompanied this reconstruction money.[80] Economic aid would be the best reinforcement for psychological resolve, and this would be accompanied by the technology of American consumerism. John Lewis Gaddis has shown through his extensive chronicling of postwar national defense policy how the United States attempted to manage development in the late 1940s, given the premise that "through loans and outright grants of aid it was in a position to affect the rate at which other countries reconstructed or modernized their economies."[81] Kennan reminded his *Life* readers that strategies like containment and reconstruction were not only deployed against the Soviet Union but were also defined against American experience.

> Surely there was never a fairer test of national quality than this. In the
> light of these circumstances the thoughtful observer of Russian-American
> relations will find no cause for complaint in the Kremlin's challenge to
> American society. He will rather experience a certain gratitude to a Provi-
> dence which, by providing the American people with this implacable
> challenge, has made their entire security as a nation dependent on their
> pulling themselves together and accepting the responsibilities of moral
> and political leadership that history plainly intended them to bear.[82]

A 1949 United Nations report, *Per Capita Income of Seventy Countries*, mapped the world through bar graphs that clearly showed the topographical connotations embedded in descriptions of both containment and reconstruction. Here the Communist countries, both the USSR and the newly formed People's Republic of China, appeared as a low plain of penury, surrounded by the higher plateau of Western allies, particularly in the English-speaking world. Above all towered the heights of American abundance, its per capita figure almost twice that of any other nation, four times that of the Soviet Union, and more than fifty times greater than that of China. David Potter would later use this map in his analysis, *People of Plenty*, in which he warned against the exportation of a democracy founded on affluence to nations that lacked a tradition of abundance.[83]

The fact of abundance was measured beyond this cartography. John Kenneth Galbraith's *The Affluent Society* addressed the main domestic task of a world order dominated by the United States: how to manage the further development of American society now that the discipline of wartime austerity and a clearly identified enemy could no longer be sustained. Events such as the blockade of Berlin by the Soviet Union in 1948 and civil unrest attributed to Communist insurgencies in Greece helped to define the Soviet Union as the enemy, almost as a necessary Other against whom to define the strength of the American character. The outline of this opposing force was thrown into sharp relief with the explosion of a Russian atomic device in 1949. Before readers could accommodate the atomic specter within the frame of photo essays, domestic commentators struggled to give their audiences a sense of collective direction at a time when it seemed obvious that world leadership required seriousness of demeanor and purpose.

Life magazine directed its readers to the responsibilities of "The American Century," as its publisher Henry Luce termed the postwar age. In the late 1940s Life tried to position itself as the explicator of Western civilization for its middle-class readers. An extensive and expensively printed history of Western civilization, later to be made into a book, appeared in 1948. During that and the subsequent year a series of articles on Life-sponsored Round Tables presented to readers divergent views on major cultural phenomena of the time. Like Ladies' Home Journal, Life performed a strategic encirclement of a domain in the name of its readership. The tone of these long articles was self-conscious, sometimes pompous, and always didactic. The organization of the Round Table operation was impressively elaborate: scholars, laypersons, and representatives from business and industry were assembled at a congenial location and encouraged to engage in two days' worth of conversation, under the moderation of Russell Davenport, a former editor of Fortune magazine, a Time/Life property.

Readers were eager to understand the workings of their own culture, now in the world spotlight, and many publications offered series catering to such curiosity. Fortune, Ladies' Home Journal, and Harper's devoted special issues or initiated long-running investigations of American traits and projections into the American future. A smaller-circulation monthly, Partisan Review, began a series of symposia titled "Our Country and Our Culture" that appealed to a clientele of intellectuals who were, at the same time, solicited for their opinions by the mass circulation press. Like the other efforts of this sort, such as the Partisan Review symposia, these Life conversations were intended to speak to, if not for, a specific reading audience and, through the influence of this group, have an effect on the general culture.

After elaborate preparation and with such lavish coverage in Life magazine, the topics for such scrutiny appear to have been selected haphazardly: the pursuit of happiness, modern art, housing, and the movies. While feature stories in the magazine substantiated a prior interest in these topics, the editorial focus on foreign policy, the United Nations, and the atom bomb made these discussions seem eccentric. However, the subjects of all four discussions acted as powerful agents of satisfaction or unrest within a burgeoning consumer culture. Not only did they indicate sources of American identity—in the Declaration of Independence, in commodities, in property, in leisure—but they addressed the necessity of differentiating among canons of taste in an increasingly mass-oriented culture. Through all four Round Tables reverberated the explanatory myths of what Life recognized as American culture. The American ideology, the almost sacramental feeling of substance in home ownership, the power of the middle-class viewer to purchase entertainment or edification, was manifested in compelling aspects of postwar American culture. And they endured. As we shall see in another chapter, through their avatars, the house, the patriotic display, the exhibition of painting, and the promotional film, they proved to be extraordinary weapons a decade later, when the American government began to wage cultural war on the Russians through the initial salvo of an exhibition in Moscow.

The results of the first Round Table, "The Pursuit of Happiness," were published in the July 12, 1948, issue of *Life*. Ensconced in the exurban, upper-middle-class splendor of the Westchester Country Club at Rye, New York, eighteen "distinguished Americans" met under the direction of Mr. Davenport and within the slowly circling gaze of a *Life* photographer to discuss this "Third Freedom." Let the organization of this Round Table stand for the complete set. Each panel contained a few recognized academics—here Erich Fromm and Sydney Hook—who were enfranchised in this public realm. The Tables tried for "balance" within a range of opinions it deemed respectable: here business leaders were matched by an official of the CIO. At the "Happiness" discussion, the lay community was represented through the 1948 Mother of the Year and Betsy Barton, a popular author and daughter of the legendary advertising man and inspirational writer, Bruce Barton. Later, at the "Modern Art" Table, Clement Greenberg and Meyer Schapiro were the designated experts. For the "Housing" discussion, builders like William Levitt stood for the business community. In the "Movies" dialogue, practitioners were represented by the reticent actor Robert Young and the voluble producer Dore Schary, among others.

The results of the Round Tables were by no means startling. The "Pursuit of Happiness" group concluded that this "Third Freedom" was "indispensable to the proper exercise of all the others, giving man the freedom to find truth in whatever terms he is able to behold it."[84] The "Modern Art" discussion dealt with the confusion of the contemporary scene by begging for the viewer's indulgence: newer forms of expression might be confusing—and modern artists should not be so pretentious about creating illegible works—but viewing art was serious business requiring attention and persistence. The "Housing" panel vacillated between homilies on the value of the American home and suggestions on how to increase production in a seller's market. From the "Movies" discussion emerged the suggestion that the film industry permit film makers to be more creative, more serious.

This is hardly revolutionary fare. However, within the texts of these reports were woven themes and techniques that reached out toward larger discussions of American culture at the time. The Tables were concerned with the construction of the myths and symbols of American identity. Participants argued about the dynamics and restraints of freedom. They assumed that they were speaking to the affluent society Galbraith described; leisure—the pleasure of new acquisitions and experiences—was a part of the cultural fabric. The Round Tables did not fear dealing with the realm of myth and symbol because they assumed that their middle-class audience typified American culture. Finally, all the discussions attempted to contain postwar exuberance within the boundaries of edification, moral rectitude, and community responsibility.

This way of looking at American culture, emphasizing the difference between action and thought, ran through both public and academic discussions. This public debate over culture and national personality enfranchised magazine writers and scholars alike, and convened a number of public round-table exchanges and university seminars. Some figures occupied seats at both forums. Not only did historians and psychologists write for academic audiences, but they debated the meaning of large cultural phenomena in a public arena. Round tables like the four staged by *Life* gained legitimacy through the participation of such experts, who enjoyed newly found prestige as cultural commentators for a large audience. During the 1950s these public intellectuals would be enveloped by a university environment invigorated by the influx of mature students with GI Bill support. At the same time seminars were convened within university walls, out of which emerged a new generation of scholarship on the American character. The curiosity that led to a softening of the border between the academy and the public allowed a psychologist like Fromm to speculate in public on broad cultural phenomena. Within the seminar, students saw that two aspects of culture—symbol and fact, thought and action—"exist on a different plane,"[85] as Henry Nash Smith put it in his dissertation. The Ph.D. candidate at Harvard echoed the pronouncements of the great social psychologist at the Table in Rye.

Like the proliferating collections of photographs, the myriad analyses of an American mind found their source in World War II. The fascination with the qualities of American life and the uniqueness of what was called American civilization, both within university seminars and at public round tables, drew from the currency of national character study, capital amassed by intellectuals in national service. The construction of a national mind had proved its utility in World War II, when instrumental knowledge was required to deal with cultures with which there was limited possibility of contact.[86] According to Margaret Mead, an early proponent of this point of view:

> Where only fragmentary materials were available—a few informants, some news broadcasts, certain sorts of literature, especially autobiographies and accounts of childhood, educational documents, films—these were analyzed to provide some kind of prediction of the probable behavior of the members of a given national group. . . .

> Anthropologists made use of their experience in the reconstruction of cultural wholes from fragmentary materials and a very few living informants.[87]

In the culture of wartime America, the nature of "informant" had changed. Observation had turned into surveillance of enemy cultures. Among the Allies, and later in the United States, cultural information became an extractive industry for analysts.

By the end of the 1940s the existence of an American mind had become a commonplace for popular and academic writers alike. The effect of The American Century upon the American character (the *Life* Round Tables) and, conversely, the projection of American values onto a newly subjugated world ("People Are People the World Over"), were preoccupations of public discourse. The ideas constructing this American world coalesced into the sort of discussion represented by both the Round Table in Rye and the seminar at Harvard. Whether self-consciously interdisciplinary or forthrightly democratic in the enfranchisement of viewpoints, these gatherings recognized that such a complex subject as the analysis of a national mind—its symbolic associations, its construction of history through myth—required more than one speaker, all voices resonating with the same, holistic construction of an American culture. A satisfying consensus was multivocal, but, like a good chorus, well-orchestrated.

Life was out to give its readers what they wanted. Discussions of housing and the movies could sell magazines, even if a debate over modern art or the third freedom became more opaque. Both the magazine and the Round Table participants were also battling for the ability to define, and then to control, middle-class taste. "The exercise of taste," Andrew Ross writes in *No Respect*, "not only *presupposes* distinctive social categories; its also helps to *create* them, in the shape of apparently 'natural' cultural classes."[88] The discussions of the *Life* Round Tables can be considered to be didactic exercises telling Americans what they should be concerned with. They can also be viewed as efforts to direct and contain taste that was backed up by purchasing power. If the activities of *Life* magazine could be termed "middlebrow," that is, if *Life* saw itself as interpreting great ideas for the expanding middle class, then these constructed debates over taste become contestations over control and what Ross terms "respect,"[89] in other words, cultural authority. The venues for these discussions become important: two country clubs and the Museum of Modern Art. It was assumed that there was a public culture surrounding the Round Tables; they also were convened in locations of power.

In order to understand the position of Edward Steichen, a "high art" photographer who had also made money through advertising assignments, formulating the *The Family of Man* exhibition at the Museum of Modern Art, or Wayne Miller, the assistant who leafed through the *Life* magazine files, one has to begin with this map of the middle landscape that *Life* had explored, discrete from the pulp of the daily press and the walls of academe, yet conversing with both realms at its borders. The battle over taste—not only a mechanism for containment and a shaping tool for postwar reconstruction but also a contest over cultural authority—was waged on this landscape. This debate, which one can see, for example, in the criticism of *The Family of Man*, was part of this larger, hegemonic struggle for domestic control of American culture. The control of, or identification with, abundance was equally important, not only in defining the newly discovered greatness of American civilization but in establishing a relationship between American culture and the rest of the world.

World War II was not the most recent war to which *The Family of Man* could respond. From June 1950 until August 1953 the United States was involved in the Korean police action, bringing both soldiers and photographers back into the battlefield after only a five-year hiatus. Although the Soviet Union was not directly involved—and recent studies have revealed that distancing itself from the conflict may have presented Soviet leaders with a strategic advantage[90]—the civil war in Korea was widely perceived as a proxy conflict between the United States and the Russians. Because this war was confined to a small peninsula, media coverage was complete, and communication with the home front was disturbingly immediate. Within the first three months of the war, 270 correspondents arrived in Korea from nineteen countries.[91] Life magazine had eleven photographers covering the action, with David Douglas Duncan and Carl Mydans heading the crew. As Duncan later commented, "there never has been a war story run continuously for so long in Life without a break and without losing a major angle."[92]

To Americans who read about Korea—the last war beyond the range of a television lens—in newspapers and magazines, this was a confusing war that generated little enthusiasm.[93] Although unrest had fomented since the end of World War II, the North Koreans seemed to attack without warning in June 1950. Quickly, they drove United Nations and Republic of Korea troops toward an enclave around the southeastern coastal city of Pusan. Then, just as suddenly, a bold landing at Inchon spurred a UN advance almost to the Chinese border, the Yalu River. When China entered the war the front retreated toward the 38th parallel, where it stalled while peace talks began and quickly stalled, too. Within a two year span, Seoul had been lost to the North Koreans, recaptured by UN troops, and threatened again by troops from the North. The war itself, like the meetings at Panmunjom, could scarcely be seen as progressing. There was American talk about the use of atomic weapons, countered by allegations from the other side that the UN troops had engaged in chemical and biological warfare. Atrocities were documented on both sides. UN bombers destroyed many of the reservoirs of North Korea, flooding out the vital rice crop and inflicting misery throughout the North. The North Koreans were repeatedly charged with brainwashing American prisoners. Finally, in August 1953 the conflict ended with little demonstrable gain and many questions regarding tactics, allegiances, and larger strategies left poorly answered. In its article on the day of the truce, Life included the remarks of an army officer about the cease-fire directive. "'It read . . . that there would be no firing weapons to celebrate the cease-fire. What the hell,' he said, looking around and shrugging, 'is there to celebrate?'"[94] The last segment of Life's thirteen-page spread on the truce chronicled the death of one American soldier on the morning of the cease-fire.[95]

The deployment of sophisticated news-gathering technology did not make the war more comprehensible. This was a conflict that hid behind masks. Life called the war righteous[96] and highlighted the international participation in the United Nations forces, but the control of the action lay in the hands of an American, as the firing of General Douglas MacArthur by President Truman had made spectacularly clear. The Russians were presumed to pull the strings, and yet soldiers encountered only North Koreans and, after the UN advance had almost nearly reached the Yalu River, the Chinese—their revolution only one year behind them and their allegiances to the Soviet Union untested. In practical terms, "our" Asians looked like "their" Asians. North Koreans were routinely referred to as "gooks," both in everyday GI parlance and in American propaganda material,[97] but the racism of that term was easily transferred to the South Korean army, which was thought of as inefficient, if not incompetent. The loyalty of civilians was always in question. Guerillas and snipers masqueraded as peasants; some women and children picked up arms and fought unsuspecting troops while others were treated hostilely by UN soldiers but proved to be as harmless as they appeared. Some American prisoners of war told stories of UN atrocities and then recanted after they were exchanged. Others acted disturbingly, as though they did not want to return. Even the cause being fought for became unclear, beyond the general assertion that Communism should be stopped. The South Korean government, headed by Synghman Rhee, was manifestly corrupt. American forces returning from the Yalu found that they had fought North Koreans in the advance and now had to protect themselves from South Korean sympathizers in retreat.

The allegiances of correspondents and photographers were tested. Because the public did not support this war as it had the just cause of the 1940s, reporters were constantly put in a position of explaining to a disunited readership what they themselves did not understand. At the beginning of the war MacArthur rejected official censorship, and yet he punished unfavorable reports of the initial UN retreat by denying the offending reporter access to stories and the means of getting them back to the States. This implicit control became so frustrating to the press that correspondents themselves asked for official censorship so they would know where they stood. There were no pools of correspondents and photographers as there had been in World War II, so competition rather than cooperation reigned. Even after the establishment of official control of stories and photographs in December 1950, the individual entrepreneurs of the press corps were harder for the military to handle than the manageable pool of World War II. The relationship between military and press quickly became adversarial. There was especial dislike for the imperial MacArthur, who played favorites and presumed to orchestrate a wartime effort that was manifestly out of control.[98]

To present-day eyes all of these facts bespeak a war more like Vietnam than World War II, a view that has become institutionalized through many American history textbooks[99] and popularized by the television series M*A*S*H. Those observers freezing and sweating, running with the troops for over a year and then observing World War I–style trench warfare for another while peace talks dragged on, were faced with day-to-day decisions on how to force a different war to make sense. Photographers employed the strategy of focusing ever more tightly on individual soldiers.[100] The Korean War became a gallery of portraits. It was no longer possible to show how a group of heroes went about vanquishing a foe. Many shots concentrated on the personal dilemmas of soldiers and encouraged viewers to empathize with them. Soldiers faced the camera strained almost beyond emotion. The circumstances of war penetrated behind the lens; correspondents had been able to cover World War II over long stretches of time but had to be rotated out of Korea as frequently as every three weeks.[101]

The editors of Life did not write about the war in the same way as their photographers saw it.[102] In their Christmas 1950 editorial, for example, the magazine lauded the virtues of the American way of life—freedom, prosperity, courage, righteousness—now at war against an enemy "who requires no choice and has only the course of enslavement." The representative soldier for them was not the grunt trying to tell good gooks from bad but the army chaplain ministering to his charges: "he left behind, and took with him, something of the tenderness and mercy of

God." He also, for the first time, packed a piece. Chaplains were armed for the same reason that many photographers picked up a carbine or a revolver: in this ambiguous terrain there was no safe ground, and the character of each inhabitant had to be questioned. Conversely, your face bespoke an allegiance that could not be mitigated by cross, star, or press credentials. Despite these new dangers, both chaplain and flock had a predictable ally: "at home and on the battlefield God does walk with us now. With all of us, that is, who will heed His presence and take His hand for the journey through whatever valleys many lie ahead." [103]

Such homilies were not apparent in the pictures that *Life* photographers sent back. In the same Christmas issue, David Douglas Duncan presented a portfolio of photographs entitled "There Was a Christmas." Duncan, an ex-marine, brought his camera close to the infantrymen as they retreated in intense cold from Changjin Reservoir to the Sea of Japan. These men were "incredibly gallant" in the way that they faced the privations of the road and the double assaults of North Koreans (and the unmentioned guerillas from the South) and the weather. There was no chaplain in these pictures, for no ministrations could have relieved their suffering. "Eyes of men who have looked at undiluted hell are not pleasant to meet soon after. . . . There is no fear in these faces and no great hatred. They were simply fighting their way out and hoping to stay alive." [104] Duncan showed his allegiance to the American soldier, who maintained his values throughout this trial. The troops pragmatically stripped all useful equipment from wreckage as they marched and humanely brought their dead and wounded out with them. Duncan did not present the same vapid parable of divine election as had his superiors in New York. "This is what it was like for those who survived unhurt, for those who were wounded and pulled through and for those whose Christmas is now forever." [105]

Susan Moeller insightfully points out that during the Korean War texts and photographs contradicted each other throughout the popular press. Editorial positions were conservative; photographers showed the futility of war. [106] She cites an evocative example from the experience of Carl Mydans on a visit to a Turkish aid station in 1951. A Turkish doctor bent over a soldier who had been badly burned. The doctor rose with his patient as the cocoon of bandages was placed onto a stretcher and faced the mountains.

> Pointing toward the darkening horizon, he turned to me and shouted: "History!" In exasperation he searched for other English words, but they would not come. "History," he shouted again and then stood jerking his fist into the air, looking wordlessly toward the purple twilight. [107]

However, when *Life* published the product of one of Mydans's visits to the Turkish troops, the inarticulate rage, the suspension of interpretation to the future, was lost in a genial recounting of the wonderful allies of the United Nations effort. From a respectful distance, the article offers soldiers from Greece and Turkey (placed happily next to each other on the page as they could not be in fact), Scotland, France, England, New Zealand, Puerto Rico ("fiercely proud of U.S. citizenship" despite the separatist enthusiasm of that island), and Australia. Statistics of all thirteen units were detailed. The subtitle of the story was "Picked men of many lands fight hard in Korea."[108]

Edward Steichen called David Douglas Duncan's book, *This Is War!*, "the most forceful indictment of the subject [war] ever put forth by photography."[109] The most famous of the Korean War photographers went into the field with his marine comrades and offered them the cover of a sympathetic lens, portraying the heroism of American soldiers in a war that offered no stable ground on which to stand. Like Steichen, Duncan assumed that pictures could demand engagement from their audience. A shot that captured the moment could create bonds of empathy that reached through the lens and reconstructed a three-dimensional feeling in the mind of the viewer. The combat photographer wanted viewers to understand the context beyond the frame. "The book is an effort to completely divorce the word 'war' as flung dramatically down off the highest benches of every land, from the look in the man's eyes who is taking his last puff on perhaps his last cigarette, perhaps forever."[110]

This Is War! contains no captions. Duncan did not presume to speak for his subjects; rather, he encouraged his viewers to think of what they would have done in similar circumstances.

> I wanted you to feel something of what I felt, and, possibly, to think
> some of the things that I thought during those dreary months before the
> pictures of the book made it possible for the men to tell of themselves.[111]

Paging through the book, one can see that these are not the faces of World War II: there is endurance rather than triumph, movement rather than direction. However, neither is this the Vietnam conflict, about which Duncan would later write. Like his colleagues from earlier decades, Duncan hoped that an evocative picture would draw viewers into the scene and demand a response.

> [T]o learn their stories, each page of photographs must be read as care-
> fully as you might read a page of written text in a novel. Asking you to
> read the story in their faces and hands and bodies, as they were feeling it
> themselves at the moment of impact, is only fair to them—and is asking
> more of you than ever before has been asked of the picture-viewing audi-
> ence.[112]

In his autobiography Steichen recounted the impact that Duncan's volume had on him, rekindling his revulsion from war at the same time that he was formulating *The Family of Man* exhibition. Like Duncan, Steichen had focused on individuals in his work in World War II, but his was not the temperament of the combat photographer. Duncan had portrayed each soldier as possessing the heroism of strong character. To do this he had stuck the camera into the action in a more threatening way than even Robert Capa could manage. Steichen watched from the distance, preferring to deal with representative moments in the life of sailors beyond the battle. This difference in temperament can be seen in the way that the two approached aerial photography. Steichen's World War I pictures had been taken out of range, from an altitude high enough to reveal the larger patterns of the combat zone. Duncan's first ride in a jet aircraft put him near the lead of a strafing run, subjected him to so much gravitational force that he felt his bile sweating through his skin, and thrust him as close to the action as a double-seat cockpit would allow. Even the actions of the pilot were telegraphed to him through the movements of the stick, ganged to the pilot's controls, poking his legs during the experience. Steichen's perspective was abstract, whether viewing the shapes of fields and villages or assessing the character of carrier pilots. Duncan immersed himself in the brotherhood of combat, in which endurance was as important as quick thought.

Steichen's sensibility was not Duncan's. Steichen contributed one of many letters to the editor of *Life* in response to Duncan's "There Was a Christmas." The most evocative picture of the spread, later to appear in *The Family of Man*, was reproduced in this section: a bundled Marine, covered with the grime of combat and escape, gazing upward expressionless as he waited for his frozen beans to thaw. Steichen's letter, identifying himself as a Captain, U.S. Navy Retired, and director of the Department of Photography at the Museum of Modern Art, commented on Duncan's accomplishment more than on his subjects. These were "wonderful photographs" which "set a new high for war photography." Duncan deserved "richly merited cheers" for the "deeply moving photographs." None of the other letters summoned up anything resembling cheers.[113]

Steichen may have held the grimy realities of this war at pen's length, but he understood the photographic assignment that Duncan had undertaken. Duncan, for his part, recognized that his own passage from Japan to Korea, and the returning cans of film rushed to New York, would be of interest to a portion of his readership. "Probably few of you who have read this book will ever be called upon to photograph a war," he begins his afterword, "Photo Data." This remarkable understatement was followed by a recognition of the democratic technology of picture taking: that the 35mm "miniature" cameras he had used in Korea were causing "a minor revolution" in the United States and Europe. Parallel to the technology of killing, advance, and retreat ran another dialogue of range-finding, instrument selection, and shooting accuracy—that of the combat photographer. The superiority of the Japanese Nikor lens on his Leica cameras was as gratifying to him as the overwhelming speed of the Shooting Star jet fighter from which he attempted to photograph. A photographer under fire in the trenches with the marines had little time to set aperture and speed, focus, and shoot. The details of each photographic volley were submerged in the wonderment that camera and lens could function at all in the climate and terrain of a battlefield demanding quick action. Here the practices of art—good composition, texture, depth of field—were dangerous.

As one might expect, Duncan's admission that not many of his readers would have his experience was followed by a "but": "since the techniques and tools employed were just about the same as many of you who are camera fans, or professionals, would use on your vacations or assignments, I thought that it might be of additional interest to you if I were to explain how these photographs were made." Even though Duncan was a combat veteran of World War II who viewed marines as his people, he acknowledged the touristic experience of photographing the war in

Korea. This was, after all, not an all-encompassing conflict; according to the United States, it was not even a war. It could be entered and escaped quickly, thereby creating the disjunctures that other photographers on general assignments felt during that period. One day Duncan was in Japan, photographing in the ocean. Two days later he was in combat. On Fridays his film, shot frantically in the rain or the snow, would leave his hands. On Mondays the mistakes of battlefield shooting conditions would be erased in Life magazine's "water temperature-controlled, air-conditioned laboratory" in New York.

Steichen valued Duncan's work so much that he created a special exhibit featuring the best portraits of the Korean War. However, this was not the war most clearly mirrored in The Family of Man. The Second World War had created the patterns and the logistics of the world photographer-tourist; the Korean War refined these already established ways of acting. World War II had presented unambiguous terrain and a clearly identified enemy personified by villains like Hitler, Mussolini, and Tojo. The Korean conflict was born of that same, earlier war but was complicated by new forces: the United Nations, the newly globalized United States, Communist China, and the Soviet Union. Most of all, Korea was an Asian war fought against and, to an extent, with, people who were disconcertingly unfamiliar to most Americans. This "police action" heightened differences; Steichen was intent on eliminating them.

We are now ready to turn to the construction of The Family of Man exhibition. We have already seen how the mechanisms for taking photographs—the figure of the photographer/tourist, the photo-gathering apparatus, the public appetite for pictures—were developed during World War II. We have examined how one particular agency, Magnum, tried to stake out (and then market) the world through a year-long series in Ladies' Home Journal. We've also seen how Life magazine tried to move beyond the stature of a picture magazine to a position of domestic cultural significance, in this case through its series of Round Tables in 1948 and 1949.

It should be clear that mass media were trying to take audiences seriously—or at least to have readers take their own culture seriously (and buy more magazines). This middlebrow landscape was Steichen's domain. Even though, as we will see, Wayne Miller had millions of images from which to select in the construction of The Family of Man, many of the photos he reviewed were shot and archived in the climate I have outlined above. Not only the material but the assumptions about how culture cohered and the exceptional status of the United States amid world cultures predisposed an outcome. The construction of the frame for these shots transcended the provenance for individual photos. Such a general control matched the congenial re-contextualization that Steichen and Miller performed in the process of assembling the exhibit. This predisposition, evident in the manufacture of The Family of Man images and encased in the Life story files that Miller examined, helped define the vocabulary with which the exhibition spoke, the audience it addressed, and the location of this statement within the public discourse of the postwar period.

PICTURING THE EXHIBITION

EDWARD STEICHEN CONSTRUCTED *THE FAMILY OF MAN* TO DELIVER A TIMELESS message to the Museum of Modern Art audience of 1955. The oxymoronic exercise of situating universal emotions in a specific historic context was given special poignancy through a direct reference to the most threatening development that could impinge on all human existence—nuclear annihilation. We will examine in detail the assembly of the photographs for the exhibition and the assumptions that guided Steichen and his crew during this process. We will look at the location for the show, the Museum of Modern Art, with an eye to how this enormous and massively popular undertaking threatened the definition of modernism to which the museum laid claim. Finally, we will examine the critical reaction to the exhibition, both the favorable reports from the 1950s and the increasingly critical response of the last twenty years. Its construction, location, and message make *The Family of Man* one of the most significant cultural productions of 1950s America.

The *Family of Man* spoke against the overt American exceptionalism that pervaded 1950s popular culture. *Life* magazine here represents a larger discourse, including the popular press, movies, television, and advertising, among other media. The exhibition assumed that people would be moved by a visual text and, in their emotional response, form a compensatory community to combat the impersonalized, highly technological conflict of the cold war. This assumption was both the exhibition's strength and its weakness. In their earnest handling of photographs, Edward Steichen and Wayne Miller, his chief assistant, produced a compelling text that continues to affect its viewers. They did not, however, indicate to what end their audience should be moved. Steichen may have thought that human empathy would break down global antagonisms. He did not, in any case, consider his job to be programmatic. So, the exhibition could pack an emotional wallop and still be overwhelmed by the structures of cold war control. *The Family of Man* has been unjustly accused of surrendering the field of action through a passive, sentimental humanism. This criticism fails to place the exhibition in the context of Steichen's reading of the times— here the 1930s, 1940s, and 1950s—in which emotion could move humans to concerted action through democratic processes. Before tracing *The Family of Man* through cultural history, we must examine the care with which it was constructed to speak to a specific audience in New York in the first half of 1955.

The *Family of Man* exhibition at the Museum of Modern Art was the most popular photographic event of the 1950s. It broke all attendance records at the museum and produced a bonus for MoMA employees. A book of the exhibition photographs, hurriedly marketed by Jerry Mason, a young, enterprising publisher, has been continuously in print ever since it first appeared in May 1955. Over 4 million copies of the familiar paperback book have been sold, but the exhibition also has been commemorated in a deluxe, hardbound volume and in millions of excerpts distributed worldwide by the United States Information Agency. Still today the book lies on many coffee tables and library shelves and is passed back and forth through the ubiquitous neighborhood enterprise, the garage sale. The exhibition aimed at popularity, and it succeeded beyond Steichen's expectations. Many who passed through the Museum of Modern Art were taking their first trip through any museum; many who purchased the book were acquiring their first volume that centered on the image and not the word.

The *Family of Man* presented 503 images—the product of 273 photographers displaying scenes in sixty-eight different lands—in sizes ranging from eight by ten inches to eight by ten feet—in a production that the photographer and critic Minor White likened to a Cecil B. DeMille extravaganza.[1] Steichen played with depth of field and peripheral vision in order to envelop the viewer in a world of images. Steichen, who was then the director of MoMA's Department of Photography, did not squander a chance to speak directly to the American people. To comment on the American dream to a mass audience had been his goal ever since seeing some of the exhibitions of the Farm Security Administration before the war. Now he had his chance, and, as we shall see, he also had a message so fundamental, so portentous, that it could not be overstated.

Steichen did not present photographs as high art. He attempted to step close to his audience, to break through the frame of connoisseurship, for a specific purpose. A survey of the history of photography was coincidental to his task—a Matthew Brady picture was included as was a Lewis Carroll portrait of his Alice. At hand for his immediate use in depicting the universal qualities of family life was the immense production of images since the end of the war. The visual vocabulary that he was to employ was formed in the exuberant age of supertourism I have described in Chapter 1. Because his purpose was to comment on the human condition rather than to construct a historical text, it should come as no surprise that the anthropology of the exhibition left critics queasy. The message that he articulated was born in the destruction of war and was magnified by possibilities of technological annihilation in the new, atomic age. The declarative sentence, "Mankind is one," whether voiced in words or in pictures, drove the formation of the exhibition.

The enterprise of preparing this exhibition preoccupied Steichen for three years. For the last two of these he was assisted by Wayne Miller, who had moved to California after the war but headed east in the summer of 1953 to be with the Captain during his biggest project to date. Through the calls for photographs, Steichen made it clear that any image would be considered. Since the net was cast wide, the available resources were overwhelming. The main source for the exhibition turned out to be the *Life* magazine files. Considering the productive engine that magazine represented and the audience Steichen hoped to attract, this was a logical choice. Such a decision, however, inflected the utterance of the exhibition in a general direction already inherent in the *Life* archives and manifested in the assignments, strategies, and Round Tables we already have encountered.

Wayne Miller entered the *Life* archives in late 1953 to discover whether or not photographs could be found that captured the concepts that Steichen had dreamed of. "To learn whether or not a *Family of Man* show was possible, we needed to know if these kinds of photographs existed," Miller remembers.[2] He searched through over 3.5 million images, filed according to assignment and collection. Many photographs had never been printed and could be viewed only on the original negative strips. Only toward the end of the war did *Life* print contact sheets of all assignments; some of the images that had been selected for the magazine had a crescent-shaped hole punched near the sprocket, signalling that they were to be developed.[3] *Life* files contained not only assignments but also collections of photographs from all over the world. Miller went through file after file, wearing out several rubber thumbs in the process. He spent between seven and nine months with the *Life* files.[4]

Steichen issued calls for photographs to professionals and amateurs. In 1952, with Robert Frank as his interpreter, he had journeyed to Europe, where he met with hundreds of photographers in eleven countries. Images came directly to the museum from all over the world. According to Miller, every day for many months one or more large mailbags of photographs arrived at the Department of Photography.[5] Miller also traveled to Washington to examine some files at the National Archives and the Library of Congress, including the photographs of the Farm Security Administration. *Look* magazine opened its files, but Miller found little that was useful to the project. Finally, Miller solicited photographic services such as Black Star and Magnum, as well as the SovFoto collection, which yielded a few 35mm shots of the Soviet Union during the war years. In all, more than 6 million photographs were surveyed for *The Family of Man*. The broad categories of the show had guided Miller's search, but he had no quota to fill.

> The emphasis we had in certain areas was not because we wanted so
> many pictures in this category and so many in that, but because the pho-
> tographs we found said something. As a result, we may have had more
> photographs in one area rather than another. The photographs themselves
> dictated the final shape, the final meaning of the show.[6]

Some photographers did not appreciate Steichen's project or did not understand what he was describing in his solicitation of photographs.

> It is essential to keep in mind the universal elements and aspects of hu-
> man relations and the experiences common to all mankind rather than
> situations that represented conditions exclusively related or peculiar to
> a race, an event, a time or place.[7]

Others were congenial, even though they were not sure how to interpret Steichen's call. The New York photographer Ruth Orkin, for example, did not submit any photographs herself but invited Miller to go through her trunk in search of appropriate photos; on her wall he found a series of five photographs of her daughter and companions playing cards that was later selected for the exhibition. A few photographers, such as Dorothea Lange, were sympathetic to the project from the start and visited the loft where Steichen and his crew compiled the exhibition.

Steichen focused the exhibition on the message he saw as contained in the photographs, not on the artistry of the photographer. The narrative strands connecting these messages, not the aesthetic greatness of each image, unified the show. In fact, from the beginning, the identity of the photographer was suppressed. As Steichen's crew received images at the loft work site, they assigned each picture a number. They maintained index cards for each of the contributors, but the staff only consulted these files when they needed an address to return a print or request a negative. Not until Steichen and Miller finally had decided on the 503 images did the staff place the names of the contributors under their images. Some photographers were offended and others pleasantly surprised as they toured the exhibition during the preview, taking a tally.

The exhibition cost more than $100,000 to produce. Most of the funds came from the Rockefeller family, which was well represented on the museum's board of trustees. Steichen demanded the highest quality reproduction possible and expended much of his budget on the printing of images. Homer Page saw to their production, but Steichen, Page, and Miller all struggled with print quality. The exhibition would contain photographs as large as eight by ten feet, and they tried to minimize as much as possible the deterioration of quality that came with such formidable enlargements. They spent many hours in the darkroom at Compo Photo and rejected many prints under this close scrutiny.

Between late 1953 and February 1955 Steichen rented a loft over a strip joint on 52nd Street. This space, in a building scheduled for demolition, gave Steichen and his staff the opportunity to sort through the photographs they had culled from all sources. Boxes of prints were brought to the loft. Some Steichen and Miller rejected immediately and returned; some they designated "maybes"; and a few the two immediately recognized as likely candidates for the exhibition. The ten thousand images of the working files of the project, containing prints from both of these categories, comprised an archive of images that Steichen and Miller continued to draw upon as they assembled the one thousand images, arranged on thematic boards, from which they would select the final 503.

Steichen invited many people to consult with him in the loft. Dorothea Lange, who had understood the project from the beginning, was among them, as was Jerry Mason, who would later publish the book version of the exhibition. Miller furnished Steichen with an impressive list of academic and public intellectuals—Lewis Mumford, Lionel Trilling, Archibald MacLeish, Robert Oppenheimer, and Margaret Mead among them. Which should he invite, Miller wanted to know. Steichen replied: "The ones I want to see are the people who in twenty years will be these people."[8] Publishers, photographers, and the museum hierarchy, especially the sympathetic René D'Harnoncourt, visited this space, which became more of a frantic workroom and less of a conversation area as January 1955 approached. The two greatest influences over the formation of the exhibition were Wayne Miller, who presented the master with a world of photographs, and Carl Sandburg, who helped shape the idea and provided the name for the project, "the family of man."

According to Steichen's own account, he had already thought of the concept of this exhibition before the war started. He had seen an exhibition of Farm Security Administration photographs in New York's Grand Central Terminal and had been taken with the idea of presenting an exhibition commenting on the American Dream to a mass audience. The 1938 FSA show made full use of the exhibition space, allowing its audience, mostly commuters, to wander among images printed in various sizes and to pick their own path through the exhibition. Individual photographs drew visitors closer, confronting them, challenging them for their empathy.

The phrase *the family of man* was supposedly drawn by Steichen from Carl Sandburg's extraction of those words from a speech by Abraham Lincoln.[9] There is more to it than that, and the complexity of the influence hints at the relationship between the two men.[10] Steichen and Sandburg were brothers-in-law; Sandburg was married to Lillian, the photographer's younger sister. The two men became like brothers, visiting each other frequently, as good relatives would, but also writing appreciative pieces about each other. In 1929 Sandburg produced what he termed the first biography of a living photographer written by a poet.[11] *Steichen the Photographer* portrays its subject as a latter-day Benjamin Franklin, rising from apprentice to master photographer because of his talent and sense of purpose; exhibiting mechanical skills in the spirit of American inventiveness; and embodying frugality, hard work, and the ability to command the respect of others, even the ferocious financier, J. P. Morgan. Steichen, for his part, took many photographs of the poet, including a multiple exposure that was Sandburg's favorite.[12] In 1966, only a year before the poet's death, Steichen edited a book-length tribute to the bard of Illinois.

It is more likely that Steichen extracted "the family of man" from another use that Sandburg made of the phrase in a long poem that he described as an interlude from his six-volume Lincoln biography, entitled *The People, Yes*. This litany of folk sayings and Whitmanesque voices from throughout the country (and beyond) contained several explicit references to the family of man. The construction of the Tower of Babel, "something proud to look at,"[13] broke apart the organic unity of this Biblical family. Without a common language, representative voices carry the force of the poem forward, through a catalogue of ills drawn from the commonplace austerities of depression-era America. Sandburg's counter to a world gone wrong was a simple assertion—the people, yes. The image conjured up of people, dignified through their fundamental, family units above the undifferentiated mass, sketched the construction of Steichen's exhibit.

> The people, yes . . .
> The one and only source of armies, navies, work-gangs,
> the living flowing breath of the history of nations,
> Of the little Family of Man hugging the little ball of Earth,

And a long hall of mirrors, straight, convex and concave,
Moving and endless with scrolls of the living,
Shimmering with phantoms flung from the past,
shot over with lights of babies to come, not yet here.[14]

It was up to Steichen to construct this "long hall of mirrors"; Sandburg had already structured the sentiment of the exhibition through his verse.

Sandburg and Steichen had worked together previously with large batches of images. In *Road to Victory* Steichen had selected 150 pictures as "a procession of photographs of the nation at war."[15] The photographer manipulated images into varying sizes and directed visitors through the display on a ramp that gave a commanding, elevated position and ensured the proper ideological reading. The poet supplied a series of captions that appealed to the patriotic resolve of the audience. Writing from the middle of this worldwide conflict, Sandburg addressed the accommodation that a twentieth-century generation of humanists had had to make to an interval of destruction.

What through war we have learned of human solidarity and national
unity, what lessons we have gained, while making war, of the values of
co-operation and humility, these we can hope to carry over into peacetime for victory in the fields of wider personal freedom and of advances
in national discipline and domestic welfare.[16]

The war now behind them, Steichen, with his collaborators, could turn to the larger, human world beyond national boundaries.

For *The Family of Man*, Steichen combined the humanism that Sandburg represented—containing rich evocations of the Civil War and Walt Whitman—with a modernist aesthetic. He employed the exhibition theories of the Bauhaus designer Herbert Bayer, who in the late 1930s had brought to the Museum of Modern Art from Germany his techniques exploiting peripheral vision, three-dimensional collage, and engineered perspectives to create an overwhelming effect on the viewer. A scale model of the floor plan designed by the young architect Paul Rudolph allowed the meticulous assembly of the elements of the exhibition's statement. Steichen interspersed among the images fragments of prose and poetry that had been researched by Dorothy Norman. The task of constructing a text from all these elements was Steichen's alone. Rudolph had provided him with the layout of the ten thousand square feet of exhibition space; Carl Sandburg was consulted frequently regarding overall themes. However, Rudolph was not connected to the project by temperament and Sandburg was not a critical reader of photographs. It was important for Steichen to be able to visualize the overall effect of the exhibition because the composition of this visual statement was his. Already twenty-one when the century started (and, one should not forget, a remarkable seventy-six when *The Family of Man* opened), he could claim a unique historical perspective on the development of photography.

Steichen and Miller pinned photographs to boards that became loaded with emotions and characteristics in the life of the family. They struggled to construct a narrative connecting these images as the mosaic began to swim before their eyes, each part seemingly interchangeable with the next.[17] They began to work by juxta-position. Wayne Miller explained:

> On one [panel] we had all the laughing people, and [on the other] all the crying people. I came in one morning and looked at them, and the crying people and the laughing people looked the same. Also, it was such an inane group of images because it had no meaning. Then we took them all down and started going through these pictures like this: put one over here and one over here, put this one where it seemed to fit. All of a sudden they came alive, because laughing and crying is in relation to something.[18]

Finally, after having winnowed the ten thousand down to one thousand, Steichen made a decision: in order to reach the necessary number of five hundred, Wayne Miller was to select pictures having to do with men and men's work; Joan Miller was to make the final selection of photographs pertaining to women and children; Steichen would reserve for himself those pictures addressing larger themes. Such a practical division of effort was as commonsensical to the three as was the gender stereotyping that pervaded the images that they selected. Steichen assumed that the family functioned according to gender-specific roles. He also believed that pictures could speak to the universal experience of viewers in their own families and, properly interpreted, could convey a large, important theme. Most significant, he took for granted that his response to photographs would represent the reaction of a broader audience. The exhibition was built on the stable message conveyed by photographs and the consistent reaction of all viewers to these utterances.

Steichen was still not satisfied that the 503 images were drawn together into a coherent visual text. Two formative decisions, made late in the project as opening day approached, illustrate the dynamics of the exhibition. One was an image showing the destructive potential of the nuclear age, which completed the socially conscious part of the exhibition. Here was The Family of Man in a nutshell: the timelessness of human emotion and the potential obliteration of time by a new capability of the human mind. A second picture, which Steichen settled upon one evening, was more lighthearted. This photograph of a Peruvian flute player was to be displayed at several stations in the exhibition. Miller placed five-by-seven, eight-by-ten, and eleven-by-fourteen prints throughout the exhibition, wherever they seemed to fit.[19] A caption from the exhibition, attributed to Plato, expressed the proper sentiment: "Music and rhythm find their way into the secret places of the soul."

This playful close-up, taken by Eugene Harris and published in Popular Photography, summoned up another universal, nonverbal language. As Miller remembers, some discussion had been made about wiring the exhibition space for recorded music, but the idea had been abandoned as distracting. Nevertheless, including another celebratory art form had appealed to the organizers in the loft. Harris had come to the loft to report on the death of Werner Bischoff. Both had been photographing in Peru when Bischoff died in an automobile accident. Harris brought with him some of his own work from South America, including the photograph of the flute player. Here was the missing accompaniment for the exhibition.

The exhibition was now complete. Steichen and Miller descended the stairs from the loft out onto 52nd Street, at that late hour enjoying its own music of the spheres courtesy of the strip joint at ground level, "and he was out there doing a jig," Miller recalled. "Here's a guy seventy-five years old doing a jig. And a drunk comes by and looks at him and says, 'I know exactly how you feel, buddy.' And he went staggering off."[20]

Let us now visit *The Family of Man* in January 1955, the night before its opening, to read the text that spoke to 1950s America. One ascended to *The Family of Man*. Winding up the stairway at the Museum of Modern Art visitors could not have anticipated what was waiting for them on the second floor: a gigantic proscenium framing the entrance to the exhibition with the undifferentiated humanity of a crowd, shot from above. The viewer was here to meet the world and have it interpreted through the poetry of Carl Sandburg and the commanding vision of Edward Steichen. Sandburg's introductory stanza, reproduced in his own, pencilled longhand, proclaimed:

> There is only one man in the world
> and his name is All Men.
> There is only one woman in the world
> and her name is All Women.
> There is only one child in the world
> and the child's name is All Children.

Steichen, more the author of the exhibition than its arranger, appealed to viewers who, like good Americans, wanted to know the pertinent statistics. How, in short, was this thing made?

> For almost three years we have been searching for these images. Over two million photographs [a modest estimate] from every corner of the earth have come to us—from individuals, collections, and files. We screened them until we had ten thousand. Then came the almost unbearable task of reducing these to 503 photographs from 68 countries. The photographers who took them—273 men and women—are amateurs and professionals, famed and unknown.[21]

The viewer was thus prepared for a vast photographic exhibition: a Lincolnesque production of the mass, by the mass, and for the mass, or so the artistry of Steichen's work proclaimed.

The Family of Man unfolded as a series of themes relating to the life of the family and depicted through universalized experiences. Steichen summarized the exhibition program:

> We sought and selected photographs, made in all parts of the world, of the gamut of life from birth to death with emphasis on the daily relationships of man to himself, to his family, to the community and to the world we live in—subject matter ranging from babies to philosophers, from the

kindergarten to the university, from primitive peoples to the Councils of the United Nations. Photographs of lovers and marriage and child-bearing, of the family unit with its joys, trials and tribulations, its deep-rooted devotions and its antagonisms. Photographs of the home in all its warmth and magnificence, its heartaches and exaltations. Photographs of the individual and the family unit in its reactions to the beginnings of life and continuing on through death and burial. Photographs concerned with man in relation to his environment, to the beauty and richness of the earth he has inherited and what he has done with this inheritance, the good and the great things, the stupid and the destructive things. Photographs concerned with the religious rather than religions. With basic human consciousness rather than social consciousness. Photographs concerned with man's dreams and aspirations and photographs of the flaming creative forces of love and truth and the corrosive evil inherent in the lie.[22]

Courtship, marriage, childbirth, child rearing, enjoyment, strife, formal education, work, old age, and death wound through a serpentine path that beckoned the visitor without commanding a specific traffic flow. Such a virtuoso performance deserved an overture. Near the entrance was a strip of clear lucite onto which pictures of courtship were suspended. Through that transparent scrim one could see the family portraits, enticing the visitor toward the center of the exhibition, and one could glimpse Ansel Adams's spectacular *Mount Williamson* on the back wall.

At this beginning point of the tour there was no choice of direction. One had to head to the right, past the courtship section and the platform, complete with a hospital curtain that earned it the nickname "the bassinet," containing pictures of birth. Around the corner, the visitor entered the central rectangle of the exhibition. In the middle, set apart by a low pedestal of crushed stone, the family photographs, suspended from the ceiling and mounted at all angles, greeted visitors face-to-face. As the viewer moved around this assembly of family groups from throughout the world, the construction was drawn into different contexts established by the photographs on the walls of the enclosure. Viewed in one direction, the world of work surrounded the family. From another angle, the frame of reference was the land. The crushed marble platform created an altarlike effect at the center of this celebration of family life.

Mount Williamson was the next logical stop. Here one could move to the right, down a cul-de-sac of families playing and celebrating at parties. One could also turn to the left, toward the most highly crafted part of the exhibition. Once again, viewers could survey what they were to experience. Along the back wall Steichen attempted to create a space dominated by curved forms that held rectangular photographs: a wheel of pictures stood immediately in front of the visitor, and at the end of the room two convex panels framed the far wall. The wheel displayed children from all over the world seemingly playing ring-around-the-rosie. The caption was John Masefield's: "Clasp hands and know the thoughts of men in other lands." The convex panels, viewers discovered, were devoted to death and mourning. Here Steichen's intent of submerging the individual in the mass was most obvious, for the panels framed a huge Andreas Feininger picture of New York's Fifth Avenue at lunch hour: individual suffering was transcended by mankind's endurance.

So far Steichen's design had allowed viewers to meander, encouraged through the exhibition by their own curiosity, which was strategically piqued by his careful construction. After the Feininger picture, however, traffic flow was much more constricted down the important left-hand wall, the most traditionally arranged section of the exhibition. Here the message of the exhibition became more didactic, less boisterous, requiring the contemplation and introspection of a more confined space. From themes relating to families, Steichen's work expanded to encompass the elements in the life of this family of man: wrongs resolved by injustice, loneliness combatted by community involvement, strife mitigated by civic responsibility. Having viewed these themes, visitors now stood near the front left-hand corner of the exhibition, in front of the last two baffles and the room containing the climax of the exhibition's text. This final sequence must be read in detail, for by this time Steichen had so focused the attention of his audience that only one statement at a time would be uttered and completely absorbed.

First, one saw a patchwork of nine portraits: three men, three women, three children. Next to this panel was a quotation from Bertrand Russell:

> The best authorities are unanimous in saying that a war with hydrogen bombs is quite likely to put an end to the human race. There will be universal death—sudden only for a fortunate minority, but for the majority a slow torture of disease and disintegration.

Walking beyond, one confronted a dead soldier, his weapon impaled in the ground above him. Beside him was a quotation from Sophocles: "Who is the slayer. Who the victim? Speak." A single overhead lamp created dramatically somber lighting and prepared the viewer for the forebodingly dark space beyond.

The viewer now stood before the single most arresting and important image of the exhibition. The only color image and the only photograph to command an entire room, it was also, curiously, the only image not reproduced in the book version of The Family of Man. It was a huge, six-by-eight-foot color transparency of a hydrogen bomb explosion, glowing red and orange in a darkened enclosure that forced the individual close, close enough to be enveloped by the cloud. The effect of the blast was produced through the new technology of a large color transparency, unfamiliar to most viewers. After perhaps 450 black-and-white images, viewers were shocked back into polychromatic reality with this reminder of life in the modern world.

Exiting from this scene, a sharp turn to the left brought one face-to-face with portraits of couples, each labeled "We two form a multitude." A few more steps into that room and a pivot to look behind revealed that the portraits extended from a wall-sized photograph of the General Assembly of the United Nations. A sentence fragment of the UN Charter gave the appropriate caption:

> We, the peoples of United Nations, determined to save succeeding generations from the scourge of war, which twice in our lifetime has brought

untold sorrow to mankind, and to reaffirm faith in fundamental human rights, in the dignity and worth of the human person, in the equal rights of men and women and of nations large and small. . . .[23]

One left the exhibition through a roomful of children at play, the last of these the reaffirming picture that W. Eugene Smith made of his two children in 1946, *The Walk to Paradise Garden*.

Walking through the exhibition the night before it opened, Miller had the feeling "that these images would come off the walls and they would move; they had a life of their own." He took a picture of his young son seemingly trying to move one of the massive boulders of *Mount Williamson*. Later, visitors to the exhibition would establish their own relationships with the pictures. Frequently, they would have their pictures taken in front of exhibition photographs, thereby contextualizing themselves into *The Family of Man*. The appeal of these pictures was international, for people throughout the world were to take their own snapshots amid the photographs when the exhibition went on tour. "There was a great sense of discovery, personal discovery," of the relationship between photographic subject and audience. "It was fascinating," Miller recounted.[24]

The placement of photographs clearly articulated the text of the exhibition; the visual effect of the collection was also finely crafted. Photographs were playfully manipulated, challenging visitors to extend their field of vision. Near the right-hand wall was a panel suspended from the ceiling. Both sides were mounted with photos of couples on swings, inviting visitors to give a surreptitious push. Steichen mounted one image in the section on home-building from the ceiling, so that the lumberjack on his springboard wielded a Sword of Damocles over the viewer. One photograph of birds in flight was mounted on a low pedestal that might be tripped over. A few photographs were mounted back-to-back, and some were used to cover the pilasters of the room.

Other technical manipulations would not have been noticed by the average viewer. Along the back wall, between *Mount Williamson* and one of the death panels, were three photographs, one of a couple, a second of a grandfather with children, and a third of a soldier returning to a party. These images began with negatives in different formats—2 1/4-by-2 1/4-inch, eight-by-ten-inch, and 35mm—but were presented in the same size and aspect ratio.[25] Equalizing the quality of prints from negatives of such different sizes epitomizes the extraordinary darkroom task that Steichen, Miller, and Page faced in crafting a technically consistent exhibition of images that were viewed through vastly different and always changing powers of enlargement.

The legibility of the text was the primary concern. When a picture by an anonymous photographer of the death slump of a lynched black man attracted great attention, Steichen had the photograph removed, but not before it appeared in the selection of *Family of Man* photographs presented in the February 14, 1955, issue of *Life* magazine. The emphasis must remain broadly distributed on the overall effect of the photographs, not concentrated on an individual photograph. Miller explained:

It was removed because he felt that this violent picture might become a focal point . . . so that people would focus on that and that would be used in press stories about the show and people would miss the point, the theme of the show being interrupted by this individual photograph. . . . That [photo] provided a form of dissonance to the theme, so we removed it for that purpose, not because we didn't think it important, but the presentation of material was dissonant to the composition.[26]

Not every attempt to draw the audience into this world of photographs succeeded. One effect that had seemed good in principle was judged by Miller as too "hokey" in practice.[27] The nine portraits beginning the climactic sequence of the text originally had a mirror mounted at the center—to implicate the viewer in this collection of world citizens. This feature distracted from the effect of the bomb room and was removed. The bomb itself received full emphasis through the use of a Kodak transparency.

Let the coda be Steichen's:

Although I had presented war in all its grimness in three exhibitions, I had failed to accomplish my mission. I had not incited people into taking open and unified action against war itself. This failure made me take stock of my fundamental idea. What was wrong? I came to the conclusion that I had been working from a negative approach, that what was needed was a positive statement on what a wonderful thing life was, how marvelous people were, and, above all, how alike people were in all parts of the world.[28]

Steichen trusted in his ability to select photographs that would speak to viewers, who would see in the images elements of their own realities. He believed that pictures could tell stories and that these utterances could be understood in the same way by mass audiences. He also assumed that emotion, kindled by the fire of sentiment, could move people to action. These beliefs predated Steichen's experience in World War II; they could be found in his review of the Farm Security Administration exhibition in Grand Central Station that had helped him decide on *The Family of Man* project. In this piece, dating from 1939, Steichen quickly moved beyond the intention of each individual photographer: "We don't know if the photographers made these pictures with the purpose of telling a story. If they did not, then their cameras certainly put one over on them." The viewer, he implied, could read through the plane of the photographer's composition to the narrative of the scene being pictured. The scene could speak directly to the viewer, with unmediated impact.

Have a look into the faces of the men and the women in these pages. Listen to the story they tell and they will leave with you a feeling of living experience you won't forget; and the babies here, and the children; weird, hungry, dirty, lovable, heart-breaking images; and then there are the fierce stories of strong, gaunt men and women in time of flood and drought. If you are the kind of rugged individualist who likes to say "Am I my brother's keeper?" don't look at these pictures—they may change your mind.[29]

Most important for the text of *The Family of Man*, Steichen believed that the emotions pictures aroused could lead to action, that, far from having a deadening effect, sentiment could affect behavior.

The FSA review indicates that Steichen had both the understanding of photography and belief in the meliorating potential of human sentiment in the 1930s, before action in the Pacific had put him to the test. His war photography heightened what he assumed to be an emotional bond between the heroic fliers on the *Lexington* and the American public that was supporting them. Now, in the 1950s, he was trusting that the ability of audiences to survey the world, in the context of a family structure presumably familiar to them and from the stance of his finely crafted panorama, could overwhelm the new technology that threatened to destroy all of humankind. For a man of exuberant sentiments and not inconsiderable ego, the ability to affect mass audiences, first in the United States and later around the world, with such a socially redeeming message was a project worth three years' devotion.

Steichen's work was rewarded with almost universal critical approval. In a special section devoted to the exhibition, *Aperture*, the 1950s' most important photographic magazine, then in its third year of publication, listed twenty-three reviews and twenty-five "mentions" in the daily press, along with an assortment of syndicated columns and magazine reviews. This was a national event, presented to readerships that could not be expected to visit the photographs in New York. A look at the twenty-page *Aperture* section shows how clearly Steichen's intentions were read by those who spoke for the exhibition's audience.

The structure of the show's argument attracted attention. Jacob Dischin, photographic editor of the *New York Times*, described the climax of the exhibition: "a large color transparency in a black-painted room which shows the explosion of a hydrogen bomb and raises questions about the future of humanity—represented in a series of faces and groups in adjoining galleries."[30] Barbara Morgan, herself a photographer, appreciated the syncopation of the images, the editing of varying sizes into a coherent whole: "The scale shift from small-to-large, large-to-small, is a breathing rhythm—the systole and diastole of the organism—[and] keeps interest pulsing."[31]

Aline Saarinen, art critic of the *Times*, commented on the nature of this interest for the masses of people that were already jamming the exhibition space on the second floor of the Museum of Modern Art. The real question asked by the collection might be: "has photography replaced painting as the great visual art of our time?"[32] The deeper question underlying Saarinen's review was whether canons of taste could contain the enthusiasm for the democratic medium of photography. If painting has become "so introverted, so personal, so intellectualized that it has lost both its emotion and its power of communication," it should not be surprising that the masses have turned to a more welcoming medium that has evolved into "the marvelous, anonymous folk-art of our time."[33] Saarinen reiterates the impatience that the 1949 *Life* Round Table on modern art had expressed: after having been frustrated before difficult works of art, people would turn to more legible but less demanding texts. The critic in 1955 was not willing to surrender a hierarchy of taste. The modernist painters had taught us how to see, she maintained, but their successors had to re-learn the ability to communicate. The immediacy of the photograph was a challenge to both the medium of painting and the temple in which it was housed, the Museum of Modern Art.

A fascinating account by Dorothy Norman focused this view of the innovation that *The Family of Man* represented. Her assignment was to comment on the selection of captions, her first collaboration with Edward Steichen. She wrote instead about the controlling relationship of her life—with Alfred Stieglitz. The comparison between Stieglitz and Steichen gave her the opportunity to contrast subtly and diplomatically two traditions of photographic aesthetics and practice still being debated in the 1950s. Stieglitz refused to manipulate his image and trusted that the truth of the photographic moment, transferred as faithfully as possible from negative to print, was the essence of the art of photography. Stieglitz's aesthetic, articulated over five decades, commanded devoted followers, including Norman, but, she pointed out, it was important to note that over the years *he had changed his mind*. The fascination with darkroom techniques of the early part of the century had evolved into the aesthetic fundamentalism of his last years. Despite his categorical pronouncements, he had always prized contradiction; he associated it with life.

Stieglitz had concentrated on the interaction between the individual and a single work of photographic art. Steichen, a public man, worked to assemble a mass audience before his highly crafted, editorial message.[34] Was there not, Norman asked, enough room for both figures in the realm of photography? Clearly, Steichen's work struck home. Visitors to the museum were so moved by the images that they made voluntary donations before they departed.[35] The message so dominated the show that many people were not aware of the traditions of the art of photography being presented to them. "What is communicated, it so happens, shakes people to such an extent that, almost paradoxically, it makes them feel as though they were being confronted by some *new* aspect of photography, even if, in truth, this is not at all the point of what is happening to them."[36] Norman used her review to unite Stieglitz and Steichen at the end of the older master's life, drawing together aesthetic and utilitarian traditions that these two photographers represented. In her opinion, Steichen could not be held to Stieglitz's rigorous aesthetics because his intentions lay in another direction. *The Family of Man*, in short "cannot be judged for what it is not."[37]

In *The Atlantic*, Phoebe Lou Adams delivered what *Aperture* called "a minority report" that chastised Steichen for constructing "a piece of sympathetic magic." She detected *Life*'s reportorial style in the arrangement of the photographs, without "the explosions of fantasy that enliven that magazine." The exhibition avoided depicting a deliberate evil that arose from intention and produced a result, even a corpse: "there are dead men, but no murderers."[38] Cultural differences disappeared into high gloss ritual woven together by inane quotations. The Western view of the photographs made every particular circumstance fit a predictable pattern. "A posed family photograph looks exactly the same whether it's African, Asian, or European. The dog may be fat or thin, but the people have identical expressions of slightly apprehensive satisfaction."[39] Even the climax of the exhibition, "the practical theater" of the bomb room, did not satisfy this critic. The explosion "looks like any other splash of orange fire" and the concluding sections only prove that "Humanity has survived the symbolic ordeal and can continue safely on the old road."[40]

Already in 1955, then, important themes had emerged in critical views. The exhibition was seen as a threat to the temple of high modernism, the museum. The collection represented a masterful job of editing—a new role for the artist that drew the medium of photography closer to television and film. Connoisseurs of the print would be offended at the ways in which photographs were manipulated, but they would have missed the point. While honoring the artistry of each image, the criterion was to portray a message through the assembled whole. The audience for this production was undisciplined in the responsibility of viewing. Indeed, the craft of Steichen the editor was to give the viewers a democratic sense of self-direction, while, at the same time, leading them through this meaningful world of images. One could follow Steichen's lead or examine the photographs at one's leisure, but, as Morgan summarized "for both kinds of viewers the life-around-trek through the show is an emotionally exhausting experience, and time is needed to assimilate the compassionate paradoxes of the message, to study the form of its dramatic unfoldment."[41]

The exhibition's broad sweep made it vulnerable to criticisms, beginning with Phoebe Lou Adams's piece in *The Atlantic* and strengthening over time as the power of Steichen's statement has dissipated, that have come to represent the entire enterprise. The exhibition has been attacked for the assumptions about cultural similarity that wove together this world of pictures and emotions. It has been castigated for assuming that photographs can be read as surely as a written text. Finally, Steichen's work has been criticized for not bearing the weight of history or stooping to the particular event in his depiction of this world family. After all, Adams pointed out, "a family quarrel can be as fierce as any other kind."[42] These criticisms demonstrate how the text of *The Family of Man* has been reconstructed by its viewers over the past four decades.

The Family of Man resolutely ignored cultural differences and burrowed to a more literally radical level where, Steichen believed, people could be affected at their roots. This led to a confused anthropology that confounded a close cultural reading of the visual text. The ring-around-the-rosie sequence, a circle of photographs of rings of children, had not explored the similarities and differences among ring games and dances. Each relatively small picture viewed its subjects from a distance, so that a reiterated form would overwhelm any particular cultural practice. The assertion through the caption, "Clasp hands and know the thoughts of men in other lands," made the assemblage resemble all the more the "People Are People the World Over" series that we examined in Chapter 1—except that here viewers were deprived of even the interpretive tool of a written text. The *Ladies' Home Journal* spread had advertised the ability of Magnum photographers to see the world; this *Family of Man* wheel encouraged the viewer to acquire a global perspective by surveying similar forms.

A more complex difficulty in the reading of cultures established by this visual text occurred in the education section, just to the left of viewers standing in front of the ring-around-the-rosie wheel. Some associations were logical enough: a small Palestinian boy writing Arabic at the blackboard was juxtaposed to the wrinkled hands of an elderly person practicing the cursive alphabet. Associations also ran toward the whimsical. A picture of the familiar, learned figure Albert Einstein was associated with his colleagues at the Princeton Institute for Advanced Study, a classroom of Czech university students, and a small boy from Allentown, Pennsylvania, at his elementary computations. By his own account Steichen was amused by the contrast between Einstein's perplexity and the boy's studious expression of accomplishment.[43]

The initial picture of this section belonged to Nat Farbman, who had gone to Bechuanaland, the present-day Botswana, on a *Life* assignment in 1949. This photograph, entitled in its original layout *The Storyteller*, shows a tribal circle dominated by an elder gesturing demonstratively, much to the apparent amusement of his audiences. This photo was intended by Steichen to introduce the theme of education and implied that an obviously tribal situation represented an earlier form of instruction. The composition of the photograph drew the viewer into the circle; the gesticulation of the elder and the reassurance of an audience at ease beckoned.

Over the decades since the exhibition, critics have come to distrust the photographic scene displayed before them. Farbman's photograph might be aesthetically pleasing, but it is an uncertain source of information, or, more grandly, of truth. Without any other knowledge of the context surrounding this circle—indeed, without the picture caption that had been expunged along with the rest of Farbman's assignment—viewers could have known virtually nothing about this photograph. The circumstances in which Farbman created his photographs, two of which were selected for the exhibition, have disappeared. The explanatory world beyond the frame contained in the notes of an anthropologist or the log of a photographer Steichen did not think important to the photograph's purpose: the man's expression, his looping arms told a story that viewers would read. As Barbara Morgan explained in her 1955 comment about the exhibition: "One does not have to be an anthropologist to see atavisms. Beneath strange hats and coats, basic customs live long."[44] For later critics the gesture has become enigmatic; the circle of listeners has become an enclosure the viewer cannot penetrate. Even the ability of the viewer to describe the scene has been questioned by the problems of representation.

Roland Barthes, an influential critic among 1950s intellectuals, pointed out the flawed assumption of commonality:

> [I]f there still remains in these actions some ethnic particularity, at least one hints that there is underlying each one an identical "nature," that their diversity is only formal and does not belie the existence of a common mould.[45]

Barthes attacked directly the faulty anthropology of the exhibition and argued strenuously for the types of pictures that Steichen had included but then removed. A picture of the lynching of a black man in Mississippi might be able to tell us something about racial intolerance in the 1930s, Barthes believed, but "[t]o reproduce death or birth tells us, literally, nothing." This was the suppression of "the determining weight of History" that so offended the French philosopher.[46] However, the composition of *The Family of Man* had its own history. As I already have pointed out, the American view of world cultures—both through the lens and in the notebook—was focused through World War II and then reinforced in the exhibition through the use of documentary pictures exemplified by *Life* magazine photographs. This view must have been irritating to Barthes, who could have seen in *The Family of Man* signs of an unwelcome Americanization of European experience, so aptly symbolized by an exhibition devoted to the primeval first family, Adam and Eve, that Steichen evoked and the New World circumstances of peace and understanding that he encouraged.

At a superficial level, the determining weight of history was absent, diffused, or, more purposefully, expunged. Each photograph's history was assiduously erased as images were accessioned for the selection process. The American family that shared the center of the exhibition space, for example, drew the attention of exhibition-goers; it appeared to be a fine, nostalgic example of what family was supposed to mean: three generations assembled before the pictures of their ancestors in the front room of a farm house. The theme of Nina Leen's story in *Life*, however, was one of dislodgment—how precisely this sort of family icon was becoming rarer because of divorce and the dissolution of the family farm under pressure from mechanization and modernization.[47] The next issue of the magazine presented the Kinsey Report, the decade's most controversial disassembly of the American family idyll.

Through its elaborate logistics of editing, the *Family of Man* project was self-conscious about the stripping of specific context that inevitably occurs when photographs are used. Steichen assumed an ineffable core of meaning in each of these shots. The irony between the context of the Nina Leen shot and its import in Steichen's narrative was one indication of the instability of images that Steichen thought to be anchored in emotion. Steichen believed that viewers would recognize what they saw and would detect a misquotation of the image's message. The exhibition was a congenial appropriation that honored the image as it displayed its testimony to human experience. In general, tracing images from *The Family of Man* back to their original uses (already removed from the experiences they depict) only increases an appreciation for Steichen's sensitivity to the photographs and sense of responsibility toward his audience, especially compared to the utilitarian editing of the weekly photo magazines. In *Life* magazine, Kosti Ruohomaa's shot of an elderly married couple on a swing was captioned: "On a child's swing near the picnic grounds Edward Rogers Castner, who ran a general store in Damariscotta, Maine, for 60 years, gives his wife a fine ride. Both husband and wife are 80 and have been married for 60 years." Steichen mounted this photograph back-to-back with a picture of a young couple caught in mid-arc (and mid-kiss) on an amusement park ride. Steichen's general point about the endurance of love was more respectful than *Life*'s own detailed caption, which highlighted the "superannuated antics of the happy ancients."[48]

The excerption performed for the exhibition was often no more violent than the original dislocation that froze an element of human experience in an image that could become a part of a narrative. Wayne Miller's selection of *The Storyteller* photograph from Nat Farbman's assignment in Bechuanaland provided Steichen with one statement for the education section. In 1949 *Life* editors had selected this negative and begun a story of their own: how the functions of the family persist, even among "primitive" cultures. The *Life* story was, in one sense, closer to the circumstance surrounding the image—the storyteller was illustrating a tale of the Jackal and the Hyena, readers were informed. The curiosity that had sent Farbman to the Kalahari was, in all likelihood, founded in the upheavals in regional politics that had brought down the Jan Smuts government in South Africa in favor of the Afrikaaner movement. The policies of the Nationalist party in South Africa, soon to rigidify into racial apartheid, came to America's attention in 1948. The possible inclusion of Bechuanaland in the Union of South Africa imperiled the friendly circle that Farbman was photographing. So these images told their own tale of racial and national politics. The photo essay had located the image within a family structure it thought of as natural.

> Admiring boys follow the grown men, who often take time to show them
> tricks of stalking and hunting. Little girls help prepare the family meals
> and go into the veld with women to learn how food is collected. . . .
> When night comes and they sit around a fire with their elders, listening
> to an old man's stories, they begin to understand that the band is a uni-
> fied group to which they belong and without which they cannot live.[49]

By stepping into history, the photo essay engaged the developing racial oppression of late-1940s South Africa. The Western frame of the photographer contains an uncomfortable history. Steichen and Miller did not respond to the specific circumstances of the scene—any response would have seemed dated—but concentrated on the emotional import of the photograph. In this case, Miller and the *Life* editors would have been in agreement with what they saw, according to what they understood "family" to mean.

Broken loose from their original contexts, however, individual photographs could be reassembled into a historical narrative through the associations of each person viewing them, a freedom that worked against the well-planned architecture of the exhibition. For example, one could remove August Sander's fine portrait of the hod carrier, part of his *Anlitz der Zeit* (The Face of Our Time) series, and make it a representative of Weimar Germany. This could be placed next to the photograph of Einstein, the most famous refugee from the Nazi regime that supplanted the Weimar Republic. The picture of Jewish survivors of the burning of the Warsaw ghetto, taken by an anonymous German photographer as they were led off to their deaths, could represent the larger holocaust of that war. Finally, a photograph of a boy heading off to school through the ruins of West Germany, book bag over his shoulder, could represent the aftermath of World War II.

Such excerptions from the exhibition inevitably resulted from the interaction between the images and the webs of associations and life experiences enmeshing each viewer in a cultural context. Countless other sets of historical illustrations could be assembled.[50] Indeed, Steichen encouraged them, trusting that the individual spark of attraction would be followed by a deeper, communal meaning that would hold his audience. It was not so important, for example, that viewers could discern that one of the children pictured in the triptych beginning the bomb sequence was a survivor of the Hiroshima attack. David Douglas Duncan's Korean War photograph of Captain Fenton, another of the nine faces, loses its immediacy—he had just learned that his company had run out of ammunition—and becomes a portrait of a haggard, helmeted soldier. Steichen believed that the viewer should be able to look each of these people in the eye and read their faces.

> Faces that are thinking of the horrible, multiplying factor, the incredible multiplying factor of the atomic weapon. Will this be? Must this be? That is written on the faces of these three women, three children, and three men.[51]

Captain Fenton sought whatever would repel the North Korean attack; perhaps he merely wanted to be anywhere else than in the midst of battle. Weariness of war and wariness of one's enemy became a more diffused and self-consciously profound emotion through Steichen's hand.

Characteristically, Steichen's own evaluation of the exhibition did not focus on individual photographs but on the overall effect.

> It is Photography (this medium that was born only a little over a hundred years ago) giving an account of itself. This is what it has done—it has made a record—a portrait of man. Feeling about people the way I do, I feel we have here an article of faith—an antidote to the horror we have been fed from day to day for a number of years.[52]

Steichen's career was devoted to adding the photographer to the list of artists who had a duty to chronicle the transcendence of humankind. His reaction to the Farm Security Administration photographs showed clearly this ability to see a relationship between particular circumstances and universal values. Elements of the 1955 exhibition also hinted at this purpose, for Steichen embedded his own families in this group portrait. Toward the beginning of the show was a picture of a woman giving birth to her son. The photographer was Wayne Miller. The woman was Joan Miller and the doctor was Wayne's father. During the final two years of work on the exhibition Steichen spent many nights at the Millers' New York apartment and would return to his house outside West Redding, Connecticut, on the weekends. Wayne was more of an adopted son than an assistant, and the Millers became his surrogate family, his connection to the future.[53] Steichen used his familiar world to stand for universal moments.

A collage on one wall of the central, rectangular space of the exhibition, one of the contexts into which the family photographs could be placed, superimposed an image of an elderly woman holding a loaf of bread on a larger picture of a field of wheat. This evocation of abundance, home, and family centered on the only picture in the exhibition actually taken by Steichen. It was of his mother, to whom he was devoted. His past was thus represented as well. Steichen's sensibility was related to the prewar eye of the Farm Security Administration photographers. In a world of quotidian concerns and gloomy wrongs, the family was the foundation, and fundamental change could best be made through awakening emotions here, at the roots, at home.

But what of "the horror"? Steichen so structured the exhibition that he only had to show it once. There were, in fact, premonitory pictures of strife and great social dislocations in the collection: the group of Polish Jews being led through the burning streets of Warsaw to certain doom, a Henri Cartier-Bresson photograph of the evacuation of Shanghai during the 1949 Communist conquest of China, the struggle of the East Germans during their unsuccessful 1953 coup. These pictures of upheaval, familiar in historic particularity to a 1950s audience, bore reiteration. The bomb, specifically the 1954 explosion of the hydrogen bomb at Bikini Atoll, was only presented once. It was both an apparition of technological doom and a glowing reminder, an attempt to recharge a symbol that had become all too commonplace to 1950s audiences.

The bomb had become familiar to American eyes. Peter Hales, among others, has traced the iconography of the atomic explosion to show how such a potent, indescribable symbol could become domesticated in the 1950s.[54] Life magazine, which had published the photograph Steichen selected, also contributed to this acclimatization. The cover of the July 4, 1954, issue of the magazine showed a suburban highway, crowded with cars. In the distance were the bursts of Independence Day fireworks. The mushroom shape of these explosions speaks eloquently of the way in which the public had become inured to the bomb. Steichen was out to resuscitate this symbol as something to be feared and combatted. The horror, like the bomb itself, could not be looked at too long or the viewer would become blind.

Steichen was faulted for his success in forcefully encouraging his audience to see the world anew. Criticisms of the exhibition's exuberant defiance of traditional taste categories came from both the right and the modernist left. Cultural conservatives, such as Jacques Barzun, faulted the exhibition for lowering a museum exhibition to the popular level and thereby submerging intellect in a morass of emotion and instinct. For him the exhibition concentrated on "the helplessness of man, and on its excuse and anodyne—his animal needs and sensual pleasures," which he specifically identifies as "kissing and caressing in public places, copulation."[55] The exhibition's problem was not that it had a fuzzy anthropology, but that it indulged "aboriginal nature" at the expense of intellect. Even the genius of Einstein, according to Barzun, was subverted through the perplexed expression on his face. The message of the collection seemed to be:

> Whatever is formed and constituted, whatever is adult, whatever exerts power, whatever is characteristically Western, whatever is unique or has a name, or embodies the complexity of thought, is of less interest and worth than what is native, common, and sensual; what is weak and confused; what is unhappy, anonymous, and elemental.[56]

The man whom Time magazine would soon place on its cover as a representative public intellectual[57] constructed a vocabulary that was revealingly dismissive. Far from being located in a smug Western view of the world—this was Barthes's complaint—for Barzun *The Family of Man* surrendered to the exotic and the primitive, groups which, like the masses in the United States, valued the senses over the intellect, the simple and homegrown over the important and the imported. Not only was the exhibition too respectful of the primitive, but it pandered to the mass, to "the unspoken demands of public opinion."[58]

Barzun was not alone in attacking the tastelessness with which the exhibition spoke to an audience that did not profess aesthetic sophistication. Ansel Adams, connoisseur of the print, was unhappy with the quality of reproduction of the photographs in *The Family of Man*. He spoke for other masters of the darkroom, such as Walker Evans, when he dismissed the seriousness of Steichen's endeavor.

> The quality of the print—of all his [Steichen's] exhibits of this gross character—was very poor . . . If a great Museum represented photography in such a style and quality, why bother about the subtle qualities of the image and the fine print?[59]

Why bother, indeed? For Steichen this was not a rhetorical question. The solitary darkroom task of manipulating print size and regulating quality had to be abandoned in the face of the larger mission of presenting the public with a thematic message.

An aesthetic criticism of the exhibition might have been justified, even in Steichen's terms, but it was also irrelevant. *The Family of Man* had subordinated aesthetics from the beginning. Wayne Miller would not have squinted at strips of negatives had aesthetics been the focus: he would have looked meticulously at contact sheets, or, better yet, at copy prints. Photographs would not have been separated from their makers, for the aura of artistry would have been essential. Thematic boards would not have been constructed, because they minimized the formal qualities of the individual print. The size of the print would have corresponded more closely to the size of the negative. Therefore, criticisms such as that of John Szarkowski, one of Steichen's successors as director of the museum's Department of Photography, appear to be huffy and defensive of the prerogative of the artist.

> Although delighted to see photography so demonstratively appreciated, many photographers were distressed that the individual character of their own work had been sacrificed to the requirements of a consistent texture for the huge tapestry of the exhibition. Only those of a philosophical disposition understood that the solution was artistically inevitable: the exhibition's basic theme—that all people are fundamentally the same—required that all photographs seem fundamentally the same.[60]

In Szarkowski's eyes, perhaps "those of a philosophical disposition" were not superior artists. They were not concerned with "texture," "uniqueness," and other qualities of the fine print. Nor, it turned out, was the orchestrator of the show, enmeshed in the politics of the Museum of Modern Art, properly respectful of the place where photographs should be hung—the museum.

The Museum of Modern Art had been designated by the participants in the *Life*

Round Table on modern art as the representative place for their discussion of contemporary styles such as Abstract Expressionism. In this 1948 seminar it was assumed that modern art spoke with an esoteric vocabulary to a tightly circumscribed audience of cognoscenti and defied the simple curiosity of *Life* readers. From the Table came the assertion that modern art was important to America's claim to world cultural leadership: "How can a great civilization like ours continue to flourish without the humanizing influence of a living art that is understood and enjoyed by a large public?"[61] Much of the *Life* article asked, in effect, for the viewer's forbearance; the fractiousness, the aggressive individualism of the artist was symptomatic of an American culture that had lost its cohesiveness. Such was the argument, generally agreed to, of Theodore Greene, a professor of philosophy from Yale.

> The modern artist feels compelled to develop his own highly individual idiom. But he does not do this out of sheer cussedness. He does it because he feels compelled to express life accurately as he sees it from a highly individualistic point of view. And why does he see it from a highly individualistic point of view? Because we are living in a highly individualistic age. Now there is nothing you can do about that directly. You have got to try to build a community, and as you build a community you will get a common language and common beliefs. Then you will get art that communicates itself more easily.[62]

Participants agreed that the necessary artistic freedom, coupled with modern, nonrepresentational forms, made for difficulty in interpreting artistic production. However, to educate the public in the rigors of reading these works would give a broader audience a valuable way of looking through the minutiae of everyday life to the struggle for meaning in the modern world. This battle *Life* considered a worthy contest for its reader. The Round Table participants showed their concern that art might have become laconic, not so much nonrepresentational as unrepresentative.

Appreciation of such modern forms as abstract expressionism demanded education, discipline, and the self-effacement of the uninitiated before the work of masters. *The Family of Man* looked past the limited number of potential recruits for this exercise and spoke directly to a general population with a visual language already familiar through the popular media. These were the same people who read *Life* magazine: viewers who recognized that a picture was worth a thousand words and who assumed that whatever reading they formulated would be replicated in other people's minds. The exhibition was indeed "an apotheosis of *Life* magazine,"[63] so long as one could strip the phrase of its dismissiveness regarding taste and endow it with the assumptions of a general viewing or reading community.

Steichen's design was flamboyant but not whimsical; what Minor White saw as a filmic extravaganza was firmly lodged in a modernist aesthetic. Herbert Bayer, a German emigre with a fine modernist pedigree, had come to the United States in 1938 to supervise the installation of the first exhibition of Bauhaus work at the Museum of Modern Art.[64] His exhibitions had introduced American audiences to radical European design theories even before Steichen picked him to design *Road to*

Victory.[65] Bayer focused on how the viewer saw an exhibition and constructed a total environment that would force the viewer to interact with his installation.[66] Like Steichen, he focused on the theme of the exhibition rather than the architecture of the building into which it was placed.[67] The designer became, in effect, the author of the exhibition, who, because of his ability to manipulate the materials of expression, could fill whatever space could house his work. Even though Bayer had moved to Aspen, Colorado, before *The Family of Man* appeared, his influence could be seen in the challenge that Steichen presented to audiences and, as it turned out, to photographers and museum curators as well.

One could view *The Family of Man* as an extension of the modernist program of the museum. Steichen broke down what Walter Benjamin labeled as the connoisseurship of the image by fulfilling the potential of the work of art in the age of mechanical reproduction.[68] He recognized that he was manipulating mere examples, prints that could be drawn in any size and in infinite number from the negatives in his possession. By not attempting to match the high-gloss sacralization of the artistic photographic print, he lessened the distance between installation and audience, eliminating the aura of high art that enforced respectful distance. All the better to see the message. In fact, it became increasingly clear that the museum itself was unnecessary: the show *could* have been placed in Grand Central Terminal. Paul Rudolph's floor plan worked well for the rectangular space available at the Museum of Modern Art. However, because of its modular organization and its lack of need for security, the show could command any space big enough to fit the 503 images.

None of the photographs had frames; wheat paste was used to fix prints to masonite, and blocking behind raised each about an inch from the wall.[69] Many prints were grouped more closely together than at traditional exhibitions. Even though early in his career he had labored to create painterly images—even picturing himself in a self-portrait with easel in hand—Steichen did not treat these photographs as ersatz paintings. Paintings would have been hung a discreet distance from each other, at eye level, so that they could have been admired seriatim. Most photographic exhibitions—Stieglitz's famous 291 installations or even the shows of such twentieth-century photographers as Walker Evans or Robert Frank—imitated this style.

Finally, one could see in the formation of the exhibition a battle within modernism—between Steichen and the individual photographers—for artistic control of vision. Steichen was the victor, and John Szarkowski's comment was a recognition of defeat. If one viewed the exhibition as Steichen's work and not as his presentation of the assembled work of others, then *The Family of Man* offered one of the prime examples of a modernist event that appealed to a mass mediated audience. There was no doubt whose consciousness controlled the various utterances of the exhibition. For a man whose career had spanned the modernist period in the United States and who had, in fact, helped to define it through his pilgrimage to France well before the Armory Show, this exhibition represented a fulfillment.

Life magazine began 1954 with a look back to the year just concluded—one of the most extraordinary twelve-month periods since the end of the war. It is important for us to examine this rosy view of developing prosperity, for this special issue sketched the contours of the middle class to which *The Family of Man* spoke. The issues raised, the sequencing of the stories, the tone established, and the photographic point of view should echo the great exhibition, then in its formative stages, if the accusation were to hold that Steichen's work was merely the magazine redux. More important, the differences between *The Family of Man* and *Life* magazine can lead us to unraveling the welter of criticisms that has surrounded the exhibition since its time at the Museum of Modern Art. Should the exhibition have been criticized because of a faulty aesthetic—that Steichen knew how to sell an artistic view without demonstrating that he was a great artist?[70] As we have seen, such criticisms missed the point of the exhibition by viewing the museum as a context rather than as a platform. Should it be accused of ideological imprecision, a fuzzy, if not flaccid critique of the atomic order delivered as a by-your-leave from a consensual point of view, circumspect because it had something to lose? The focus on the bomb, to which we will return, showed that many contemporary critics have paged through Steichen's book without examining the rhetoric of the exhibition that so affected 1950s audiences. Should it be relegated to the dangerous and swampy middle ground of a 1950s battle between elite and popular culture? Let us turn to the January 4, 1954, issue of *Life*.[71]

The tone of this retrospective view of 1953 was the same as that enveloping the prints Miller examined: American circumstances were never better. Families lived in their own houses and enjoyed the prosperity of their industry. Material circumstances showed a preeminent nation still on the rise, and it was clear that the national culture was properly focused. "What we had done in 1953 was more than any nation had ever done. More people were employed, more buildings built, more paychecks raised than in 1952. The whole machine was geared to one job—feeding, housing, defending the U.S. family" (p. 2). Having attended to the welfare and security of its citizens, the political and economic genius of this country could be exported to other parts of the globe, specifically to Europe. Finally, through the ingenuity of men (and, possibly, women) the future development of this new world power was guaranteed, as a reassuring look ahead to the bicentennial year of 1976 portended.

The rhetoric of the issue was founded on the family, five examples of which were examined in some detail. An Arkansas family, headed by an insurance salesman, had prospered well enough in 1953 to buy a car. *Life* approved of "keeping the money in circulation" (p. 7) and kibitzed as Mr. Rector bought his wife a more extravagant diamond pin instead of a single-stone ring for their anniversary. Across the country, the Waterman family in Bakersfield, California, built two pools in the backyard, one, almost as an afterthought, just for the children, as a reward for a boom year in the agricultural chemicals business (p. 11). Both these families had earned over $20,000 for 1953, more than twice the national average.

Even families of more modest means had done well. A Georgia family pulling in only $5,000 nonetheless had enough leisure time for the man of the house to attend several model airplane meets out of the state and, in fact, follow his hobby to an international event in Yugoslavia (p. 8). The Denver household, earning slightly more than $10,000, did not reserve much money for entertainment outside the home but did splurge for its first television set in 1953 (p. 10). Only an Illinois farm family was portrayed as suffering financially—the decline in farm incomes in the early 1950s was undeniable after the relatively prosperous war years of full production—but even here Mr. Brown "had enough left over to pay half the $1,500 material costs for a trim little weekend cottage he and his father-in-law built" (p. 9).

None of the wives worked outside the home, proclaiming each family as middle class. Only two women supplemented the income of their husbands, but all contributed to the household through the domestic labor that signalled their containment.[72] The husband's role—that of the newly "domesticated man"—was limned in cartoons and accompanying text: because he now focused his attention on the home, the suburbanite husband was interested in power tools and in the supplies of the shade-tree mechanic and backyard builder (pp. 41–42). Teenagers were not left out of the picture. They were members of the "Luckiest Generation," part of a small cohort of depression-era babies who could have their pick of jobs in an economy that had expanded by 8 percent in the preceding year (pp. 27–28). Surrounding this locus of stability was a world under construction. "All across the U.S. people were coming upon familiar country fields and finding housing projects there, upon suburban street corners and finding brand new factories" (p. 31).[73] Such factories received laudatory attention in a photo essay showing that architectural style enhanced a healthy profit margin.

"Looking ahead 10 years, 25 years," the editors crowed, "there is nothing to hold us back" (p. 3). Certainly, nothing appeared on the eastern horizon. The map summoned up by Life showed the same terrain as David Potter was to describe in People of Plenty. The average American earned three times more than his English counterpart, six times more than an Italian, eleven times more than a Turk (p. 46). Underdeveloped countries were poor almost beyond comparison, if not redemption. The Life article devoted to the world economy was actually directed toward the Old World and seems oddly prescient in its advocacy of a united European market, then visible only as a coal and steel tariff agreement among selected countries. Viewed from forty years' distance, the tone seems all wrong, gloating, if not naive.

> To get enough food and raw materials to live in its accustomed style, Europe has had to rely more and more on the only source where their supply has greatly increased: the U.S. and Canada, dollarland. To make this harder, Europe's old investments in North America, once an easy source of dollars, have been largely liquidated. Britain, before the war the world's largest creditor, is now its largest debtor. Europe is like a great ship that used to stand in the roads surrounded by dhows, san-pans and lighters but is now soughing and listing by a New York dock (p. 48).

America, the new world power, must learn from its predecessor on the world stage, Great Britain, and spread the wealth, the article maintained, because only then would the United States be able to sell enough of its goods abroad.[74]

The language of the issue assumed economic growth, just as the indices of prosperity throughout the postwar volumes of the magazine were to be read through the accumulation of things. More than a million homes were built in 1953; the $34.7 billion spent on construction was mostly given over to industrial and commercial buildings, "impressive testimony to the faith industrial America has in its own future" (p. 31). Color televisions were licensed by the FCC in late 1953 for mass production in the year to come, and the world's first plastic sports car, the Corvette, brought a European thrill of driving within the grasp of the middle class. And if one were too carefree, a dent could be repaired with a blowtorch (p. 71). One Milwaukee teenager could "pick up enough money in odd jobs to buy stocks, all his own clothes, and a 1946 Plymouth as well" (p. 28). The American male, even the domesticated one, was the most essential producer of all.

> The average U.S. man used to wait until after his 24th birthday to get married. Now he goes to the altar when he is 22. As a newlywed he used to rent an apartment. Now he buys a house. He used to wait for several years before having his first child. Now after three years of marriage he is the father of two (p. 42).

This vocabulary celebrating abundance within particular American circumstances was foreign to *The Family of Man*. Connecting family members were the bonds of emotion, not the flow of goods and the pressures of a national economy. Man, woman, and child played roles within the family, but these were not specific to the affluence of the United States. Steichen was not interested in "dollarland." On the contrary, he frequently went to what was just then being christened the Third World for his examples of family life. Although he was not able to extricate himself from the values of his culture, Steichen was self-conscious about American power. His object was to erase the topography of economic inequity and depict man (and woman) without surrounding goods, with only the qualities of their souls, which, as we have seen, he assumed to be the same the world over.

Overt signs of power were handled differently as well. After having presented the American family, the *Life* issue offered an article on national defense. *Life* did not look back toward Korea but ahead toward the cold war against the Soviets. Armaments expenditures were hefty—11 percent of the nation's earnings in 1953—but the airplanes and missiles were considered worth the money. Furthermore, an early-warning system in the faraway Arctic, housed in "pressurized globe[s] of neoprene and Fiberglas" (p. 20), was being built to protect the American home and assure families that they did not have to move from the city to the less-developed suburban rim out of fear of enemy attack. This one article stood, like the Second Amendment to the Constitution, as a show of force among the happy reassurances and guarantees of American life. Steichen's portrayal of the bomb was carefully anticipated and segregated from the celebration of family life contained at the center of the exhibition. This was no afterthought: the power to destroy completely was a potential in the human mind rather than a problem to be fixed with technology and money.

By 1953 *Life* had learned to live with a bomb to which Steichen could not be reconciled. The March 30 issue featured an article entitled "A-Bomb vs. House" that described in split-second detail the horror of an atomic explosion, yet, for all its chronicling of the destruction of two model homes in the Nevada desert, the layout did not have the focused eloquence of Steichen's apparition. Two $18,000 sacrificial houses were blown apart by a nuclear blast that was witnessed by soldiers and ordinary citizens in trenches and by Civil Defense officials via television.[75] These two structures came as fully equipped as model units on a suburban tract. In fact, both had been furnished with synthetic inhabitants to recreate completely middle-class life: a family group in the living room, two small fry at quiet mischief at papa's back, and auntie, for some unexplained reason, still in her beach shorts and halter. And upstairs in a bedroom, a blonde asleep.[76]

What the remote control cameras documented shocked the technically informed Civil Defense witnesses, who saw clearly, unrealistically, in freeze-frame, the fundamental disintegration of matter. *Life* gave its readers a play-by-play of one house's demise in stills drawn from the filmed footage.

> At 1 7/8 seconds the concussion tears the roof off, rafters and all, causing it to balloon upward from the front of the house. The air is filled with flying lumber. By 2 1/3 seconds the first house on the American continent to be destroyed by atomic energy had been reduced to char and radioactivated kindling.[77]

A close-up survey of the remains confirmed what the camera portrayed: the destruction had been complete. However, one family dismembered, one blonde knocked askew, could not portray the scale of the bomb's destructive potential. By focusing on the particular, even the symbolically loaded family with a surplus blonde in bed, the panoramic scope of the atomic theater was lost. "To suggest with such scanty material the power of an atomic weapon was a good deal like trying to stage *Ben Hur* with a solitary chariot," *Life* acknowledged.[78]

The eyewitnesses to the event did not gain this sweeping recognition of destructive potential by their enforced, two-mile separation from the event. One woman commented: "I really didn't mind it at all. I rather suspected something much more violent." Even a Civil Defense observer, huddled in the forward trenches with army troops, was not impressed. *Life* commented that "he was inclined to rate the A-bomb as something between a heavy hand grenade and an artillery shell." No one was allowed to get closer than one mile after the explosion because of radioactivity, but a close perusal through field glasses revealed that

> When the damage was finally added up, the total was equivalent, in the judgment of an old police reporter, to what might be expected, in terms of cars, of a Fourth of July weekend on the Pennsylvania Turnpike, and, as regards houses, to a three-alarm fire.[79]

The test, which had been arranged to promote preparedness, was a failure because people had become inured to the mushroom cloud. *Life* could see this clearly and moralized to its audience: "When the first nuclear device exploded at Alamogordo, observers had the sense of being close to the infinite. Now it is depressingly plain that the bloom is off infinity's rose."[80]

As Peter B. Hales has insightfully pointed out, by 1953 Americans had anesthetized themselves to the destructive power of the mushroom cloud by inventing an atomic sublime. While recognizing the disintegration masked by the cloud, the beauty of the elemental chain reaction—the weird colors captured by the camera and the seemingly purposeful growth of the cloud to overwhelming heights—drew viewers to it.[81] This tension between horror and fascination was reflected in the focus of *Life* articles pertaining to the atom. From 1946 through 1955 most articles focused on the science of the nuclear reaction rather than on the destructive capabilities of the bomb. Only in 1946, when Hiroshima and Nagasaki were fresh in readers' minds, in late 1949 and early 1950, after the Soviet Union had exploded its first nuclear weapon, and in 1951 were there more articles about bombs than about the atomic reactions that could become, in President Eisenhower's phrase, "atoms for peace."[82]

The camera, a tool that had to be subdued by text, proved to be a potent weapon in reviving the power of the mushroom cloud. Occasionally, the magazine published evidence of a new technical accomplishment: the first successful test of an atomic artillery shell or the capturing of the first one-millionth of a second of a nuclear blast with a special camera.[83] Captions gave the technical details; pictures presented a more threatening experience. In the case of the artillery blast, for example, the distance between the familiar cloud and the military witnesses was foreshortened through the use of a telephoto lens. Don't worry, the magazine was compelled to reassure, we are not as close as we appear to be.

The best example of this dual view came after the first hydrogen bomb explosion was broadcast on American television in early April 1954. This test, code-named Operation Ivy, had incinerated an atoll in the Pacific and was clearly a new experience, scientifically and aesthetically. The scope of the reaction was so broad that even the head of the Atomic Energy Commission admitted that it was scarcely under control.

> A.E.C. Chairman Lewis Strauss informed a stunned nation that one
> H-bomb could incinerate a whole city, although he did cancel out the
> irrational notion that the tests had got out of hand and were liable to
> blow up the whole planet.[84]

A close-up photograph showed a "poisonous cloud surging up into the stratosphere, turgid with the remnants of Elugelab Island."[85] Merely hunkering down, as the citizenry was conditioned to do in case of an atomic attack, would not do the trick. The government had not blown up a couple of houses and created a one-mile hazard zone; it had caused an island to disappear and lethally contaminated everything within a four-mile diameter.

Life readers already knew that this new bomb could not be contained. The March 29 issue of the magazine had documented the misfortune of the Japanese fishing vessel *Fortunate Dragon*, which had had the bad luck of appearing downwind during the test.[86] Even though the ship was outside the danger zone, it was showered with radioactive ash, the remains of the atoll. Sailors lost their appetite and became ill, all the while suppressing what they had heard in Japan to be the effects of fallout. They barely made it back to Japan with their load of radioactive tuna. The picture of one fisherman was black and white, but the description was vivid enough to paint in the colors. His "face [was] almost black with blisters and a pus-like substance had flowed from his eyes and ears."[87] And within two weeks television viewers and Life readers had seen up close what the Japanese crew had witnessed as a glow over the horizon. The possibility of destruction had at once become human and overwhelming.

Life quickly reestablished textual distance on this test by including in an April 12 article maps of five cities with suggestions as to evacuation plans. The view, strategic, elevated, and detached, restored a feeling of command to Life readers. Significantly, this was one of the few forays by the magazine into postwar cityscape. A lot more would have to be known, Life admitted, about the urban forms and about their services, such as transportation and hospitals. Because of the denseness at the core and the expansiveness of suburban rings, urban citizens "would have to be drilled like an army."[88] Thus, a reaction to the anvil head of the new cloud, one hundred miles in diameter, was rationalized by literally putting the explosion in perspective. This disengagement occurred throughout the magazine's prose. An editorial in the April 12 issue pointed to the proper attitude.

> A world of two malevolent collosi is one in which none of this nation's
> political ideals can make itself at home. It is not a world of law nor is it a
> world of pluralistic balance in which freedom can thrive. It is a desperate
> world of survival, which requires us to be steadfast, but it also requires us
> to be politically creative, so that this world can change.[89]

The Family of Man made its audience concentrate on the bomb. Significantly, it had chosen a picture from Life magazine that had documented the disturbing Operation Ivy test. Steichen had gone to the expense of reproducing this photograph in color at the Kodak laboratory in Rochester; he wanted to capture the elemental emission of colored light that had so overawed viewers of the Pacific island explosion, even as it had transfixed the Japanese fishermen six minutes before the sonic evidence of the explosion had overwhelmed them. Furthermore, the glowing cloud in the exhibition was not shaped like the familiar, symmetrical mushroom; the H-bomb had created an aesthetic disjuncture, and Steichen made use of it before it, too, had been digested.

By the time Steichen's exhibition appeared, Life was busily cocooning the elemental annihilation of the hydrogen bomb with technical concerns. New weapons were explained as they were developed, and pictures of bombs became reflexive. There was as much fascination with the problems of taking pictures under such circumstances as with the subject. Destruction was elided into "radioactivity," a Life index category that first appeared in 1953 and consumed more and more attention as the decade progressed. Meanwhile, the nuclear geopolitics of the cold war absorbed more editorial attention from a magazine that knew a potent enemy when it saw one and recognized a friendly administration with which to ally. What Steichen saw did not depend on either the technical ability to see inside a bomb or a knowledge of nuclear reactions. He felt the horror and was sure he could convey it to a large audience.

Steichen focused on the urgency of his message. He looked beyond the specifics of class, taste, and education to the power of the collective entity, "the people," to reassert compassionate control over the affairs of men and nations by rediscovering common human bonds cutting across all classifications. The audience for the exhibition, whom Steichen assumed to be "the people," neophytes in the museum world, was, in fact, a burgeoning group remarkable enough to have drawn the attention of critics of popular culture, who adapted a familiar terminology to describe it. This crowd in search of culture was the middlebrow. In the April 11, 1949, issue of Life, the magazine, with the help of Harper's managing editor, Russell Lynes, attempted to map out the "everyday tastes" of postwar culture.[90] Using the familiar designations of "highbrow, middlebrow, and lowbrow," a grid helped readers discover that a proclivity for avocado and tomato differentiated their middlebrow salads from a more austere, highbrow concoction. Highbrow people did not wear hats, even in town, and preferred to read "little" magazines and avant-garde literature sitting in their Eames chairs. A balsam-stuffed pillow was the sure sign of lowbrow tastes. The highbrow dealt in original works of art, criticism of criticism, and the global thoughts of the shaggy sophisticate. The lowbrow picked out a chair for its comfort rather than its aesthetics and did not begrudge highbrow culture, so long as he (a lover of coleslaw, Westerns, and beer was definitely a he) did not have it inflicted on him. The middlebrow was bent on improvement of both mind and material circumstances and his or her acquisitiveness was an embarrassment to the highbrow and an annoyance to the low.

The February 1949 Harper's article to which this Life piece referred characterized the earnest middlebrow family and their emblematic possessions:

> a world of new two-door sedans, and Bendix washers, and reproductions
> of hunting prints over the living room mantel. It is a world in which the
> ingenuity and patience of the housewife are equaled only by the fidelity
> of her husband and his love of home, pipe, and radio. But it is a world of
> ambition as well, the constant striving for a better way of life—better fur-
> niture, bigger refrigerators, more books in the bookcase, more evenings at
> the movies. To the advertisers this is Americanism; to the highbrows this is
> the dead weight around the neck of progress, the gag in the mouth of art.[91]

Life articles, however, attempted to coax the upper middlebrow into complexity. The 1948 Round Table on modern art was Life magazine's "major pedagogic effort on behalf of modern art," and the article on the three brows attempted to recruit the upper middlebrow to an appreciation of serious culture.[92] The Round Table and profiles of modern painters, most notably Jackson Pollock, attempted to make the motivations, if not the expressions, of artists understandable.[93]

As a mass culture phenomenon housed in an institution of high culture, The Family of Man occupied ambiguous ground that destabilized these taste categories. It was enshrined in the same building with a great and demanding collection of modernist works, but it attempted to speak to the same audience that read *Life* magazine. One can see the Photography Department's attempt to reconcile the museum with its new visitors through the exhibition's appeal to different cultural constituencies. For example, Steichen and Dorothy Norman drew the written texts that were interspersed throughout the exhibition primarily from high and folk cultures. The exhibition anointed itself with the "seriousness" of elite writers but associated these recognized names with unfamiliar utterances from preliterate peoples and a few excerpts from novels from the best-sellers list. On the one hand there were aphorisms from the venerable Greeks:

> As the generation of leaves, so is that of men. (Homer)
> Music and rhythm find their way into the secret places of the soul. (Plato)
> Who is the slayer, who the victim? Speak. (Sophocles)

On the other hand there were sayings from a number of Native American tribes, including:

> Before me peaceful,
> Behind me peaceful,
> Under me peaceful,
> Over me peaceful,
> All around me peaceful . . . (Navajo Indian)
> Behold this and always love it! It is very sacred, and you must treat it as such . . .
> (Sioux Indian)

Quotations from the Bible, the Bhagavad Gita, and Lao-tze were balanced with Maori, African, and Russian folk sayings. William Blake appeared, and so did John Masefield, William Shakespeare and St. John Perse, Montaigne and George Sand, and Thomas Jefferson and Tom Paine. The only living persons whose thoughts were excerpted for the exhibition were Bertrand Russell and Albert Einstein, both of them anointed with the Nobel Prize.

The verbal embellishments of *The Family of Man* were secondary to the photographs, and few of the images that were selected to represent the medium for this show were in themselves icons of the art of photography. *Migrant Mother* by Dorothea Lange certainly qualified, but it was relegated to one of the baffles along the left-hand wall and not given a prominent spot. W. Eugene Smith's concluding photograph would have been recognized by many, but it would perhaps have summoned up the 1954 advertising campaign for General Electric, which had featured *The Walk to Paradise Garden*, and not the artistic stature of the photographer or his creation. Aside from these few familiar images, the photographs were not presented to overwhelm the audience with their artistry. In fact, they were brought closer to this audience through the much-publicized methods of their production, all the better to convey Steichen's message.

The exhibition presented photography as a doubly democratic medium: not only could anyone read a photograph, but anyone could produce one worth showing off, maybe even inside a museum. Steichen had advertised that both professional and amateur photographers were represented in the show. Even though most of the images were produced by professionals, the aura of amateur participation was important. Some of the work of the professionals resembled the snapshot of the amateur: Ralph Crane's seemingly candid shot of a couple on the beach, Gary Winogrand's rapid-fire capturing of a male bather playfully throwing his female companion into the water, Robert Doisneau's pictures of lovers in Paris. No doubt, the easily available technology of photography also allowed the amateur to mimic the craft of the professional. The sharp focus of almost all *The Family of Man* photographs revealed their intentionality and their artfulness. There were few snapshots in the exhibition, but the artifice of spontaneity was important for the construction of a world family album.[94]

Steichen prospered in this middle ground between art and craft, aesthetics and information. He had turned to fashion photography and advertising assignments in the 1920s and comfortably employed artistic methods in a career shaped by the culture of pre-World War II consumption of goods, images, and celebrities. His 1940s experience in the Pacific had given him the opportunity to speak to the broadest audience possible; he had found the single event of the decade that transcended all cultural classifications, where technique could transmit a patriotic, forthrightly important message. Now, in the cold war era, he sought to reestablish this middle ground in a world divided into competing ideologies. He fought against an Us and a Them by asserting that there was a common humanity, a We ("We two form a multitude"). His effort was obscured by the fact that he assumed that, at some level, everyone would want to become like us: his was an American vision of a one-world order. This was not his conscious intention but was embedded in his assumptions about human nature.

Steichen did not engage in the job of clarifying cultural forms as did critics in the weekly and monthly press. His homilies drove the critic Dwight Macdonald to devote an acerbic footnote to the exhibition in the middle of his important essay, "Masscult and Midcult." The heat was apparent five years after the fact.

> The editorializing was insistent—the Midcult audience always wants to be Told—and the photographs were marshalled to demonstrate that although there are real Problems (death, for instance), it's a pretty good old world after all.[95]

He associated this earnestness with the Book-of-the-Month Club, or the Film Department of the Museum of Modern Art, which had stooped to honor a Hollywood producer, or, in another essay, with the popular Great Books program of Mortimer Adler and the Encyclopedia Britannica. Like Adler's shelf of tomes, this erudition could now be sold by the foot. "The chief negative aspect," he observed, "is that so far our Renaissance, unlike the original one, has been passive, a matter of consuming rather than creating. . . ."[96]

Dwight Macdonald attacked midcult from above: the Book-of-the-Month Club, the PTA, earnest symphony societies, and reading groups—all were signs of the jejune aspirations and acquisitiveness of the suburban, middle-class order. The art critic Clement Greenberg supplied a term, *kitsch*, for the appropriation of aesthetic forms by the uninitiated (which term Macdonald adapted for his own use), and re-inforced his critique with the Marxist vocabulary of class analysis. In an article published during *The Family of Man*'s tenure at the Museum of Modern Art, Leslie Fiedler argued for the value of popular culture, the product of lowbrow taste.[97] In validating such semiliterate forms of culture, however, Fiedler created an enclave for those who preferred comic books to Shakespeare. The real enemy, as far as he was concerned, was those who ventured over the line into other taste categories. New universities, he complained, were institutions where degrees could be purchased. Here Classics Illustrated was not cartoon entertainment but a study aid.

Steichen fought against the containment strategies articulated by these critics.[98] His sentimental humanism assumed that the perils to world order, national hatreds, and injustices were ephemeral when compared with the enduring facts of human nature. He therefore created in *The Family of Man* an expanding middle ground that ignored Manichean cold war ideologies and entrenched canons of taste by forcing them farther off to the side. It was not his purpose to fight against high culture, nor was he out to pander to the taste of the vulgar. The photographs included were neither pretentiously imitative of art shots nor graphic in their sensationalism. He was indifferent to both in his attempt to exhibit a visual message with the broadest possible vocabulary. In service of this goal, any material became fair game. The exhibition defied class-oriented categories by ignoring differences caused by class. Its architecture and its narrative were crafted to gather everyone in.

Joan Shelley Rubin has reminded us recently that scholars have "reified and perpetuated the conventional dichotomy between 'high' and 'popular' culture, overlooking the interaction between the two."[99] Andrew Ross's study of intellectuals and popular culture, *No Respect*, hits even closer to the mark: the ability to classify, to bracket an amorphous middle with a clearly identifiable high and low brought to the analyst the taxonomic power of cultural authority. More than taste was being objectified. As Russell Lynes commented:

> Highbrow, lowbrow, upper middlebrow, and lower middlebrow—the
> lines between them are sometimes indistinct, as the lines between upper
> class, lower class, and middle class have always been in our traditionally
> fluid society. But gradually they are finding their own levels and confining
> themselves more and more to the company of their own kind.[100]

By attempting to describe these basic cultural elements, Ross asserted, intellectuals were striving for the power of the cartographer, the geologist, the namer of parts. Lynes's consciousness of this control, expressed before the 1950s began, accounts for the sardonic view that this avowedly upper- middlebrow editor sketched of intellectuals who attempted to control without participating. There was, in fact, a widespread rejection by these intellectuals—among them Macdonald and Fiedler—of the middlebrow culture. The classifications that developed into a working vocabulary for the description of culture came to be considered natural, creating a hierarchy of taste that, too, seemed to be stable, predictable, and, in some cases, deliciously lamentable.[101]

The defining of class boundaries gave more than cultural control to the critic or a voice to the editorial combatant. As artists in the 1950s discovered, embellishing the figure of the alienated intellectual paradoxically also helped make a living. Bradford Collins has suggested that abstract expressionists contributed to the image of their own alienation from mainstream culture because a newly evolving commodity, the career of the Bohemian artist, demanded an oppositional persona. The *Life* magazine feature, photographed by Nina Leen, on the "Irascible Group of Advanced Artists" who had refused to participate in a juried show at the Metropolitan Museum of Art represented both a protest against that institution's antimodernism and a willing co-optation that increased the artists' celebrity through the *Life* feature.[102]

Russell Lynes, who had some experience dealing with the Museum of Modern Art, showed in his 1954 book, *The Tastemakers*, how a cultural phenomenon could migrate from one classification to another. The *Life* grid had shown high-, middle- and lowbrow manifestations in contemporary culture. His revision for the 1954 volume, which carried his 1949 essay verbatim, classified creative works over time. Here a work by Whistler appeared in all categories: first as "*Arrangement in Grey and Black, No 1* (Highbrow—1870s and 1880s)," then as "*Portrait of the Artist's Mother* (Middlebrow—1910s and 1920s)," and finally as "*Whistler's Mother* (Lowbrow—1940s and 1950s)."[103] Consciousness of technique yielded to a biographical identification, which, in turn, surrendered to the meager shorthand of the mass reproduction. Neither the museum nor the artist could predict the appetites of consumers of culture.

The Family of Man self-consciously placed itself in the public realm and sought to be taken seriously. In the same way that David Riesman's *The Lonely Crowd* provided a vocabulary for character types in postwar prosperity—inner-directed, other-directed, autonomous—the exhibition provided a way of seeing things: the nuclear family attempting to live out the implications of this pun in a new world in which to survive meant to discover the enduring elements of human behavior. In self-consciously striving for status as a cultural expression, the exhibition should have been subject to the categories, proposed by intellectuals, that attempted to describe the middle class's ascendancy in the 1950s. However, as a complex cultural text that was read by intellectuals, museum goers, and book purchasers, *The Family of Man* both epitomized and transcended terms such as *middlebrow*, *midcult*, and *kitsch*.

The exhibition did, in fact, draw many of its themes and its photographs from *Life* magazine, in search of the same audience for the museum exhibition as appeared at the newsstand every week. This does not trivialize *The Family of Man*, because, as we have seen, the magazine responded to many of the defining concerns of middle-class life in the first half decade of the 1950s: prosperity, nuclear war, a public culture, even the construction of a vocabulary for discussing broad aspects of the culture. Steichen refined this point of view throughout the exhibition and sharpened it by presenting a nuclear blast in quite literally a different light. If we are to examine the middle-class culture of the 1950s as more than a collection of urges gratified, longings for gender equality deferred, and national might indulged, then *The Family of Man* should be required viewing.

The cover of the February 14, 1955, issue of *Life* displayed a photograph by Wayne Miller of his family. Inside was a nineteen-picture spread on *The Family of Man*, accompanied by one installation shot of the family portraits. This was, the magazine proclaimed, "the most ambitious photographic exhibition ever held." The logistics of assembly were once again repeated to verify this point. The scope of Steichen's vision was suggested by the captions in the *Life* layout, each of which named a human quality or emotion and identified a place where a person experienced it: "Compassion in Korea," "Withdrawal in an Ohio Insane Asylum," "Tribal Instruction in Bechuanaland." Page headings surveyed some of the larger themes of the exhibition: "Harmony in work and play," "Loneliness—even among many," "Tensions turned to dread and hate." Steichen's accomplishment was clear: "portraying the emotions which all members of the human family share, no matter in what country or at what stage of civilization they live."[104]

The preview of this photo essay about a photographic text, appearing just over the table of contents, retold the story of the exhibition's assembly: how Steichen had gone to Europe to seek out photographers, how Wayne Miller had labored through the *Life* files, how Steichen had been exhausted by the whole process, how he had finally found a way to shape these 503 images into a coherent text and had danced a little jig in front of the nightclub on 52nd Street.[105] The magazine was less explicit about how it had rewritten Steichen's text through its selection. All but one of the temporal references in *The Family of Man* were removed. Only one photograph included a preposition that implied any sense of time: Henri Cartier-Bresson's picture, captioned "Panic as Communists Approach Shanghai." The *Life* selection ended with another Cartier-Bresson picture, "Prayerful meditation by the morning light in Kashmir," taken from the convex death panels. Andreas Feininger's photo, captioned "Anonymity in a Fifth Avenue crowd," appeared much earlier, as one of two pictures on loneliness. Steichen's construction of death and transcendence was transformed into a homily on piety—"Fellowship in silent faith" was the heading on the concluding page. With the exception of the Shanghai picture—one that had originally appeared in *Life*—none of the pictures along the socially conscious left-hand wall were selected. The bomb was nowhere in sight, nor was the bomb included in the book version of the exhibition.[106]

This book, the enduring record of the exhibition, was published by Jerry Mason, who had approached Steichen in 1954 about the possibility of such a volume. The older man was skeptical of Mason's ability to land the project with a publisher but supported the effort. He had brought several publishers to the loft, but none had expressed any enthusiasm for the mass appeal of what they regarded as a picture book. Mason came up to the loft to examine the final stages of the work in progress and saw to it that the book appeared before the exhibition closed at the Museum of Modern Art. While Steichen and Leo Lionni produced the final dummy, Mason committed his own money to publication costs and sought a distributor. Wayne Miller remembers that Steichen offered advice regarding the quality of the cover of the paperback—suggesting that a coated stock might be used so that pictures could be put inside front and back covers. This would cost an extra $500, Mason estimated, which Steichen himself was prepared to pay. Mason declined the contribution and paid for the additional quality himself. Without Mason's enterprise, Wayne Miller summarizes, there would not have been a book.[107]

The volume faithfully represented the content of the exhibition. With the exception of the bomb picture, all photos were reproduced—the Peruvian piper once again acting as a leitmotif. Mason published the book himself through his firm, Maco Press, but it was quickly picked up by Simon and Schuster. During most of his career, Mason developed projects and then handed them to established publishing houses with whom he shared profits. He concentrated on layout and on identifying volumes that would be attractive to both a publishing house and the public. *The Family of Man*, his first large project, showed that he had a fine sense of his market.

However, a book cannot replicate such an exhibition. Were this a traditional photographic display, a book would have done it justice: the catalogs of Walker Evans, for example, replicate in the size and the visual relationship to the viewer the exhibitions they commemorate. *The Family of Man* images, however, were not made to be viewed one at a time, or even in the rectilinear groupings of a two-page spread. Depth of field, peripheral vision, the relationships among images of greatly different sizes, not to mention the restricted ability of the reader to meander through a large number of images regimented by sequential numbering and glued to an inflexible spine, made the experience of paging through the book very different from confronting the images at the Museum of Modern Art.

The exhibition spoke directly to the audience of 1955 and was destroyed. The book, designed to commemorate the look of the exhibition, had history in mind and has endured, but, ironically, it had lost the reading that tied Steichen's work most closely to its audience. The bomb was not there. One can only speculate why, since both Steichen and, more recently, Mason, are now dead. Miller's explanation—that a color picture was not practical in a black-and-white volume retailing for one dollar—is commonsensical but tantalizingly incomplete. Since the bomb was represented in all of the traveling versions of the exhibition, it cannot be that Steichen was retreating from his view over the edge of human rationality into the crater of annihilation. On the contrary, it could be that he avoided constricting a representation of fundamental annihilation to the rectangular confines of a book layout in which it could be compared to other images. In any case, the bomb was left out.

The decision that brought *The Family of Man* its millions of sales lay it open to criticism, particularly as viewers became more familiar with this retelling than with Steichen's original statement. In fact, one can look in vain through contemporary criticisms of Steichen's work for any recognition that there had been a nuclear argument in the arrangement of the photographs just before the invocation of the United Nations. To see the specter of the bomb in this volume—filling in this visual elision—is to place it more securely in 1950s America and to recover some of the demonstrable effect that it had on its viewers.

The Family of Man has suffered from its own success. It spoke earnestly to the middle class of the 1950s, to what Steichen considered representative citizens who could be persuaded to change their view of the world. In doing so, it became enmeshed in the battle of definitions that consumed cultural criticism. It assumed that a story could be told through photographs, and that this narrative would be clear and consistently interpreted by the viewing public. Inevitably, *The Family of Man* was subject to reinterpretation during and after the Vietnam War, when critics such as Susan Sontag, Jonathan Green, and Allan Sekula paged through the book that became for them an anthology of 1950s middle-class sentimentalism and insensitivity. The book representing Steichen's work used sentiment as an active force in drawing the world together; this offended Sontag, who saw in Steichen's work a tradition of anesthetizing viewers to the pain of reality.[108] For Green, to picture reality was to show the unseemly, to root beneath facades.[109] The insensitivity transferred to Steichen by Sekula and Sontag, in particular, was framed by a view of Third World exploitation taken from Southeast Asia.[110] Steichen's anthropology was anathema to these critics; his point that people were the same underneath all cultures disturbingly approached the assertion that all cultures different from ours were to be subjugated or erased.

The Family of Man used the material available to it to speak to an audience it considered representative of a democracy newly emergent as a world power. Its sense of human characteristics was formed by the photographer/world tourist, dominated by the generalizations of a man approaching the end of his life, and tempered by the experiences, both reassuring and horrific, of the recently concluded war years. Steichen responded directly to the most important threat to humankind—nuclear weapons—in a truly global theater. To criticize the exhibition from the perspective of the 1990s, with all that we have come to know about the ambiguity of photographs and the power of technology to subjugate cultures around the world, is too easy. We need to be able to account for the legitimate seriousness with which the exhibition approached its task and for its impact in 1950s culture. This impact can be traced throughout the world, although, as we shall see, the nature of the message, and the purposes of the messenger, made for a cacophony of reverberations.

Edward Steichen aboard the aircraft carrier Lexington, *Pacific Theater, World War II. Photo: National Archives.*

Steichen and some of the 10,000 photographs from which the final selection for The Family of Man *was made.*
Photo: Homer Page.

Steichen and his chief assistant, Wayne Miller, formed a close, familial relationship. Photo: Homer Page.

Joan Miller helped select photographs relating to women and children. Photo: *Wayne F. Miller, courtesy Magnum Photos.*

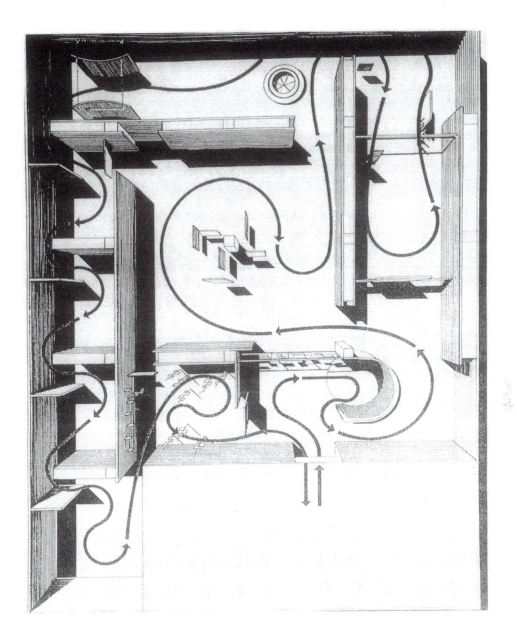

The floor plan for the exhibition in the Museum of Modern Art, 1955.
Viewers were led through symbolic moments in the life of the family and then introduced to themes
in private and civic experience. The exhibition broke all attendance marks at the museum.

Family portraits formed the center of the exhibition. Photo © 1955 by Ezra Stoller, Esto Photographics.

The ring-around-the-rosy carousel of children led to the convex death panels and the anonymous crowd of Fifth Avenue beyond. Photo © 1955 by Ezra Stoller, Esto Photographics.

The nine portraits of the last baffle on the side wall prepared viewers for the solitary death of a Korean War soldier and the thematic climax in the room beyond. Photo © 1955 by Ezra Stoller, Esto Photographics.

Viewers moved from the room in the front lefthand corner to confront portraits mounted at right angles to the wall. The presentation reinforced the message, "We two form a multitude": the photographs were mounted on a picture of the General Assembly of the United Nations. Photo © Ezra Stoller, Esto Photographics.

Page 182 from The Family of Man. The book version of The Family of Man thinned the texture of the message as it flattened the presentation into two dimensions. Photo courtesy Museum of Modern Art, New York.

Pages 94–95 from The Family of Man. This ring-around-the-rosy layout encouraged readers to view the world in a single glance. Photo courtesy Museum of Modern Art, New York.

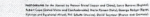

by JOHN GODFREY MORRIS

PEOPLE ARE PEOPLE THE WORLD OVER

"People are people the world over." A Ladies' Home Journal series (1848–1949) used a similar layout to satisfy the browsing curiosity of readers in family life throughout the world.

Institute for Advanced Study, Princeton. Eisenstaedt. Life

Allentown, Pa. Nina Leen. Life

Institute for Advanced Study, Princeton. Ernst Haas. Magnum. Vogue

125

Page 125 from The Family of Man. The book retained some of Steichen's favorite juxtapositions, such as this one between a self-assured youth and a perplexed master. Photo courtesy Museum of Modern Art, New York.

Bachuanaland, Nat Farbman Life

The little ones leaped, and shouted, and laugh'd

And all the hills echoed . . .

William Blake

Page 35 from The Family of Man. The captions, chosen for the project by Dorothy Norman,
set up contexts that asserted universal truths for some, but, for others, were founded on faulty anthropological assumptions.
Photo courtesy Museum of Modern Art, New York.

The exhibition's import was amplified by its use of three-dimensional space. Visitors could see through the introductory lucite panel to the family portraits and Ansel Adams's Mount Williamson on the back wall. Photo: National Archives.

The photographs received families in a personal embrace. Here Wayne Miller's son plays with the crushed marble below the family portraits. Photo: Wayne F. Miller, courtesy Magnum Photos.

The exhibit also encouraged discussion of larger questions. This Wayne Miller photograph of his family is the only published representation of the hydrogen bomb picture. Photo: Wayne F. Miller, courtesy Magnum Photos.

From the beginning, The Family of Man was a media event and Steichen became its most illustrious publicist, granting interviews in the exhibition space. Photo: Wayne F. Miller, courtesy Magnum Photos.

chapter

THE FAMILY OF MAN ON THE MOVE

three

BETWEEN 1955 AND 1962 THE FAMILY OF MAN WAS ON THE MOVE. IN SEVERAL international editions it appeared in thirty-eight countries and was seen by over 9 million people. It became a complex touristic site. As we have seen, the exhibition was assembled from the photographs of a newly available world and responded to the curiosity of an American middle-class public about distant lands. Its bags packed or, to sharpen the analogy, packed in bags, the installation itself played the part of the tourist: it visited Lebanon shortly after marine troops had performed a well-publicized landing at Beirut; it toured Yugoslavia as an emissary to the renegade Communist leader, Marshall Tito; remembrances of Hiroshima included as propitiation, it stopped in Tokyo and at Ground Zero itself; when Vice-President Nixon debated Premier Khrushchev in Moscow in 1959, it was on the periphery of the crowd.

This grand tour was underwritten by the United States Information Agency (USIA), which contributed its worldwide logistical network to the seven-year effort. The Family of Man was already a valuable exhibition when it was presented to this agency. We must examine this work as a commodity in the cultural diplomacy of the postwar period, a context little related to photography but intertwined with the message of Steichen's collection. To assess the cultural capital of the exhibition, we must see the economy in which it received its worth—the fledgling bureaucracy of the USIA. We also must remind ourselves of the person who saw most clearly the use and value of these photographs in both the host country and in the dangerous domestic context of anti-Communist enthusiasms and congressional investigations— the foreign service officer. Finally, we must trace, as best we can, the course of The Family of Man throughout the world.

This exercise is not limited to following the enthusiastic circulation of the version that we have so closely examined at the Museum of Modern Art. The Family of Man was reproduced in four full-size versions. The first to be displayed began its life at the Corcoran Gallery in Washington, D.C., and then departed for Western Europe. Later in 1955 Guatemala City premiered a second copy, which made a stop in Mexico City before being sent to India.[1] These two full-size versions and the anticipated expense of two more at a reduced scale cost the agency slightly more than $180,000.[2] The smaller versions, however, graduated to full replicas as the success of the exhibition spread, and by summer 1957 a copy could be seen in Scandinavia or in Central and South America. Even these four were not the only collections on tour. Under a Museum of Modern Art contract with a Tokyo publishing company, one full-size and two smaller versions toured Japan. These copies were produced in Japan with negatives furnished by the museum. The museum also circulated two smaller versions in North America, one staying mostly east of the Mississippi, the other starting in Dallas and heading through Omaha toward a lengthy stay in Canada.[3]

Steichen periodically received memoranda from both the museum and the USIA that attested through impressive statistics to the overwhelming success of this elaborate tour. The exhibition had made ninety-one stops in the thirty-eight countries visited by 1962. In Japan, 621,000 people saw one of the three versions, including 28,700 during a two-week stay in Hiroshima in October 1956. Over 1.5 million Indians filed past the photographs in the subcontinent. The stop in Belgrade brought 275,000, more than half the population of the city, to The Family of Man. Head counts in the United States were similarly impressive: 37,600 in Minneapolis, 116,214 in Dallas, 113,991 in Cleveland, and a whopping 311,686 at the Museum of Science and Industry in Chicago.[4] Glancing over these memos, Steichen must have seen verification of his assumption about the worldwide appeal of his photo collection. A staff member had a more sardonic response. The photographs, she penciled in one of the margins of a page of statistics, had been everywhere "except Antarctica."[5]

The measure of the exhibition's success lay in more than admission figures. Printed copies of the pictures were equally popular. The USIA distributed magazine-format previews of the exhibit in advance of each showing and in many countries gave The Family of Man book gratis to leading citizens and to those who caused the turnstile to reach a significant number. In the City Museum of Amsterdam, for example, books were handed out to the 10,000th, 25,000th, 50,000th, and 100,000th visitors. Still, it was reported through Washington to Jerry Mason, 4,414 books were sold and they "could have sold up to 11,000 if available." In the Netherlands, as in all countries, there had been extensive press coverage from "practically all newspapers, some giving it full page and front page coverage, including favorable treatment by the left wing and Communist dailies."[6]

This still was not the extent of the USIA's effort or the exhibition's return. In October 1955 the USIA in Washington announced to all posts the availability of a four-and-a-half-minute filmed introduction to The Family of Man, shot during the exhibition's stop at the Corcoran Gallery. This program, showing the gallery, the installation, and a portion of Steichen's introductory speech, was intended for local television broadcast. The segment was available in English or in a silent version so that local announcers could dub in their own narration. A five-minute lecture was also available in English, with Steichen's voice lowered at intervals for local translations. Or the entire presentation could be obtained in Spanish, French, German, Dutch, Japanese, and Tagolog.[7] Later that year, a longer USIA film appeared, drawing an admiring description from a 1957 Museum of Modern Art memo.

> The USIA has made more than 300 prints of the 26-minute black-and-
> white "Family of Man" film, which is available in both 16mm and 35mm. In

addition to the English language, the audio part of the film has been translated into the following 22 languages: Spanish, Portuguese, Persian, Hindi, Tamil, Teluga, Bengali, Urdu, Turkish, Arabic, Greek, Serbo-Croat, German, Italian, Japanese, Danish, French, Icelandic, Dutch, Norwegian, Swedish and Finnish. Of the more than 300 prints, 115 are in English and the rest in these foreign languages. To date the film is being shown in commercial theatres in Mexico, Bolivia, Honduras, Chile, Uruguay, India, Netherlands, Pakistan, and Kenya. The film is being screened in 70 overseas countries.[8]

The languages used in the clips and the twenty-six-minute film sketch a strategic map of the non-Communist world, as seen by the USIA: Western Europe, the best allies against the new foe; Latin America, the traditional sphere of influence; and countries in the great gap between NATO-member Turkey and the recently subdued and occupied Japan. This area included a former colony, the Philippines (Tagolog had appeared next to Japanese as an Asian linguistic priority); countries being courted or influenced by the United States, like Iran, where the shah had been reinstalled recently; and the emerging nonaligned countries, represented by India or, shortly before *The Family of Man* reached its capital city, Indonesia.

The exhibition was not designed with the USIA in mind; however, the agency did not have to coerce changes in the exhibition, just as it did not have to screen the talks of the willing academics whose foreign tours it began to sponsor in the 1950s. The connection between the photographs and the overseas information bureaucracy was no doubt aided by Nelson Rockefeller, whose family supported the museum and who had supervised the information/propaganda link with Latin America during World War II. Taken on its own terms, *The Family of Man* must have been an attractive commodity to the agency. The exhibition was made available at a particular moment in the USIA's brief history and fulfilled a welcome role in the way the agency defined itself. Steichen surrendered control of the photographs and became an interested spectator, occasionally rendezvousing with *The Family of Man* as it toured the world.

From around the world, public affairs officers in American embassies cabled back to Washington their appreciation for what *The Family of Man* had given them. As we shall see, the collection of photographs responded so well to both local circumstances and demands from Washington that reports from Berlin to Beirut were uniformly positive. Only a handful of the evaluative reports from public affairs officers in individual countries survive, and so we have an imperfect view of the exhibition's long tour. Even if more of these cables had been archived, we would not be able to reconstruct the specific message that each embassy was trying to portray or to decipher the complex reading given the photographs by individual viewers who had stepped into this universe of images from their particular cultural circumstances. The best that we can do is to trace the dislocation of the exhibition from both its original site and its grounding rhetoric. In order to do this we must examine the agency that put the photographs to such good use.

As was the case with *The Family of Man*, the origin of the USIA lay in World War II and the aftermath of American dominance and prosperity. Like the exhibition, the structure of the agency was determined during the early 1950s, and, before the exhibition was exported, it was subject to criteria of taste and utility inherent in the distinction between *culture* and *information* within the USIA. By the time Steichen's installation left its first stop in sweltering Washington for its foreign tours, the agency had established lines of authority, bolstered by a bureaucratic rhetoric and sharpened by confrontations with Congress that overpowered what *The Family of Man* had to say.

Steichen's photographs could not compete with the aggressive marketing of America throughout the world. The expanding network of corporate, cultural, and governmental systems made the American way of life a familiar, if not attainable commodity. We are accustomed to seeing this global influence through corporate products or through the lens of foreign-policy objectives. Cars and television sets, American marketing techniques, American military bases, and doctrines emanating from the White House are familiar indices of the stature of a world power. Cultural commodities were handled in the same way. Through the Architectural Advisory Panel of the State Department the commissioning of designs for American embassies became exercises in binational cultural diplomacy. The European Recovery Administration sponsored both Hollywood film distribution and its own series of documentaries, through which European allies were to interpret both idealized American life and their own developing aspirations. In each of its exhibition sites, the USIA refashioned Steichen's work to fit the structure of this internationalized Americanism. The particular domestic exhortations and appeals of the exhibition were lost amid the contexts of individual display environments. The sophisticated aesthetics and the directness of the message about family life made the collection a valuable commodity in the commerce of cultural diplomacy. The beauty of the photographs, the skill of their arrangement, and the celebrity of Edward Steichen made an expansive and useful comment about the culture from which *The Family of Man* sprang.

The USIA deployed the exhibition for almost a decade to good effect throughout the world. Such a cultural commodity also fit the evolving role of the agency extraordinarily well; in short, it spoke well of both the culture that produced it and the agency that displayed it. Steichen's work had its worth within Washington bureaucracies unaccustomed to the strategic imperative of portraying American society to foreign audiences. The USIA had to explain to a domestic audience why an agency devoted to providing information about American life and civic values was necessary. Congress examined the ideological purity of the message delivered in especially excruciating detail during the first three years of the decade, when the fledgling bureaucracy of the Information Agency was vulnerable to attack. The agency charged with projecting American values abroad was formed under the harsh scrutiny of congressional committees that questioned the intentions of this new messenger. Finally, the exhibition's message about the universality of family life reflected well on the characters of those who delivered this message. The exhibition was as popular with the USIA as it was with the audiences who saw the photographs.

During World War II the government production of "information" was handled by two offices that anticipated in their different purposes the schizophrenic sense of mission of the USIA in the 1950s. The Office of Strategic Services (OSS) engaged in active psychological warfare against the Axis. This was applied through culture studies: how to use local knowledge to insinuate, dissemble, and persuade in the service of a cause recognized to be just. The Office of War Information (OWI) gave friendly civilian populations an account of war activities. The model for this function was the British Broadcasting Corporation, which managed to be informative and patriotic at the same time. The OSS embraced propaganda; the OWI professed to hold the term at a news reporter's arm's length. The OSS could issue disinformation; the OWI reported facts, with a pro-Allied twist. Both portrayed the struggle between the Allied and Axis powers as a battle between good and evil. It was the OWI that prohibited the picturing of individual American war dead until late in the war and did not allow cameras to personalize these casualties by showing their faces. Neither office was dispassionate; uniting them was a conviction that American virtue and heroism were under fire.

Information about both foreign and domestic cultures continued to be a valuable commodity after 1945, when one enemy took the place of another. With the end of the war came the demobilization of the war apparatus, including the two offices. OWI officers were given the opportunity to continue in the State Department's information service, and many from the OSS joined the newly formed Central Intelligence Agency. The new enemy and a form of warfare based on ideology increased the need for an information agency to represent the United States government abroad in this cold war—the first such peacetime effort in American history. The battle with the Soviet Union was fought on the ground of European reconstruction and in the confusing crazy quilt of emerging Third World nationalisms. The weapon was persuasion. When American congressmen examined Europe during the formative years of the late 1940s, they found a massive Soviet propaganda campaign all over the continent.[9] Until the 1950s the federal government downplayed its role in portraying American culture abroad, but private groups and industry coalitions were simply no match for a centralized Soviet effort. The 1948 Smith-Mundt Act led to the 1952 creation by the United States government of the International Information Administration (IIA) as the arm of the State Department that would project American interests abroad. The idea, as one commentator has put it, was "to 'sell' America."[10]

Selling America may have established an appropriately capitalistic metaphor for this new competition with the Soviets, but the vocabulary of the pitch gained its power in the consummate hard sell of World War II, "when terms like 'freedom,' 'democracy,' and 'the free world' could be used without a trace of cynicism or self-consciousness and with the expectation that they would strike a responsive chord."[11] Even those in the IIA who believed in the soft sell—in merely portraying the ways in which American interests were shared by people all over the world—were tied to the loaded vocabulary of early-1950s America. As Frank Ninkovich, an astute commentator on post–World War II cultural diplomacy, asserts, "the State Department, by conscripting the principle of freedom, repudiated the distinction between the world of politics and the world of ideas."[12] All branches of the IIA devoted to the media, informational programming, and educational exchanges were employed in projecting American freedoms onto the world.

Nowhere in the IIA was this mission more vitally felt than in the International Broadcasting Service, whose Voice of America, which received almost 25 percent of IIA appropriations, insured that a mixture of politics and ideas was broadcast throughout the world, particularly behind the Iron Curtain. The rest of the information apparatus plodded along. For several years, through the final months of the IIA, programs and policies were set in Washington and then distributed to an increasing number of embassies and consulates around the world. In 1953, just before the USIA was formed, the procedure was reversed, and individual country plans and regional desks insured a more direct appeal to Washington offices. The switch in policy was given an appropriately military description: the IIA had switched from the shotgun to the rifle approach. All the while the Voice of America beamed overhead, lobbed from a battery of offices in New York toward an increasing number of shortwave sets in emerging nations and through the jamming efforts of the Soviets. Before the formation of the USIA, the role of information had become doubly ideological within the federal government. The message abroad was orthodox rather than representative. The bureaucracy at home was subjugated to the jingoistic scrutiny of anti-Communist crusades.

Enter Joseph McCarthy, during the year of his ascendancy, 1953. During February and March of that year, the Voice of America was subjected to televised hearings by the Permanent Subcommittee on Investigations of the United States Senate, with the junior senator from Wisconsin presiding. The Republican Party had just attained the majority in the Senate, and this was the first inquisition under McCarthy's direction. The timing was propitious for the high drama that this showman would create. The Korean War was hardening into compromise. Ethel and Julius Rosenberg, convicted atomic spies, were staving off execution dates through appeals increasingly backed up by international protests. And, through seeming clairvoyance, the McCarthy hearings reached their climax on the day that Joseph Stalin's death was reported in American papers.

The Voice of America, a ripe target, had been prepared for attack by McCarthy's investigators Roy Cohn and David Schine, who had held their own upscale inquisition by dragging suspects and sympathizers to Schine's suite at the swank Waldorf-Astoria Hotel in New York City. Meanwhile, three committees were meeting to discuss the reorganization of the IIA. The President's Advisory Committee on Government Organization, headed by Nelson Rockefeller, the President's Committee on International Programs, chaired by New York investment banker William Jackson, and a subcommittee of the Senate Foreign Relations Committee, chaired by Senator Bourke Hickenlooper of Iowa, were reaching conclusions that would result in the creation of a separate agency, the USIA, in August of that year.

At the same time, away from Washington, the New York headquarters of the Voice of America held refugees from what were then called the Captive Nations of Eastern Europe, many of whom were strenuously anti-Communist. This staff reported to superiors in both New York and Washington who were politically more liberal and, in any case, not consumed by the cold fire of day-to-day propaganda warfare with the Soviets. Some superiors had begun their careers in the OWI, which had, in fact, employed leftists because of their disdain for the Fascist enemy. Such employees were subject to the accusation of premature anti-Fascism—that their early revulsion of the Right must have been balanced by an equally extreme conviction on the Left. The Voice also was made vulnerable by the conflicting missions of the IIA. The complexities of handling both information and propaganda within an agency that was virtually unknown to most Americans portended high drama, as McCarthy's subcommittee feasted on the testimony of liberal administrators, with appetites whetted by anti-Communist informants within the offices of the Voice.

With the announcement that he was investigating "mismanagement and subversion"[13] in the Voice of America, Joseph McCarthy convened his subcommittee in mid-February at the federal court in Foley Square, New York City. Spring had come to New York. Outside crocuses bloomed a month early; inside McCarthy, behind a battery of klieg lights for the television cameras, was quick to turn up the heat. The purported focus of the investigation was the proposed placement of two transmitters—Baker East and Baker West—in zones of the country that did not present the best atmospheric conditions for penetrating the Eastern Bloc with radio waves. After having heard only five witnesses in executive session, McCarthy announced that "there are some people in the Voice of America who are doing a rather effective job of sabotaging Dulles' and Eisenhower's foreign policy program."[14] The battle was joined. The Voice administration produced studies by electrical engineers and statements of effectiveness from IIA staff members from Washington. Cohn and Schine had lined up an array of Eastern European employees who complained of incompetence, indifference, and obstruction.

The March hearings moved to Washington and got closer to the real point of the exercise: the exposure of supposed Communists and fellow travelers in the IIA. Highlight of the six weeks of hearings in both locations, all of which were covered by the *New York Times* as front-page news, was the grilling of Reed Harris, who at the time was the interim administrator of the IIA. The exchanges between McCarthy and Harris started out "bristling and explosive"[15] and ended up ruining Harris's career.

Harris was a good target for McCarthy. As a student at Columbia University in the early 1930s he had flirted with leftist groups. His contributions to the student newspaper, the *Spectator*, became so prickly that he was suspended from college. He had had the gumption to suggest that college football had turned into a "semi-professional racket" for the entertainment of hard-drinking alumni. In 1932, between the time of his suspension and his reinstatement, he wrote a book, *King Football*, which expanded on this theme and took a variety of jabs at Columbia and what Harris considered to be the class interests it served.

Harris entered the hearing room thinking that he was defending the loyalty of two IIA employees who had been smeared by McCarthy. He found himself impaled on his own pointed utterances of twenty years before. He attempted a general recantation of his former beliefs but was forced to return, again and again, to the subject of *King Football* and its violation of the American way. Even though his job demanded that he gain quick control of an administration so unwieldy that it was soon to be transformed, he was given the additional homework of proving in writing by chapter and page citation from his published work and his resumé that he had re-constructed his life as a good American after the calumny of *King Football*. McCarthy promised him all the time he needed to respond to accusations made during the hearings, and then cut him off with innuendo, unanswerable implications, and extensive quotations from the still-offending volume. Harris survived the hearings but resigned soon thereafter.

The effects of these hearings on the IIA and on its legacy for the USIA were profound. First of all, the IIA found itself unable to describe succinctly to domestic audiences what it was doing in foreign venues. This was the ironic result of the decision that the IIA was not to become a domestic propaganda agency; all of its effort, by law, was to be directed abroad. For Americans, there was relatively little information about the information agency that they were paying for. For the USIA there would be an explicit, if ultimately ambiguous, mission statement uttered by the president himself around which a domestic explanation, suitable for citizens and congressional committees, would be crafted.

Second, the IIA found itself threatened by the ambiguities of the term *propaganda*. Were they to wage a war of words against the Communists, or were they to form alliances through the power of reason and common sense? While the hearings were underway, a collateral scandal broke that answered this question, for a time, in favor of a sanitized account of what the American version of these habits of thought might require. Overseas libraries, the intrepid Cohn and Schine had discovered, contained works written by leftists and Communists. This was, in fact, true. As a matter of policy, favorable impressions of the United States written by such noted radicals as Howard Fast were included in American libraries in Europe. With McCarthy brandishing *King Football* in Washington, the State Department issued a new edict that all suspicious volumes were to be removed from foreign libraries. In their panic not to be sullied by offending thoughts, some librarians burned books rather than store them. The State Department order was quickly rescinded, but the succeeding policy made it very difficult to accession library material that was in any way questionable. The intersection between information and propaganda could create career-threatening collisions.

Third, McCarthy seemed to be unstoppable. President Eisenhower did not like the man or his tactics, but, as the *New York Times* remarked at the time, the Chief Executive was loathe to intervene in the Senate's investigative prerogative unless the stature of the executive was being threatened.[16] In 1953, at least, McCarthy avoided this misstep. John Foster Dulles, on the other hand, was quite sympathetic to McCarthy's cause and, as has become apparent, supplied the subcommittee's investigators with classified material from State Department files.[17] Dulles was eager to separate himself from the administration of his Democratic predecessor, Dean Acheson. While McCarthy held forth in Washington, the secretary of state publicly fired a China hand, John Carter Vincent, even though the foreign service officer had been exonerated by Acheson of accusations of disloyalty.[18] With the selective help of the department being investigated, the hearings widened and became more ominous. "No greater series of victories by a Congressional body over a senior Executive department in so short a time is recalled here," the New York Times reporter asserted. And this was in February, when the hearings were only half over.[19]

The question of where all of this would stop was asked by more than just IIA employees. New York Times editorials at first admonished McCarthy to stick to a virtuous intent—to extirpate waste in an inefficient bureaucracy. Getting rid of the disloyal "should be a relatively minor thing."[20] Soon the editors began to complain about McCarthy's style. Witnesses were called only if the chairman thought "they have any information of value." Otherwise they were silenced. On February 24, before the move to Washington, the Times called the hearings an inquisition.[21] By the twenty-seventh it had become a carnival, one with a nasty ringmaster: "There has . . . been evident a disposition to appease Mr. McCarthy, which, apart from its moral implications, is a manifest impossibility."[22]

Television played an important part in this carnival, and the newspaper criticized this newly powerful medium. Again the Harris episode served as illustration. ABC, the American Broadcasting Company, was due to carry two hours of testimony during the morning of March 5 and cut Harris off before he had had a chance to respond to the lengthy harangue from McCarthy. There was some question as to where to fix the blame. The network said that McCarthy had notified them of the extended session too late to make technical accommodations; McCarthy remained silent about his motives. The fact was that at 12:30 p.m., Harris was abandoned in favor of a call-in quiz show. "This episode showed more clearly than anything else how both Senator McCarthy and television are putting show business considerations above the minimum canons of fair play and responsible journalistic behavior," Jack Gould, the Times's media critic, intoned.[23]

The point, however, could not be missed by readers of the popular press: none of these objections fazed McCarthy. In fact, what really slowed down the investigation was a human sacrifice. On March 5, Raymond Kaplan, a Boston electrical engineer, took his own life rather than testify before McCarthy's tribunal. The suicide note, leaked to the New York Times by an anonymous senator before it was seen by Kaplan's family, began with a lengthy defense of the placement of the now almost forgotten Baker East and Baker West transmitters and ended with the author's chilling decision to remove himself rather than see himself and his family hounded for the rest of their lives.[24] Soon thereafter, with no conclusion reached, the hearings mumbled to a stop.

What had been gained? The IIA had been revealed as "a child of misfortune almost from birth," as it was put in the New York Times.

> Its whole reason for being is one that is strange and somehow suspect to Americans when they are not at war. It is frankly and simply a propaganda organ—this country's principal weapon of psychological warfare against communism.[25]

In some minds it had been sullied from the beginning. Thanks to the hearings the IIA's effectiveness was called into question even by its advocates. Ironically, the one accomplishment of the McCarthy hearings was the cancellation of construction of improved broadcast facilities. Symbolically, the Voice of America had become an embarrassment, its very name an ironic jab at the principles it was instructed to articulate. A European correspondent to the *Times* wrote:

> Many European newspapers give their readers the impression that Washington officials are living under a kind of terror not unlike those experienced in Europe at various periods. In neutral Switzerland the handling and evaluation of Washington news about Congressional committee investigations have become almost indistinguishable from the handling and evaluation of news about purge trials in Communist countries.[26]

There had been at least one significant victory of this congressional committee over the executive branch and one compromise that offered employees of the IIA little comfort. Early in the cycle of hearings, an order from the secretary of state deprived employees of their discretion as to whether to testify before the committee or not. Whatever shelter executive privilege might have offered was removed, and IIA personnel were left unprotected in the glare of the television lights and the heat of McCarthy's indignation. The senator was less successful in getting legal access to State Department security files, one of the main objects of the investigation. Nothing was released to him at first. His response was to make unsubstantiated accusations about IIA personnel and then prohibit witnesses from referring to the content of these files, even in summary form. This was Harris's original offense: to have received authorization from State Department superiors to say that certain employees had been declared not to be security risks. Later in the hearings, specific documents were allowed to be drawn from these files and shown to the subcommittee as corroboration of statements by witnesses but could not be distributed to the public. Whole files could not be released to the likes of Schine and Cohn. At least on the surface the department had kept the subcommittee out of the file room, while, at the same time, establishing an economy of paper and leaked information down Pennsylvania Avenue.

The Hickenlooper committee report quickly gave the IIA a knockout punch, with the other two commissions reluctantly standing at ringside to count out the battered fighter. But all the preparatory work, the hard shots to the belly, as it were, were delivered by McCarthy. As one historian of the USIA put it, the new agency took a year to recover from the pounding that was delivered during the first three months of 1953.[27] From this troubled beginning, the USIA, which came into being on August 1, 1953, had to assemble the identity and the rhetoric that would carry it through the rest of the decade.

The practice of cultural diplomacy brought the same hazards as experienced by other professions in the ultranationalism of the early 1950s. The examples of ruined careers and questioned loyalty must have balanced the need for serious thought with the urge for self-justification as the new bureaucracy was being formed. The ironies were overwhelming: on the one hand a predatory congressional committee demanding a narrow definition of Americanness, on the other the mandate to speak for the culture; on the domestic side a use of media that was profoundly un-American, abroad the concern for how these media could portray the variety of American life in unfamiliar circumstances. Such a web of information and propaganda, intent and justification, warranted caution from those who hoped to make a career of speaking for America.

The agency's explanation of itself changed according to circumstances, but the rhetoric and vocabulary it used became established early on and persisted, despite frequent changes in leadership. The information service had four directors and two interim directors between 1953 and 1957. Robert Johnson took a leave of absence from the presidency of Temple University to head the IIA in 1953. Before the end of the year, he turned the new Information Agency over to Theodore Streibert, a broadcasting executive. For a brief time in 1957 the USIA was headed by Arthur Larsen, a former undersecretary of labor. Only in 1958 was the agency put under the direction of a career foreign service officer, George V. Allen. After 1958 the agency's voice became more measured and diplomatic, yet the discourse had not changed since the early days.

The experience of one man who entered the IIA at a critical time illustrates life in the complex gravitational field of 1950s geopolitics and postwar Washington bureaucracies. Martin Merson accompanied Robert Johnson to Washington in the early spring of 1953 for what he thought would be the short transition from the IIA to an independent agency. In *The Private Life of a Public Servant* Merson recounts the frustrations accompanying the maneuvering among IIA, the White House, and the State Department in the climate of the McCarthy investigations.

The McCarthy imbroglio was as chaotic viewed from inside the IIA as it had appeared to observers from *New York Times* accounts. Merson saw Reed Harris return from his testimony and resign his interim directorship a burned-out hulk. The result of this "one-sided televised hearing"[28] was the destruction of a fine career. Merson cited the same testimonials to Harris's character that had been entered into the hearing record by the accused. Both appeals were, of course, after the fact: the character being attested to was no longer capable of defense. The immediate result of the Harris episode was the demoralization of career IIA officers.[29]

Merson dined with the notorious junior senator, whom he found to be quite pleasant, ideological obsessions aside. He also had audiences with the less congenial Cohn and Schine, who drove home the irony of cold war cultural diplomacy: "To say that I was as apprehensive as a Soviet citizen must be when the secret police raps on the door is not overstating the case."[30] At one such audience, he found himself enveloped in a bizarre conversation about whether the American composer Aaron Copland should be blacklisted or not. Discussing an effective reorganization of the IIA did not appeal to McCarthy and his cronies. "Their joint aim apparently was to kill the agency, in which case the location of the burial plot was of secondary interest."[31] Finally, Merson recounted, the IIA "was looking directly to McCarthy [rather than the State Department] for policy. It was quicker that way."[32]

According to Merson, the State Department was eagerly awaiting the development of a separate agency to replace the troublesome IIA. In the meantime, the Information Administration was left to the ravages of the House Appropriations Committee, a member of which had said to Merson's boss, Dr. Johnson:

> [Y]ou seem like a very nice man. We've heard nothing but good things about you. But your agency is full of Communists, left-wingers, New Dealers, radicals, and pinkos, and the best thing you can do is to take the funds you have on hand, liquidate it, and go back to Temple.[33]

Through a procedure christened by Merson "Operation Emasculation," the State Department kept for itself educational exchange programs, "the heart of the agency," mostly, according to him, to appease Senator Fulbright, after whom the most famous of these programs was named.[34] Beyond this Merson sensed, at best, the disinterest of the State Department. The covert sharing of security files with the McCarthy committee was obvious at the time: details of the lives of IIA employees were openly discussed in the twilight world of McCarthy's circle by both employees of the committee and hangers-on from the press.[35] As far as Merson could see, John Foster Dulles offered them no protection. The secretary of state issued enigmatic statements about the future of the IIA and allowed Appropriations Committee hearings to proceed so aimlessly that no one had "more than a vague idea of what the information program was attempting to do."[36] At last, just as Merson left government service in the summer of 1953, the newly formed USIA received the mandate "for promoting better understanding. . . . free and clear of stifling State Department red tape"[37]—what Johnson and Merson had wanted all along.

Johnson and Merson had temporarily entered into the IIA out of loyalty to a president they considered to be a war hero. From the beginning of their time in Washington, however, they were disappointed by the Eisenhower administration. The terms of Johnson's appointment were misrepresented in the initial press releases. The executive branch did not protect the IIA from McCarthy. Merson, echoing *New York Times* observations, attributed this to Eisenhower's reluctance to anger Congress. The administration's unwillingness to circumscribe congressional prerogatives was a "terrible price to be paid for compromise with what was essentially evil."[38] Furthermore, the White House did not even free the IIA from the interference of an element of the branch of government theoretically under its control, the State Department. While awaiting the study that would make recommendations on the reorganization of the IIA, Johnson's weakened, "semi-autonomous" agency was ravaged by State.

> It [the IIA] had, for instance, no security division, no cable transmitting facilities. Overseas it was housed in our embassies and consulates. It could make no news releases without State authorization. State could, and did, dig into IIA's funds.[39]

Merson and Johnson approached the elder statesman of the Republican Party, Herbert Hoover, but found that Dulles and McCarthy had tainted the former president's view of the IIA. To Merson's relief, the findings of the Hickenlooper committee proved to be "a model of balanced, thoughtful presentation,"[40] and he and Johnson could leave the new agency in the hands of Theodore Streibert, former head of the Mutual Broadcasting Network, with clear consciences.

Contemporary accounts amplify Merson's frustrations. Before they left office, Johnson and Merson commissioned Leo Bogart to do a survey of the operating assumptions of the fledgling Information Agency. Presented to Theodore Streibert in 1954, the policy study was stamped "classified" and shelved; it was not published until the 1970s.[41] Bogart's survey was viewed with some distrust by Streibert for reasons that make it all the more useful for examination today. Rather than quantify opinion, Bogart and his associates took a more narrative approach, allowing USIA personnel to speak directly through the study in the form of long, unattributed quotations. The authors tried, unsuccessfully, to give the study the aura of statistical validity by characterizing the relative prevalence of the many opinions expressed. What was viewed by the agency as a flawed methodology was, in fact, interesting ethnography; by allowing employees to speak, Bogart presented a most useful glimpse into the working culture of a new federal agency.

Merson's account of ideological struggle at the home base in Washington was thus extended into the field. As one respondent commented, "Nobody will say whether the agency's fundamental objective is opposition to Communism or the Soviet Union, or the defense of the positive role of the United States abroad."[42] The rhetorical complexity of defending a positive position was felt in practical terms by those whose job it was to interpret American culture abroad.

> A democracy must embrace a multiplicity of theories, unlike Communist society with one 'Bible' of working philosophical, social, and political theories. It is impossible to achieve an anti-communist or non-communist 'gospel' because the Free World encompasses too many different cultures and philosophies.[43]

Given the congressional demand for orthodoxy, this was a potentially hazardous statement. According to Bogart's commentary, there was no consensus about whether political action or cultural persuasion was the central mission of the USIA.[44]

Respondents extended this confusion through the operations of the USIA. For example, the agency could not decide whether to focus on the masses or the cultural elite, particularly behind the Iron Curtain.[45] In lieu of differentiating scripts according to the depths of allegiance to Communism in the audience, the agency, through the Voice of America, selected broadcast programs that were the most blatantly anti-Communist. These were "a common denominator" that could be used because "anti-Communist propaganda is the same everywhere."[46] At the same time, those sensitive to reactions in Western Europe observed that Europeans did not respond well to being hectored by American "information" concerning the evils of Communism.

> People in Europe do not want to be educated by us except about America. They would let us talk to them about Chicago but not about Moscow. It is not only that there is a positive interest in hearing about America, there is

a positive resentment about having us talk to them about a good many subjects outside of our borders, including communism.[47]

You have to be subtle when discussing Communism, one informant responded. In the context of ideological purges in Washington, subtlety was neither possible nor healthy.

Looking from outside the agency at the project of presenting American "information" abroad did not lessen the tension inherent in the agency's charge. Studies of this aspect of cultural diplomacy frequently made reference to the American advantage: "Our objectives are *constructive*. We want to build. The Soviet objectives are *disruptive*. They want to tear down."[48] Or, more eloquently:

> We are in a sense the ideological propagandists of all time, telling everybody that freedom, prosperity and social equality are attainable realities for one and all. . . . Having conducted the world's oldest experiment in political and social freedom, we have an instinctive feel for the new surge toward freedom in the rest of the free world.[49]

The problem, summarized another observer, was that "we tend to go to the extreme, thus becoming predominantly negative, *against* something but for nothing."[50] The resolution of this debate lay in the realm of tactics rather than strategy. One could be forthrightly anti-Communist or engage in rhetorical contortions. Behind malleable tactical decisions lay the larger, inflexible strategy of Manichean cold war ideology: us vs. them, the free world vs. the Communist world.

At many levels, the situation was more complicated than this. Strategy, tactics, the rhetoric through which policy was articulated, even the definition of and provenance over terms such as *freedom* and *liberty*, had to be examined. Before turning to these larger questions, let us not forget the individual USIA officer in his (and, only later, her) foreign post. This person, constructed by his bureaucracy as a representative American, would be the one who would view the opportunity to present *The Family of Man* in his country with a relief mixed with gratitude.

> Contrary to much popular folklore, the Cultural Affairs Officer is not set apart from the struggles of the cold war. He inhabits no ivory tower. In some countries it would be more correct to think of the Cultural Affairs Officer as a hard-hitting political infighter. He is sometimes successful in this because he is not seeking in his activities immediate political advantages. On the other hand, he is dealing with a host of personal contacts and with those elements in the life of a nation which vibrate warmly and more genuinely—a people's music, art, books, theater. Creation of a genuine climate of mutual understanding about these elements of national culture affords a long-term influence difficult to evaluate and dangerous to underestimate. The Cultural Affairs Officer is dealing with schools and education (including adult education); with the entire spectrum of the flow of intellectual life in the country to which he is accredited; in the broadest sense he is reflecting the American people's way of life through

American ideas wrapped in human beings and through the product of America's creative talent.[51]

The struggle that the State Department faced in the early 1950s was not only between Us and Them, but between different conceptions of who we were and how we should be portrayed abroad. As Frank Ninkovich has pointed out,[52] the foreign service debated whether cultural diplomacy or information should be its central function. The former was associated with the traditional role of the diplomatic mission: the concert of the philharmonic orchestra or a reading by a prizewinning novelist, followed by the tasteful reception at the ambassador's villa. This was the sort of occasion that William Faulkner, for one, so dreaded when he thought of going to Stockholm to accept the Nobel Prize in 1949. Art, theatre, literature, dance—the elements of elite culture could be offered to the upper strata of host countries as proof that Americans were sophisticated and civilized, certainly not the jejune materialists of Soviet caricatures. Information, on the other hand, brought with it propaganda, the quick response to daily happenings made possible by the newer media of radio, newspaper wire services, and, later, television. In this world one wanted a quick-thinking operative more than an orotund diplomat.

The question that we have encountered among 1950s intellectuals and cultural commentators became even more basic when applied to the projection of American culture abroad: how to describe American culture to a domestic audience became how to define culture strategically in an international context. This definition of culture was instrumental; it furthered the foreign policy objectives (and international commercial aspirations) of the American government. Americans (even diplomats) indulged in popular culture, but what one carried abroad should be only the best. Intellectuals devised the categories of the three brows to give themselves the power of the taxonomist; diplomats filtered items of American culture to be exhibited abroad according to an elite standard of taste. American culture became contrived. Pack away the comic books; brandish Faulkner and Hemingway instead. High culture became a potent commodity; however, one also had to be aware of what would change the dynamics of the host culture in ways favorable to the United States. Here American popular culture and the avalanche of American goods proved to be very useful.

Hollywood, for example, had already reentered Europe at the end of World War II, literally following the troops as they moved toward Berlin. Not only was the glamour of Hollywood's America shown in film after film, but the government's Bureau of Motion Pictures, established during the war, assisted with script ideas and distribution schedules.[53] The Marshall Plan increased the appetite for economic goods and created the syndicated newspaper features, documentary films, and reading rooms in American culture centers that solidified the predominance of the United States in the postwar order. The weight of the mass media—the same forces that could make the beer-drinking lowbrow happy in what Leslie Fiedler had already called illiteracy—could help the American cause abroad, even as the personal culture of this same lowbrow would be camouflaged by generalized appeals to American democratic principles.

This appeal to foreign audiences through mass media did have its drawbacks. Since the beginning of World War II, radio had been used as a way of projecting America abroad. Before war's end, the OWI's Voice of America was broadcasting information and propaganda to the world in forty languages twenty-four hours a day.[54] The media used to serve American interests abroad could be employed against the Information Agency at home. The McCarthy hearings were begun as a purported investigation of the efficacy of radio transmissions overseas, and the domestic damage had been done on live radio and television. As we have already seen, the opportunistic senator deprived Reed Harris of his ability to speak to a television audience. Attention could be turned to the disadvantage of the IIA, as when Cohn and Schine visited the American libraries of Europe, and it could provide domestic opponents a way of making points with an electorate eager to cut the federal budget. Information could work against culture, a telling aspect of diplomacy in a period known for its anti-intellectualism. In 1947, a major art exhibition, *Advancing American Art*, was not only criticized but investigated by Congress because some of its offending, modernist works had been produced by political leftists. Finally, as the abolition of the art exhibition program resulting from the controversial 1947 show demonstrated, internationalists and cultural conservatives within the State Department could unite in their fear of a program that would threaten the managerial control of a newly centralized overseas cultural and informational program. It was no accident that the first permanent overseas information program was established only after *Advancing American Art* had been turned over to the War Assets Board for disposal as surplus property.[55]

Removing *information* from *culture* in the foreign policy apparatus of the government shows that separating aspects of American life according to taste categories was not just the preoccupation of a grid in *Life* magazine. Reacting to day-to-day happenings in an expanding international sphere of influence was the job of one set of government employees—public affairs officers. Maintaining the stature of American culture remained the task of the State Department, through its ambassadorial representatives. The USIA, therefore, handled the press and the school; the State Department kept the opera house and the university lecture hall. As we shall see, such an artificial definition, established with the Eisenhower administration's reorganization plans, would not hold up in practice. As the decade wore on, it became more logical that the public affairs officer, assisted by the cultural affairs officer, would have to deal with such a hybrid event as *The Family of Man*. Elements of culture could not be categorized according to a bureaucracy. And each officer who had read pulp fiction, attended a concert, and appreciated *Life* photographs when the magazine arrived in embassy libraries knew this.

Within the agency, the USIA's independence must have been greeted with equanimity rather than celebration. The agency received jurisdiction over "information" but also inherited the tradition of propagandizing that linked it to OSS and OWI operations in World War II. Furthermore, the agency was still doubly yoked to the Department of State. In the field, the public affairs officer, the highest ranking USIA employee at most embassies, was under the jurisdiction of an ambassador, whose role had been strengthened through postwar reorganizations of the foreign service;

at home the director of the USIA received policy mandates from the secretary of state. The USIA was to engage in the operation of American foreign policy, not in its formation. Because the agency was, in effect, the medium through which information about America was projected into the world, it could be direct, rather than diplomatic. Nonetheless, through its association with (and location in) American embassies and its connection to the State Department, the Information Agency became enmeshed in the paradoxical cultural diplomacy of the cold war.

The pronouncements of this diplomacy came from bureaucratic structures that were far more elaborate than they had been before the war. This important reinforcement was necessary to carry the weight of the newly preeminent power in the world. The construction of this framework and the building of a cultural diplomacy was "necessary not only to nationalize cultural power, but to rationalize it."[56] A contradictory rhetoric was deployed by American diplomats in the cold war against the Russians and, after Korea, the Chinese, that masked this American national power in the name of internationalism and invoked New World idealism in the defense of free world practicalities.[57] Because of this stature, the USIA, or United States Information Service (USIS) as the agency was known abroad, became enmeshed in cultural diplomacy, whether it was separate from the State Department or not.

Before World War II, a great deal of this depiction of American culture abroad was undertaken by private groups and American tourists. Seemingly common values—freedom and individualism, for example—were considered to be universals that could be understood by people who were basically the same. After the war, the State Department advocated a freedom of information policy, the particularism of "peoples speaking to peoples," that brought an American understanding of the world order to foreign audiences, many of whom did not have the technological means of responding.[58] Enough of the traditional American belief in the power of ideas remained that a forthright capitulation to propaganda was impossible. However, the ideological force behind the new diplomacy of information and culture was the power politics of a national foreign policy that recognized its enemy. The paradox of a young country invoking the ideals of its enshrined tradition while contradicting these high principles with self-serving actions reveals an ideological confusion that lay at the center of official American diplomatic discourse. "Because a direct transition to power politics was out of the question, the only alternative was an ideological detour in which, paradoxically, a determination to abide by tradition was the precondition of its abandonment."[59]

In Frank Ninkovich's analysis, the ideological structure undergirding cold war discourse contained three axes. First, ideology might be seen as "a culture's intellectual style," an anthropological conception of culture. Adherents to this view would see "a causal connection between intellectual liberty and a democratic social order."[60]

A second, sociological form of ideology encouraged a delusion: the unitary idea of America marketed abroad by USIS personnel inadequately reflected the complex social realities that citizens experienced at home.[61] When tested, American loyalty to the ideals of its constitution were frequently found wanting, as we have already seen in the McCarthy hearings. A reading of cold war liberal discourse, of which Arthur

Schlesinger's *Vital Center* is only one example, shows that principle could bow before rationalized expediency. This acquiescence might have been the measure of the center's dominance rather than its vitality, for many liberals were presented with Hobson's choice: either they could speak up and be rejected by this "complex social reality" that circumscribed acceptable thought, or they could remain silent. In either case, they surrendered their power.[62] An argument over taste categories was safer than a direct debate over American ideology.

The third use of ideology Ninkovich classified as symbolic, as a way that a culture used to deal with revolutionary social change.[63] America had become a world power, but its conception of itself was as a developing nation. This "ideological distortion" led to "cultural self-delusion," in this case the conviction that Communism must be fought by the free world, with the United States in the lead. "If Communism had not existed," Ninkovich intones, "something like it would have to be invented." No matter how it could be defined, the ideology of cultural diplomacy presents us with a congeries of contradictions.

> Ideology was both a means of disguise and a source of comforting reassurance: disguise, because it concealed the unwelcome dynamics of power and institutional change; false reassurance, because it furnished traditional justification for novel and otherwise questionable activities. It rationalized, legitimized, and concealed underlying political and structural transformations, the existence of which originally gave rise to the need for ideological thought. It allowed the United States to undertake policies that it had to adopt, but could not otherwise justify. To put it somewhat perversely, ideology provided a means of violating American beliefs while continuing to defend them.[64]

To these three conceptions of ideology should be added the stratigraphy of the levels of culture. As we have already seen, intellectuals disenfranchised at the overtly political level attempted to control the vocabulary of cultural description. Every foreign service officer, an interpreter of a complex culture to a foreign audience, was put in a position of using the parlance of the domestic commentator—many of whom were available for USIA-sponsored lectures abroad—while supporting the foreign policy mission of the State Department. One system of power could work against the other; all these ideological vectors were uniquely, and disconcertingly, theirs.

The matrix holding these forces together was configured before the agency was established. The formation of the USIA was a part of a general reorganization of government that occurred at the beginning of Eisenhower's first term. Reorganization plan number eight, submitted to Congress on June 1, 1953, split the Information Agency off from State Department administration. The director of the agency would report to the National Security Council, emphasizing the fact that USIA was an operational, not a policy-forming body. However, Eisenhower's message to Congress accompanying the plan also reasserted "the primary position of the Secretary of State within the executive branch in matters of foreign policy."[65] Furthermore, the message encouraged the USIA to develop "subordinate levels" that would be parallel to those on the organizational chart of the State Department.[66] The agency thus began its life with divided responsibilities. When expressing official government policies, it was responsible to the State Department, "to assure accurate statements of United States official positions on important issues and current developments."[67] Beyond conducting the business of American foreign policy, the agency's role was unclear.

Defining the gray realm of mission and responsibility became the subject of National Security Council meetings during the month of October 1953. On October 28, with the Security Council's guidance, Eisenhower, through his press secretary, released the following statement.

1. The purpose of the United States Information Agency shall be to submit evidence to peoples of other nations by means of communication techniques that the objectives and policies of the United States are in harmony with and will advance their legitimate aspirations for freedom, progress and peace.
2. The purpose in paragraph 1 above is to be carried out primarily:
   a. By explaining and interpreting to foreign peoples the objectives and policies of the United States Government.
   b. By depicting imaginatively the correlation between United States policies and the legitimate aspirations of other peoples of the world.
   c. By unmasking and countering hostile attempts to distort or to frustrate the objectives and policies of the United States.
   d. By delineating those important aspects of the life and culture of the people of the United States which facilitate understanding of the policies and objectives of the Government of the United States.[68]

This delphic pronouncement was read with great care in the agency and served as the foundation for all official rhetoric in the following years.

Theodore Streibert, who had just become the director of the USIA, viewed this statement as "a public 'masthead' " for the agency[69] and returned a letter to Eisenhower giving his understanding of what the chief executive had just said. He concentrated on the areas in which he had the most leeway, items 2b through 2d. The agency, he asserted, would create a connection between "the legitimate aspirations of other peoples" and the goals of American foreign policy. This was the nationalization of internationalism that Ninkovich saw at the heart of American cultural diplomacy in the 1950s.

> Under this new mission, avoiding a propagandistic tone the agency will emphasize the community of interest that exists among freedom-loving peoples and show how American objectives and policies advance the legitimate interests of such peoples.[70]

Streibert's USIA would "not misrepresent a given situation" and would avoid a "strident or antagonistic tone." However, it could not free itself of the information vs. propaganda dilemma that had befuddled all of its predecessors. Streibert was now down to item 2c, the defense of the positive, the confrontation with the Other Side.

The new approach will be harder hitting than previous more diffuse approaches because it is based on the idea of getting across a message that will be convincing. Facts, and comment associated with facts, are more compelling than accusations and unsupported assertions on a wide variety of issues.[71]

Harder hitting on whom? Streibert did not yet address directly the strategic dilemma of whether to attack Communism in its homeland, its satellites, or the waiting battleground of developing Third World nations. The consciousness of accusations of American braggadocio and shallowness implicit in the last sentence of Streibert's statement indicated a delicate operation sensitive to cultural difference and existing stereotyping of Americans, tactics associated more with the periphery of Communism than its Soviet core. No matter where it was projected, the message of the United States would be founded on what Streibert identified as fundamental beliefs.

These include belief in a Deity, in individual and national freedom, in the right to ownership of property and a decent standard of living, in the common humanity of all men, and in the vision of a peaceful world with nations compromising their differences in the United Nations.[72]

American culture, as seen from abroad, consisted then of economic conditions, political ideals, and attractive character traits. There was no mention of the expressive aspects of a vibrant culture in which people actually lived, embodied in the programs and exhibitions that the agency would sponsor.

Streibert clarified his intentions in a subsequent letter to an undersecretary of state. Here item 2a, the function of the USIA as a part of the foreign-policy apparatus, became more important as the portrayal of culture was subordinated to national purpose.

Although our publicly assigned mission does not explicitly point to our role as a weapon of political warfare, the current conflict of interests between the United States and the Soviet Union, in which each seeks its aims by methods other than the use of armed force, constitutes political warfare. The activities of USIA, as an instrument of national policy, must be viewed in light of this fact.[73]

The rest of the memo defined the instrument, or weapon, that the USIA contributed to the cold war. The agency would not present "all facets of American life" but would "deliberately foster certain general assumptions about the U.S., and preserve an overall consistency." This was information with a purpose, news with a consistent narrative, a comforting reassurance to right-thinking foreigners that Americans were not just like them but just like they hoped to be. The trick was, then, to offer both reassurance and strength, enticement and possible retribution. Streibert recapitulated the American beliefs he had pledged to Eisenhower but added the following:

The military strength of the U.S., its economic system, its standard of living, its technical development and productive capacity make fruitful and effective subjects of propaganda if presented without self-praise and in ways which show U.S. capacity to resist aggression and to give powerful assistance in the creation of a peaceful world order.[74]

The parallel construction, creating a sheath around the equal weapons of military, economic, and technological might, created a powerful quiver for the USIA.

Streibert refused to resolve the dilemma of whether information or propaganda was at the heart of the USIA's mission, assuming, as did many of his predecessors, that most facts, forcefully presented, would support American foreign policy objectives.

> We further seek to avoid the ready application of the propaganda label by the tone and character of our output. This means that we avoid exaggeration, implausibility, and broad generalizations not convincingly supported, as well as strident polemic, blatant self-justification and shrill invective. We must preserve constantly in our output a general tenor of reasonableness, objectivity, and moderation.

Through words such as tone, character, and tenor, Streibert backed away from the objectivity of informing people of the news and focused more on the character behind the voice delivering the message. The best form of personal persuasion was disarmingly to act like Americans. He ended the memo by unmasking his intentions: "We are no less engaged in propaganda because we are to minimize the propagandistic."[75]

Much of USIA rhetoric over the rest of the decade followed the patterns, established through the initial conversations in 1953, of examining both message and messenger. The USIA promoted "the deep morality characteristic of the U.S." by showing that America stood for "positive values, including the positive freedoms—freedom to learn, to debate, to worship, to work, to live and to serve."[76] The projection of positive values became the promulgation of political change in vast parts of the world.

> What the U.S. means by peace . . . is a *peace by change*—a free Germany, reunified in the context of NATO and threatening neither East nor West, eventual liberation of the satellites, a world freed from the violence and subversion of international communism; and a free and expanding world economy. This is peace with justice and freedom, not between rival blocs but between nations acting in the true interests of all peoples. Our information program must clarify this distinction and make it stick.[77]

This conflation of political and economic systems, grounded in the cold war division of the world into us and them, the consolidation of terms such as peace, justice, and freedom in the cause of the United States, and the appropriation of the ability to read correctly the desires of people in other cultures, was typical of American rhetoric in the 1950s. The reminder of the function of the USIA in making the message stick proclaimed the utility and the loyalty of the agency.

In 1958, even the more measured George V. Allen reiterated these views in his first appearance before the Appropriations Committee as agency director. We must combat the Communists where we can, Allen said, by using the most powerful values we can summon to further "evolutionary changes within the Communist orbit." First, there was the power of our economy, "in which virtually all United States families share in ownership benefits and responsibilities." Then there was the example that the United States, the first of the nations to emerge from colonialism into world leadership, could offer.[78] In an appearance before that same committee a year later, Allen summarized this advantage.

> Fortunately for ourselves and for others, our national interests coincide with the interests of a large proportion of mankind; the desire for liberty, peace and progress. I would not be so bold as to say that the real image of America can become a guide to all—but it most certainly should be an example to many.[79]

Eisenhower's mission statement in 1953 was quickly digested by the agency and became a part of its strategic definition of itself during the decade. References to this press release, embedded in testimony or visible in prepared statements, permeated the conversations between USIA personnel and members of Congress. Eisenhower's objectives were constantly reiterated in cables to USIS posts and in discussion points that accompanied both news summaries and releases of public statements from the State Department or the White House. Individual reports from cultural affairs officers or public affairs officers made reference to these goals. The reports on The Family of Man, then, were only one set of examples of a discourse that constantly circled back to its point of origin.

The tactics employed abroad by USIS remained consistent, as well. Ordinarily, the USIS staff liked to be in control of the marketing of an American image to the world, whether such projects were attributed to the American embassy or unattributed productions of groups not perceived as being associated with the embassy of the United States. The agency constantly flirted with the distinction between commissioning from existing groups projects to be completed within the host country without publicizing a connection to the embassy and using money actively to dissemble, confuse, or distract. Perhaps this was a vestige of the primordial split between the OWI and OSS. Most definitely, this presentation of the United States abroad was founded in Eisenhower's statement and the push-pull impulses of positive and negative portrayals of information and/or propaganda that coursed throughout the agency.

In any case, the two impulses—to be ingenuous and crafty at the same time—could be found in the day-to-day commerce of the agency. A representative anecdote, taken from a 1954 biannual report to a National Security Council that would appreciate such a story, shows the pleasures of the gray world of unattributed material.

> In Denmark, for instance, a widely-distributed publication promoting support for NATO and pegged to NATO's Fifth Anniversary was prepared by a Danish organization in collaboration with the USIS staff in Copenhagen. The publication was so well regarded that the Danish government

called it to the attention of elements of the U.S. Department of State which were not familiar with the project. Equally impressed, the Department of State drew it to the attention of USIA, with the suggestion that the agency might wish "to utilize it in some way." A project maintained throughout as an indigenous operation had come full-circle.[80]

More generally, and more generously, the agency was as sensitive to what would play in the cultures surrounding USIS posts as they were conscious of the "natural" appeal of the message they were promulgating. "The chief advantage we have," George Allen remarked, "is that we have a better product to sell, if you want to put it in commercial terms."[81] Of course, we first have to portray accurately who we are; Streibert, speaking in 1954, knew that credibility was a foundation.[82] Then we can appeal to the common desire the world over for peace. Allen advised that in order to sell "human liberty, freedom, and dignity," we have to get to the man on the street.

> If you can deal directly with peoples, you are tapping a resource which may be tremendously important in achieving what the whole American policy and effort is trying to do—establish a durable and peaceful world.[83]

This was the strategy that put *The Family of Man* on the road. As we shall see, it also placed Richard Nixon in a Moscow vegetable market to press the flesh scarcely a year after Allen's advice.

"You know," Theodore Streibert remarked to the Foreign Affairs Committee in 1955, "in advertising and in public relations work you need constant reiteration."[84] But, as the drummers used to say, you had to know the territory. While the USIA put great stock in universals that penetrated the local circumstances of all people, the agency dealt with a United Nations of cultures, not assembled in one building but distributed in ancestral lands and disputed territory. Thus, the USIA entered into the new, postcolonial definition of culture that was a focus for American writers, culture critics, and photographers. What is striking is how much of this cultural awareness was turned inward toward the American message being promulgated rather than outward toward the audiences listening to the USIA.

Toward the end of the agency's first year Streibert wrote all posts a directive that both summarized an operative definition of culture and revealed the long-standing feeling of cultural inferiority of Americans looking back to the rich traditions of Europe. Here, as in so many other pronouncements of cultural policy, the Soviets were transformed into Russians and the Americans revealed as Europeans at heart.

> We cannot spend millions of dollars, as the Soviets are doing, to finance and publicize trips of our most famous artists. But we certainly can create an awareness abroad of the long cultural heritage of the United States, growing out of the European tradition and contributing something more to it, a heritage which is worthy of our role in the world today.

This "long cultural heritage" was not founded on the ephemera of popular culture but on an enshrined high culture. It was important, therefore, that the USIA display

American refinement. At the same time, Streibert came to the same assessment as many domestic commentators on the highbrow: this form of culture was demanding, not welcoming. The more representative forms were not elite and were made to be marketed, primarily at home, but also to be presented to immediate effect abroad. It was in the best interests of the USIA to define culture broadly, even if the word was made synonymous with spirit.

> Culture is a broad term, which encompasses not only scholarly and artistic fields but all significant manifestations and aspirations of the spirit of America, from athletics to political controversy.[85]

Any definition of culture for the agency would have to be instrumental; that is, it would have to result in programming in the field: performing artists, exhibits, lectures by academics and noted personalities, even tours by athletic teams and exhibitions of sports new to foreign audiences were a part of the traffic between Washington and more than two hundred posts. These events could be viewed as demonstrations of positive attributes of this "American spirit"—a kind of international audition, or preening, of a constructed American character well aware of the spotlight being trained on it. Those selected to play to the light, whose tickets were paid for by USIA, were well aware of their role. As the president of the Federation of Modern Painters and Sculptors said in 1956:

> Cultural commodities, if they may be called that, cannot be mass produced nor augmented by automation or technological ingenuities. They spring from the hearths of our communities where the weapons of future cultural cold wars will be forged.[86]

The commodities of high culture could counteract the constant accusation of American shallowness. An appreciation of the day-to-day values of American life, a broader definition of culture, could be accomplished through a more intelligent use of USIA personnel as representative Americans. Person-to-person contact, the hallmark of cultural persuasion in USIA programming, could be extended to the sustained field work of operatives who were increasingly differentiated from their State Department colleagues. George Allen, a former ambassador to India and Iran, knew the value of long-term visibility under skeptical eyes.

> The United States is made up of people of all races and religions, from all parts of the world. This is an advantage that no other country has. We can draw on peoples of all races, who are highly qualified and skilled, to carry on our program.[87]

Support for the USIA overwhelmed congressional suspicions, and voices challenging the existence of the agency were summoned up so that they could be successfully rebutted. A 1958 hearing before a subcommittee of the House Foreign Affairs Committee began with a long excerpt from a speech that Walter Judd of Minnesota had delivered on the floor of the House. He had uttered the criticism that had followed the agency for the first few years of its existence, that it was not doing "a good job of telling our story—it is weak, half-hearted, unconvincing." In fact, the Republican congressman continued, "it is hard to believe so second rate a job could have been done in this field, unless someone planned it that way."[88] The subject of this hearing was familiar—the resurrected radio transmitter project, Baker East and Baker West—but by this time the suspicions of the Communist infiltration, intimated by Judd's tirade that resonated with the history of McCarthy's 1953 inquisition, could be addressed directly. The times had changed, George Allen implied in his testimony before the subcommittee. Few former OWI personnel had been fired for security reasons—only fourteen in the preceding five years.[89] The Voice of America was now only a small part of the information operation. He was now confident enough of the loyalty and demonstrated utility of the agency that he could forthrightly explain the demise of the transmitter project.

> I judge from an examination of the record that perhaps the predominant
> consideration in reaching this decision was the severe congressional criti-
> cism leveled at the project by the Senate Permanent Subcommittee on In-
> vestigations.[90]

Some congressmen assumed that the USIA had not changed since one totalitarian foe was replaced by another in 1945, but by 1958 the USIA's understanding of its role was far more sophisticated than that. To be sure, Soviet initiatives had to be countered and current events defined, but the projection of American character, as epitomized and interpreted by USIS officers, was more effective in the long run. As an enduring strategy, the portrayal of a complex American culture had the greatest impact of all.

The Family of Man ideally suited all facets of this complex function. According to Allan Sekula, a critic of *The Family of Man*, the exhibition entered willingly into the cultural warfare against the Russians. He cites a cable from Indonesia in which the public affairs office at the American embassy gratefully noted that the exhibit outdrew a Russian circus, complete with performing bear.[91] This oversimplifies the impact of the exhibit abroad, in both the embassy bureaucracy and the host culture. Since the formation of the cultural and information programs after World War II, such exhibitions had created an American presence where other, more overt displays had been impossible, and were measured against their Communist counterparts. Cables comparing American and Soviet events were common after 1945. In 1947 the controversial *Advancing American Art*, for example, was praised by the embassy in Prague because it had not only forced the Soviets to create their own art display but had vanquished its hastily assembled competition.[92] The path of *The Family of Man* around the world shows how the message that Steichen had so meticulously crafted could be reconfigured to meet local circumstances in the portrayal of universal qualities. Not only was the exhibition's message acceptable, but its appearance helped define a visible function for newly independent USIA officers. If the exhibit participated in the cultural cold war, it was as an ingenuous conscriptee.

In advance of the exhibition, thousands of pamphlets, in effect catalogs for the exhibition, were distributed, and many copies of the entire book were presented to prominent individuals and important institutions. Foreign service officers contacted members of the press and cultivated schools. In all of the locations for which reports still exist there was a preview of the exhibition to which opinion leaders were invited. This followed the standard practice of the agency, as outlined by the biannual report submitted to the National Security Council just before *The Family of Man* hit the road. In order to achieve the maximum effect abroad from cultural events, the report stated, the agency should engage in:

> the production of special pamphlets, leaflets and posters, and special film, photo and radio coverage; the purchase of tickets for opinion-forming individuals and groups; and the travel of artists to enable them to appear non-commercially before university students and labor and other groups.[93]

The Family of Man, however, was not a USIA production.

The reports from public affairs officers indicate clearly that the exhibit fit well the established vocabulary we have explored. First of all, it was immensely popular—"the best record of any similar cultural exhibition held in Hamburg in recent years," the consulate in Germany reported. It had received 43,308 visitors in a month, including 3,520 on the last day.[94] Secondly, it was easy to publicize. Articles were published in the USIS-sponsored magazines; some of these were so profusely illustrated that they stood in the place of an exhibition catalog. The *Family of Man* film was shown in movie houses and classrooms. Press previews of the exhibition were given and dignitaries invited. All of this was standard procedure for USIA events, but there was a special appeal to *The Family of Man*, one that emanated from the circumstances of world tourism in which the images were collected. A report from Yugoslavia summarized the advantage of finding a picture taken in a Croatian town, Sisak, in 1949:

> Close liaison with the Sisak [newspaper] enabled us to collect fourteen of the individuals who appeared in the photograph. And on November 7th USIS Zagreb arranged for these individuals to visit Zagreb to meet newspapermen and press photographers who had been called in for the occasion. The visit of the Sisak group to Zagreb resulted in two lengthy articles in the local press accompanied by photos of the group at the exhibit. This exploitation was of considerable usefulness in developing further interest in the exhibit.[95]

By representing sixty-eight countries, the exhibit gave innumerable opportunities for such stories, and photos of inhabitants examining representations of their cultures became a leitmotif in USIA press photographs.

The appearance of the exhibition in the Netherlands was typical of the passage of the photographs through Europe. Queen Juliana stood admiringly before the exhibit when *The Family of Man* came to the Stedelijk Museum (City Museum) in Amsterdam in spring 1956. Over the next several weeks she was succeeded by over 100,000 of her subjects, a larger percentage of the population than anywhere else in Europe, the Dutch magazine *Foto* proclaimed.[96] Among these were many amateur photographers, and from their magazines, *Focus* and *Foto*, we may get a glimpse of the exhibition's impact on the interested viewer. Contemporary viewers were more sophisticated than they have been given credit for; through their criticisms we can read a deep appreciation of *The Family of Man*.

The *Focus* reviewer characterized this as an exhibition organized for American viewers: "in my opinion it is a typical view of American sentimentality and romanticism." However, the reviewer also recognized that each of the photographs, many of them not remarkable, in his opinion, for their artistry, was a statement that fit into a larger story. His example shows the effectiveness of the show. He chose the picture by the Dutch photographer Emmy Andriesse, one in the section entitled "We two form a multitude." This photo, set with the other six in this series, completed a sentence. "The entire exhibit consists of such sentences and these sentences form the complete story."[97] The question then became: did this story overcome the sentimentality and romanticism of its American origins? In other words, would the exhibition transcend its nationality and become a universal statement? The verdict of both magazines was in the affirmative. For *Focus* this could more aptly be called "the epic of the human" than "the family of man."[98] *Foto* stood even more eloquently on the side of Steichen's collection.

> It appeals to our people, from young to old, rich to poor. In one word,
> if you can ever speak about the universal, then this is it. This is not specif-
> ically a photography exhibit, nor an art exhibit. The exhibit must be seen
> from a humanitarian viewpoint. It is a question not of what is on it, but
> of what is in it.[99]

This was, in sum, "the monument of the unknown photographer."[100]

Both magazines commented intently on photographic technique. Both were interested in the difference between posed and unposed photographs and were concerned with the license that photographers might take with unsuspecting subjects. Much was to be learned from the exhibition. The ring-around-the-rosie sequence, mounted in the Netherlands on a movable carousel, offered the possibility of creative arrangements of photographs. The text of the exhibition encouraged all photographers to put together their own stories. Finally, the catalog could be used as a textbook of technique and aesthetics.

> The greatest value is the catalog with its nearly 500 reproductions, a uni-
> versal bible for everyone rich and poor, believer and nonbeliever, in one
> word a volume with images of everyone for everyone. Steichen has cre-
> ated an event for which humanity can only be thankful.[101]

Dutch amateur photographers, in appreciation, sent Steichen, an avid gardener, a selection of the best flower bulbs.[102] The exhibition was so popular that it returned to Rotterdam several years later and became a part of the *floriade*, a gigantic flower exhibition put on once every decade.

These favorable reports promised a good program for any embassy. During the 1950s *The Family of Man* was enthusiastically received as an evocative expression of America's view of world cultures. Behind USIS reports from throughout the world one can envision the same dynamics of programmatic utility and broader cultural support that we have already viewed in the Netherlands. The exhibit garnered "the right kind of people," the opinion leaders that USIS was told to influence. From a Beirut report: "Those who attended the exhibit were comprised mainly of students, artists, cultural and press leaders; in other words, the educational, media, and diverse religious elements were the components of the exhibit's audience here."[103] What each audience received was a useful view of the United States; examined from the perspective of the internationalist relying on the cumulative, legitimating effect of cultural events, the exhibition was a signal accomplishment. An inelegantly translated excerpt from a German newspaper accompanied the USIS post's account of the twenty-five news stories, pictures and notices that appeared in Hamburg newspapers.

The pictures have been collected according to their contents. However, the majority has also a strong artistic expression in their compositions. As a result of this the exhibition has taken on an importance which today only very few artistic ventures enjoy: to enjoy the eyes and to appeal to the conscience and the heart of the people.[104]

The Bonn embassy summarized this successful event: "There is little doubt that the success of the exhibit contributed to U.S. prestige and to an identification of the U.S. with values highly prized and deeply held by the German viewer."[105]

The sole dissenting evaluation in the 1950s, directed to the State Department and not USIA headquarters, hints at what objections the conservatives in the agency may have had: The Family of Man was too international in its orientation and defied the managerial control of the USIA through its origins at the Museum of Modern Art. These "Afterthoughts on the Exhibit 'Family of Man'" reflected on the Mexico City showing of the photographs in late 1955, one of the first appearances of the exhibition outside the United States. Underscored near the beginning of the cable was the admonition that "this exhibit is not a USIA creation." Its expense did not result in demonstrable propaganda benefit. The impact was emotional and therefore not measurable, especially with regard to the fundamental charge given the USIA: explaining the actions of the United States government, the beliefs and values of the American people, and the manifestation of these values in American foreign policy.[106] Eisenhower's mandate to the USIA, then more than two years old, resonated in these criticisms. As far as the public affairs officer in Mexico City was concerned, for exhibits such as this one the best criterion might be "how does the emotional experience of the visitor translate itself into political motivations and affect his attitude toward all other aspects of the USIA message?" The agency, in short, should exercise direct control over the content of American products offered to specific foreign audiences.

For this public affairs officer the message of the exhibition contradicted American policy objectives.

The leit motif of the exhibit is the brotherhood of men. Surrounding the exhibit the United States Government promotes the idea of the brotherhood of men. On the level of idea alone, there is nothing in the exhibit that could not be promulgated equally by libertarian and anti-libertarian doctrines. . . . That is to say, the idea is one which the Communists might also have sought to propagate exhibitwise.

The writer continued with an accurate assessment of the exhibit's intentions and the limits of its utility to the Information Agency.

> The idea as presented in "The Family of Man" was made to appear as apolitical as possible. People all over the globe are born, fall in love, marry, have children, suffer and die. There is nothing in this idea which argues against life as it is lived behind the Iron Curtain. The reporting officer can attest from direct witness that behind the Iron Curtain people are born, fall in love, marry, have children, suffer and die.

In the universe of world virtue, according to the exhibition, the United States did not stand front and center. The foreign service officer also recognized Steichen's appeal to the United Nations, his abhorrence of the nuclear bomb, and the dissonance of this message with American foreign policy: "The idea that the fission bomb may be just one other cause of death is nowhere suggested; instead the atom bomb becomes the brooding presence darkening man's mind, threatening its extinction. It is posed as an ultimate, a finality . . ." Beyond these strategic concerns over world command, the writer in Mexico City objected to the flattening of terrain, the opening of borders, encouraged by the photographs.

> The ideological struggle today is not over the question of whether or not man shall live; it is over the question of *how* man shall live. . . . The exhibit "The Family of Man" imputes value and dignity to man on the simple ground that he is a man, and it says he is a man anywhere and everywhere, even today, with half the human race in bondage to an anti-humanist doctrine and a large portion of the rest of it living in squalor.

The exhibition, he noted in conclusion, had been very popular with the Mexican people.

By the time of the Kennedy administration, the welcome for *The Family of Man* had cooled. The photographs appeared in Kabul, Afghanistan, in 1962 and did quite well, "perhaps an average of 2,500 per day," the public affairs officer reported, despite the fact that a small cyclone had passed over the American exhibit shortly before opening day, necessitating frantic carpentry.[107] Symbolically, the photographs had also been passed over. A sharpened national consciousness placed this American view of universal qualities into the frame of reference of the viewer's own experience. The most popular American attractions of this Independence Day Fair showed the projection of national tastes from a Third World audience back to the American display.

> In addition to the exhibit, USIS showed motion pictures on its outdoor screen at the exhibit area. The titles shown were: *Arizona Sheep Dog, Bear Country, Copters and Cows, Jumping Horses, Follow the Sun, Invitation to New York,* and *Transcontinental.* As always, the crowds for these showing were huge. Not

only was every inch of space within the grounds packed and jammed with Afghans, but they stood 30 and 40 deep outside the grounds, outside the range of the amplifiers and nearly out of sight of the screen.

More significantly, the ethnic and religious consciousness of this and other Third World locations[108] had enveloped the general statements of *The Family of Man* with the particularities of history, custom, and contemporary life. The public affairs officer noted that the Soviets had brought in a Tadjik dance troupe that was received with warm enthusiasm.

> Without doubt, the Soviet artists made a strong impact on a somewhat select group of Afghans, and they were praised and publicized in the press; but much of this impact can be attributed to the strong similarity of the language and culture of Afghanistan and Tadjikistan.

At least for the time being, the Soviets could make inroads into Afghanistan using a compelling, ethnic appeal.

The Family of Man spoke to the world of the 1950s. Its political message was directed to a domestic audience faced with the dilemma of nuclear weapons but limited by the horizon of a pre-ballistic-missile world. Steichen's visual statement quickly became framed outside the United States by local circumstances and world events. The crates of photographs blended well with the mission and the ethos of the USIA, and Captain Steichen received copies of reports that must have sounded like appreciative postcards recording the visit of an old friend on a sightseeing tour. The exhibition had its own trajectory, which came back to ground in the explosive terrain of the emerging Third World of the early 1960s. The next chapter traces the downward path of the photographs, simultaneously a triumph and a sign of the exhibition's decline, in the midst of the audience most difficult to recruit—Moscow in 1959.

chapter

THE FAMILY OF MAN IN MOSCOW

four

THE MOST IMPORTANT STOP OF THE INTERNATIONAL TOUR OF *THE FAMILY OF Man* was Moscow, where a special pavilion was constructed for the collection. Despite the varied circumstances in which Steichen's text was exhibited abroad, this appearance was so significantly different that the Captain himself appeared at the opening on July 25, 1959. The photographic exhibition that had been created to break down the suspicions of a rigidifying cold war had finally penetrated the capital of the other side. Ironically, by this time the potency of the collection's message had been diminished. The power of sentiment was no match for the technological race with the Soviet Union and the space-age suspicions of the post-sputnik era.

By decade's end, the development of a Soviet space program supported by the technological sophistication of intercontinental ballistic missiles had directed this distrust into a dangerous and ritualized contest. The weapons here were national ideologies, traditions of technology, and, above all, the productive capacities of national economies. At the Moscow exhibition, arguments were conducted through the aggressively immediate medium of television and were invoked in the name of the people by government representatives. The Moscow exhibition was the site of the famous Kitchen Debate between Richard Nixon and Nikita Khrushchev; controlling competition short of war, not unifying humankind around notions of family, was the objective. This new contest thrust *The Family of Man*, both the exhibit and its message, into the background.

The Family of Man hit the road when the USIA was scarcely two years old. By the time the Moscow exhibition opened, the agency had had six years of experience interpreting American culture abroad. Furthermore, the number of programs defining the American character had grown as the United States became more accustomed to its international stature and as its adversary was drawn closer to New World shores through the technology of weaponry and communications. During the second half of the decade, the State Department spent an average of $20 million per year on construction abroad, as much in one year as had been spent in the entire period from 1900 to 1945. Hundreds of new structures proclaimed America's stature and resolved to engage the Soviets in a war of diplomacy.[1]

By the end of the 1950s the United States government had institutionalized the strategy of presenting ideas through things. American goods, treated as tangible products of New World civilization, were displayed around the world through the International Trade Fairs program, established in 1956 and administered through the office of Harold McClellan, an assistant secretary in the Department of Commerce. The further division of labor reflects the stratified conception of culture that we have already seen in government agencies. The USIA was to handle publicity and information, and the State Department would provide cultural programming for these installations. The object of the new program was not just to give a proper venue for marketing American goods abroad, as McClellan explained in 1956.

> Our concern . . . is to leave an impact that is a proper one and one for which the program is launched, that is, understanding and appreciation of the American system, the American way of life, what it offers, and what the true attitude of the American people is toward the free-world countries and others, and what might be achieved if this understanding were reciprocated.[2]

We have already seen that American cultural diplomacy was drawn more tightly under the control of the State Department after World War II, as private initiatives were overwhelmed by the intensity of a complex world order. In the realm of international commerce the government also played a role, although a collision with an entrenched American value had to be avoided. McClellan was aware that the International Trade Fairs program was not to interfere with private enterprise. Businesses did not need to be subsidized by his program: he proclaimed before cost-conscious congressmen that fairs should exhibit types of products and provide producers a way of talking to potential consumers rather than subsidize particular companies. Besides, he asserted, businesses should not be perceived as being directed by the government: "We don't want to appear as they do in Russia, that the government is the business agent and the people do what we say."[3]

International trade fairs included more than displays of industrial or consumer goods. Book exhibits or collections like *The Family of Man* could be scheduled; live performances would draw in large audiences. This was familiar USIA logic: show foreign populations that the United States was a cultured country and one would assuage many of the fears about this new superpower. In Burma, for example, a performance by the Martha Graham dance troupe at a trade fair just after a visit by the Soviet leadership helped in portraying American concern for the Burmese people. This fair stated a double message: that the most affluent country in the world could support both a stunning array of easily available things and a vibrant (elite) culture. Such appearances by marquee performers served another, subtle purpose. Even as they attracted large crowds into the large central building of the trade fair—frequently a well-traveled geodesic dome—cultural events assured audiences that even though Americans were proud to show off their abundance, they were not consumed by materialism.

> This program helps to correct a distorted picture of this Nation by demonstrating that the United States can match other countries in the tra-

ditional performing arts, has made effective contributions of its own to the mainstream of culture, and is willing to share with other nations its artistic and spiritual treasures as well as its material goods and services.[4]

Here, in short, was a way of packaging a view of the United States in a manageable domain. Inside the gates of the trade fair, the United States was a supermarket (a frequently recreated institution in these venues) of consumer goods. The national economy was not dominated by the arms race but was aimed at placing more conveniences in the hands of more of its citizens. American technology—represented by television and the movies—had penetrated the cultural realm but was held in balance by an enduring concern for the higher pursuits of artistic appreciation. The fairs presented an American world of unlimited possibilities, controlled diversity, and an orderly market, reflecting with the enfranchising checkbook and the increasingly common credit card the logical extension of the voting booth in a capitalistic democracy.

The epitome of the commercial-cultural approach to international persuasion came with the 1958 World's Fair in Brussels. As Howard Callman, commissioner general for the American pavilion at the fair, predicted in testimony before Congress in March 1957, visitors would see all facets of American life without leaving Belgium. There would be an American supermarket, "not to sell merchandise but to show the Russians and the Czechs and the Poles and these people how many hours of work it takes to buy a pair of pants or shoes or lettuce or a bottle of catsup, translated in working hours . . ."[5] Other displays would focus on the American worker, "how the individual invests in American industry—he is the stockholder." The theme of rapidly progressing American technology nurtured by capitalism would be stressed, from the stagecoach and railroad to the television and the peaceful use of the atom, the overarching theme of the fair.[6]

Callman continued into the realm of culture: "But one of the most important things, in my opinion, will be to show the typical American type of culture that we have, and we have a unique culture." The leap in his next sentence revealed what culture meant in such an international context. American culture, he defined as "starting with Indian and primitive art right up to date: sculpture."[7] The catchpenny realism of the supermarket would, in theory, be balanced by the lofty ideals of the sculpture display. On the ground, in a Western European city, such success was difficult to achieve. The organizers complained that they were outspent by the Soviets ten to one, and tourist comment, voiced by ordinary Americans and congressional junketeers, was, at best, mixed. A congressional committee investigating why a $4 million expenditure would have brought such desultory results discovered specific problems and criticized the design of the carousel-like pavilion. The most ominous reading of this Whitman Sampler of American goods and cultural tidbits was that displays of the high and the low—the exalted and the money grubbing—had made American civilization incomprehensible rather than vibrantly attractive.

International events were to provide Harold McClellan, now a private citizen, with another chance to show American culture and American goods abroad: the 1959 American National Exhibition in Moscow. The Moscow exhibition sprang from a bilateral agreement between the Unite States and the Soviet Union signed in 1958. The Russians were to have the services of New York City's Coliseum and the Americans were to build an exhibition space in Moscow. Both events were scheduled for the summer of the following year, presenting the American organizers with a tight schedule to construct the first real opportunity to present the American way of life to Russians, without interference, the agreement reassured, from the other side. There was not even time for a separate appropriation by Congress. President Eisenhower authorized $3.3 million of U.S. Mutual Security funds for the effort.

The exhibition was designed to demonstrate the joys of American consumption: "how America lives, works, learns, produces, consumes, and plays; what kind of people Americans are and what they stand for; and America's cultural values."[8] Thus, the massive production of the post-World War II American consumer economy became an arsenal for this display of the might of appetite. As Felix Belair of the *New York Times* anticipated, "The purpose here will be to show the abundance of the American economy as it is broadly shared by all the people, the immense variety and great freedom of choice and the conveniences available.[9] The widespread abundance of American life was "irrefutable truth," according to the exhibition organizers. From this foundation could be built the apparently pervasive democracy and the ease of living that, in the eyes of Americans preparing for their invasion of Moscow, made the benefits of the American system manifestly superior.

The attention of the Russian audience must be held on items that were representative of the culture in which such goods were so common. Major exhibition elements were selected, therefore, for their symbolic, typically American character. The American single-family home was indispensable. The six-room structure to be deployed in Moscow—three bedrooms, one and one-half baths, "L"-shaped living/ dining area, and kitchen—was similar to $12,000 homes being constructed in the suburban boom near New York City. Herbert Sadkin, president of All-State Properties, which prefabricated the home on Long Island, predicted that envious Russians would not believe that this was truly middle-class housing and suggested that pictures of people at home in suburban subdivisions be placed inside.[10]

People were chosen as carefully as goods. Representative American families were selected for the fashion show to be presented at the exhibition, among them the R. Ted Davis family of Milburn, New Jersey, chosen to represent the suburban ideal. Mr. Davis was active in the Explorer Scout program and was an usher at the Episcopal Church. Mrs. Davis was a Sunday school teacher and an active PTA member. Their three children were distributed among high school, junior high, and grade school. The interweaving of church and school, the value placed on activities that drew the nuclear family together, marked the Davises as exemplars of the burgeoning middle class of the late 1950s. All the Davises were learning Russian in preparation for a "summer trip that will be anything but typical."[11]

A committee supervised by the Whitney Museum chose a spectrum of American art from the preceding thirty years, a problematic exercise because the politics of art in the 1950s was thoroughly enmeshed in the cold war struggle in which the overall exhibition was enlisted. Since the 1947 controversy over *Advancing American Art,* few art exhibits had been sponsored by the government, out of concern for domestic criticism. That such a risk would now be taken demonstrates the importance of showing two strata of American culture, the commercially successful and the elite. And the anticipated objections did come. Charging that more than half of the sixty-seven paintings and sculptures had been executed by artists with records of "affiliation with Communist fronts and causes," Francis E. Walter, Democrat of Pennsylvania and chairman of the House Un-American Activities Committee, subpoenaed several artists, Ben Shahn among them, for well-publicized inquisitions.[12] This controversy reached President Eisenhower, who, in a summer press conference, supported the display by stating enigmatically, "I am not going to be the censor myself for the art."[13]

In order to defuse this HUAC inquiry into the relationship between politics and aesthetics, additions were made to the gently modernist display of art. To the show that appeared in Moscow was appended a selection of eighteenth- and nineteenth-century paintings. Despite the protests of conservative congressmen, the show contained all the works that had originally been selected—an achievement noted by Lloyd Goodrich of the Whitney Museum, one of the curators of the show: "The Administration's decision to stand firm marked a great and encouraging difference from similar past incidents."[14]

Close scrutiny was given to the ideological force carried by a particular house, a specific family, an array of aesthetic experiences. The selection of actual goods to be displayed in the suburban home and the model apartment at Sokolniki Park was left to the discretion of George Nelson and Co., the interior design consultants for the exhibition. Nelson's staff scoured Macy's and other New York department stores for appropriate objects. Having been screened by the buyers at these establishments, these consumer items needed no further proof of purity.[15]

Harold McClellan directed the exhibition staff and delegated responsibilities in an interdepartmental pattern that must have been familiar to him from his time heading the International Trade Fairs program. Staff supplied by the USIA contributed to planning the exhibition and controlling its message. The State Department helped with the negotiations that brought the first American exhibition to Moscow. The Commerce Department assisted with the procurement and shipping of goods to Moscow.[16]

Because this was the first beachhead in enemy territory, extraordinary care was given to managing this American space. All the while dealing with several federal agencies and hundreds of interested businesses, McClellan consulted experts whom he thought might be able to help the exhibition reach the Russian people with the American message. On January 8, 1959, for example, McClellan convened a round table consisting of his staff, the exhibition's designer George Nelson, USIA Deputy Director Abbott Washburn, and several representatives of the press, Daniel Schorr (CBS), Marvin Kalb (CBS), Whitman Bassow (UPI), and E. Clifton Daniel (*New York Times*).[17] The transcript of this one preserved conversation should give us an idea of other consultations.

There was to be no censorship, McClellan reported.[18] The director, like his USIA colleagues, placed his faith in the persuasive power of information. The first task, therefore, was to establish credibility through the introduction of some abstract themes—the story of American science, labor, or education.[19] Then the object was to inundate the visitor with products that the average American could afford.

> We don't want to show them we make bigger stuff. We want to show them we make things they don't know about, that the average guy will be tickled to death to have, like trailers, farm machinery for a small unit farm in the U.S., but are not known in Russia.[20]

A supermarket, containing the consumable analog to randomly accessible bits of information, would also be part of this deployment, particularly the frozen-food section, which was armed with convenient delicacies unknown in Russia.

It was important to show both quantity and quality, Daniel Schorr pointed out. If a television set or an automobile were hauled out as a single curiosity, Russians were not likely to be impressed: equally functional Russian models could be shown, but, "theirs are models and prototypes which they are just developing but which are just not available in numbers." He continued with an observation that has relevance to the situation in Russia decades later.

> The reason I mention the supermarket is that the one great crying need in Russia is for better service. Their distribution system plods along. People are constantly irritated by not being able to buy things that are theoretically available without queuing up. . . . We must convey a sense of distribution, service and availability. Simply showing one Chrysler or one Chevrolet car in itself will not impress the Russians unless some way can be found to show with it the statistics on how many people have Chevrolet cars.[21]

The portrayal of American geography could vary—Russians should see both palm trees and snowy scenery—but the ubiquity of consumer goods should remain as an organizing principle.

As we will see, the American government kept elaborate statistics about their Russian visitors. In return, Americans were told to expect careful scrutiny from the outset, at least on the part of the masses, who were expected to ignore official disdain. The Russians, Clifton Daniel pointed out, would arrive with their notebooks in hand.

> These Russians will be very precise; they will write down figures in notebooks. They like figures and we should give it [sic] to them. But be prepared for them to be critical and if you don't have the answer, they'll get mad. They'll want to know the facts and figures; that is the way they have been brought up. You have to have everything there. Don't count on them missing a trick.

The debate that was intended for this exhibition started with the initial seduction of consumer goods and continued through pencilled calculations in the notebook of the Russian visitor who would carry this germinating knowledge into the home.

They may be regimented but they do have minds, they will have questions and they'll want the answers. You have got to have the answers, no matter which field it is in, such as how many automobiles are owned by Americans—even if they don't necessarily believe it. But if you tell it to them, they'll write it down in their books. Soon you'll have them arguing about it, they will be at each other's throats and pretty soon the whole damn system will collapse.[22]

In such an ideologically charged debate, one had to anticipate rebuttal. One probable source of hostile questions would have to do with race. The strategy for dealing with this issue was to defuse it by diffusing it: don't single out great African Americans, integrate the mass. As McClellan commented, "If you want to show a lot of people going into a supermarket, pick an area where there are a lot of colored people. Do not just say colored and white people mix. You've got to show them doing it. You have got to have that point made indirectly."[23] Seeing was believing. Despite the widely reported school desegregation riots in Arkansas and the turmoil of the nascent civil rights movement, a well-chosen picture would allow the organizers to reconstruct the vision of an America of harmonious difference and equality for all.

The Family of Man did not figure into the initial plans for the Moscow exhibition. Only in February 1959 was the collection of photographs added, and the debate over the inclusion of Steichen's work shows the great distance traveled since the Museum of Modern Art debut. The Moscow exhibition's advisory board had argued successfully for the photographs, "feeling that . . . its political and humanistic overtones made it a very appropriate part of this exhibition."[24] The immediate problem was assembling a pristine copy for Moscow. Two versions had already been dispersed, two well-traveled sets were on the road in Asia and Scandinavia, and the freshest set of photographs, the Museum of Modern Art original, which had circulated through major museums in the United States, had been seriously damaged by water while in storage in Lebanon. The subject of discussion among museum and USIA staff members and the exhibition organizers was not the efficacy of the display (or its artistic merit, for that matter) but who was to pay for its installation.

The negotiations that brought Steichen's visual text to Moscow reveal the interlocking channels of power that dominated cultural diplomacy in the late 1950s. Abbott Washburn, the USIA deputy director, went from the International Program of the Museum of Modern Art to the Rockefeller Brothers Fund in search of about $35,000 for a new copy of the photographs. No matter where he went he found himself asking the same people to support the project. Nelson Rockefeller had been president of both the museum and the Brothers Fund. Furthermore, during World War II he had worked with the Office of Inter-American Information, a predecessor of the USIA, had presided over the reorganization of the executive branch of government that produced the USIA from its predecessor, the IIA, and had served for over a year as special assistant to the president for cold war strategy. Blanchette Rockefeller, his sister-in-law, was the president of the museum's International Program, and Porter McCray, that program's director, sat on the advisory board for the

Moscow exhibition. McCray was, of course, directly familiar with the debate over the inclusion of *The Family of Man* (he had opposed it because he thought the purpose of the exhibition was "to show off America"[25]).

The connections among the three institutions were more than personal. Before the USIA's formation, when cultural diplomacy was still negotiated between the State Department and private groups, the Museum of Modern Art had received $650,000 from the Rockefeller Brothers Fund to present American art abroad. This they did with the blessing of the government, which saw the opportunity for American representation at important international shows like the Venice Biennale without the inevitable inquisition about the Americanness of modern art that would result from direct government involvement. *The Family of Man* had not been a part of this program but had been purchased directly by the USIA—four times over—from the museum. The museum and the agency also were linked by the necessity to classify *The Family of Man* within a taxonomy of cultural forms. As we have seen, the exhibition's success challenged the museum's sense of audience and its definition of modernism. The agency viewed the photographs through the proprietary lens of an instrumental definition of culture, and yet there was no doubt that the presence of Steichen elevated the reception of the show to the formal attire that the State Department held as its prerogative.

The discussions among Washburn, Charles Noyes of the Rockefeller Brothers Fund, Porter McCray, and the harried Harold McClellan during late February and early March 1959 show what sort of cultural commodity *The Family of Man* had become. The International Program turned down Washburn's request for funding because "they felt that their role was to do things that the government and others weren't willing to do. The Family of Man is not controversial, nothing difficult about it, it is an established show and has a reputation on its own."[26] Noyes's initial reply to Washburn was hardly more encouraging. The Brothers Fund, he said, would be "allergic" to a proposal for the entire $35,000.[27] On the same day of Washburn's phone call, March 5, Noyes had lunch with Harold McClellan. Noyes's recapitulation of their conversation shows how anxious the director of the American exhibition had become. There was no USIA money to be had for this worthy purpose, but McClellan:

> wanted, nevertheless, to make it perfectly clear that, come hell or high water, the exhibit was going to be included and it was going to be in absolutely A-1 condition. He would not tolerate any second-rate operation. He didn't know how, but he was going to find the necessary funds somewhere or other.

Noyes viewed preparing the photographs as the government's responsibility.

> I pointed out that apparently the only reason there was a need for funds was that the Government hadn't taken proper care of one set, and furthermore, after the Moscow Exhibition was over, the exhibit would still have substantial value for the Government and could form the basis for future tours of the same nature.[28]

To McCray he had confided more pointedly that the fund would be underwriting an exhibition that would have service to the government long after the one-time investment in the Moscow display. This hardheaded negotiation over who was to pay and who was to profit was masked by the final request, which made a by-now typical obeisance to The Family of Man. The project was granted $15,000 "because of artistic excellence and because it expresses very effectively America's underlying interest in humanity everywhere."[29] The attached budget revealed the extent of compromise: the government provided $40,000 in mounting, lighting, and staffing costs in Moscow; the museum received the grant from the fund, less than half of the original request; the plastics industry donated the display pavilion, valued at $50,000. The copy that appeared in Moscow, the fifth and last copy to be circulated by USIA, combined newly developed prints with salvageable remnants from Beirut and undamaged recruits from the Scandinavian version.

Steichen's work appeared in Moscow through one last recognition of its sentimental message. Now it was subsumed into a larger text, crafted for a new audience that both echoed and transcended the construction of The Family of Man. McClellan's staff examined millions of products for their appropriateness to the exhibition's goal. Steichen and Miller had used a similar procedure in preparation for The Family of Man, but with a different intent. The two photographers assumed that these images transcended ideology by presenting universally recognized symbols that gained their attraction not through the longing after possessions but through the recognition that the life of the viewer was within the domain of the photograph. The American exhibition workers chose goods for Moscow to embody ideology, so that the items would become metonymies, symbolic of a national culture. The object of Steichen's work was to show similarity: couples from all over the world united in bonds of love or loyalty—"We two form a multitude." The Moscow exhibition spoke words of harmony, but assumed difference, a dissonance between what the United States was and what Russian audiences had been told. This was the ultimate deployment of our information against their propaganda.

Both exhibitions had sought outside advice. Steichen had brought individual consultants into the loft on 52nd Street: Dorothea Lange, the most sympathetic of the photographers, Jerry Mason, the prospective publisher of The Family of Man book, and Carl Sandburg, for example. McClellan, borrowing from the corporate world that the Moscow exhibition was intended to represent, convened round tables as boards of advisors. The bomb helped shape the syntax of both efforts. The 1955 photographic collection aimed at being disarming: atomic attack would become unthinkable. The 1959 exhibition did not go even as far as disarmament: the retaliatory capabilities of both sides should sublimate mutual enmity into a commercial war, coincidentally, more favorable ground for the United States.

The Family of Man and the Sokolniki Park installation also demonstrate the interlocking influence of American modernism. George Nelson, who dealt with both building design and the display of American goods in Moscow, was as greatly influenced by Herbert Bayer as Steichen had been, particularly by the Bauhaus designer's concept of expanded vision.[30] Unlike Steichen, Nelson worked in Bayer's domain;

both had accepted modernism and were engaged in applying these principles of perspective and design to the world of industry. Bayer and Nelson had also dealt with the modernist architect Paul Rudolph, designer of floor plans for both *The Family of Man* and the *Good Design* 1952 exhibition at the Chicago Merchandise Mart, a layout to which Nelson referred approvingly.[31] Bayer's view of the purpose of an exhibition was also Nelson's: "an exhibition has a story to tell. The story begins at the entrance and ends at the exit, and it should be seen—just as a book is read—in its proper sequence."[32]

Where Bayer spoke of stretching vision along both a horizontal and a vertical axis, Nelson wrote about "the enlargement of vision."[33] In his elaboration of this concept, we see a kindred spirit to Edward Steichen. In both cases—Steichen's collection of photographs and Nelson's design for the Moscow exhibition—we can see how easily the intention of the designer can be appropriated by the ideological structure surrounding the work of an individual. Nelson believed that the modern world had been transformed by the atomic bomb. The feeling of being dislodged was exacerbated by an almost palpable paradox.

> The Bomb was programmed, designed, built, and exploded by people who presumably knew exactly what they were doing. It is, I think, this new sense of intellectual mastery over the physical world that is making us so acutely and unhappily aware of the world over which seemingly we have no mastery at all.[34]

According to Nelson, people viewed the world "atomistically"—"everything is seen as a separate, static object or idea."[35] Thus traditional relationships would not work in a newly dynamic world where the static energy based in a stable universe had been split into kinesis. Relationships among things became more important than the things themselves. This was translatable to foreign relations, according to Nelson, and also accounted for the disappearance of the author in much of modern art and sculpture.

> It is no coincidence that at the peak of his self-consciousness the individual dissolved into an almost incomprehensibly abstract network of relationships and that the same thing happened to his concept of inanimate matter. Both developments, you will note, tended to substitute transparency, in a sense, for solidity, relationships for dissociated entities, and tension or energy for mass.[36]

As individuals became accustomed to renegotiating relationships constantly, they would learn to cooperate. It was to this new, postwar individual that architects and designers had to address themselves.

> Ideologically he may be taken in by the propaganda pumped into him so persistently wherever he lives, for he is still a bit green, but every major development in his very dynamic world, whether under capitalism or communism, in peace or war, will act to foster him as a type.[37]

The philosophy of the Moscow exhibition's designer, then, was to talk around or over the level of ideology to the common attributes of post-atomic man. This would have struck the author of The Family of Man as not only sensible but as a brave reliance on the goodness of humankind in dangerous times. However, the aesthetics of both Nelson and Steichen were overwhelmed by the American space deployed in the heart of Moscow.

The exhibition's ideology was deeply embedded in the rhetoric of display. On one level, the presentation in Sokolniki Park was restrained: overtly political propagandizing was downplayed. On a deeper level, the exhibition was profoundly ideological—all the more so because the particular logic of capitalism was presented as straightforward fact, as second nature. The text of display spoke to a post-sputnik world of international competition. Crafted with the ingenuity of American business, headed by a former president of the National Association of Manufacturers and government official accustomed to internationalizing American nationalism, the exhibition addressed the world of peaceful coexistence with a partisan force that reduced the actions of the people to the pronouncements of their representatives. The weight of this argument, and the celebrity of the contest, submerged The Family of Man in a world order it had warned against just four years before.

The exhibition's view of the United States was carefully crafted during the first half of 1959, so that when the buildings opened in Sokolniki Park in July, Russian visitors were presented with a rigorously legible arrangement, seemingly impartial in its portrayals of the facts of American life, setting up a debate with the presumed propaganda with which this space was otherwise surrounded. Two significant voices made this debate explicit. Richard Nixon and Nikita Khrushchev toured this American platform, recognized clearly what was being fashioned there, and debated its meaning. However, the harmony of the display had already been disrupted implicitly by elements of the exhibition like The Family of Man, which fought through the careful control to speak of their own contradictory histories. Before sampling the debate or exploring some sites of contestation, we must examine the product of this half-year of consultation: the American National Exhibition in Moscow, as it presented itself to the visitor in July 1959.

Advertised as "a corner of America in the heart of Moscow,"[38] the exhibition commanded an acute, open angle of Sokolniki Park. The center of attention was a gold-anodized geodesic dome, two hundred feet in diameter. Traffic was funnelled into this circular "idea" building and then enticed into the large exhibition hall, which spread an array of American consumer goods from more than five hundred companies before the 2.7 million Russian visitors to the six-week exhibition. This division between thought and goods replicated the organization of the Brussels World's Fair installation. An outside area, located mostly behind the exhibition hall, presented automobiles from Detroit, the tract house from Long Island, and a multi-screen film introduction to America from Walt Disney. Six stands dispensed free cups of Pepsi to the weary, and a secluded hi-fi exhibit, surrounded by trees, allowed visitors to sit and collect their thoughts with musical accompaniment.

The American organizers had predicted correctly that this would be a popular exhibition. In preparation for the deluge, seventy-five Russian-speaking American guides had been enlisted to answer questions and fill the notebooks that Mr. Daniel had told them their audiences would bring. A voluminous *Training Book for Guides* was constructed, so that these Americans could satisfy the Russian appetite for those facts that would bring home the ideological intention of the exhibition. The guides received preliminary training in Washington, and the *Training Book* oriented them to both the space and the structure of the exhibition. This hastily published introduction furnishes us with the clearest impression of this self-consciously American place.

Rimming the outside of the dome was a gallery of "lifesize photographs of prominent Americans" accompanied by explanatory four-foot panels in Russian[39] that provided "a composite picture of Americans and their contributions to mankind's welfare in nearly all fields." Inside the entrance of the dome, framing the material beyond, was a message from President Eisenhower. Around the interior circumference of the idea building were displays of eight broad themes governing the production and consumption of ideas in the United States: "Education, Medical Research, Agricultural Research, Labor, Space Research, Nuclear Research, Chemical Research, and Basic Research."[40] Each area was marked by a different color of light that reflected off the facets of the ceiling like a rainbow or a kaleidoscope. Occasionally, the lights in the dome would be dimmed and a seven-screen film introduction to life in the United States would be projected overhead. Even before walking into the center of this American hemisphere, visitors were challenged to look up, beyond the horizontal, to planes of action that impinged on the limits of vision.

One item of particular interest inside the dome was a computer—an interactive feature. The fashioners of the exposition had learned something from the 1958 Brussels World's Fair, in which the United States had also been represented by a geodesic dome and a computer. In Moscow the more sophisticated RAMAC "electronic brain" from IBM would answer over four thousand questions about the United States and, in this age of electronic surveillance, keep a tally of the most popular inquiries. In Brussels a smaller array of possibilities had been presented to visitors through the computer, and a prominently displayed voting booth had allowed them to pick their favorite president. RAMAC encouraged the Soviets, in effect, to vote for their view of the United States by selecting from questions either hostile or friendly. The formal voting booth in Sokolniki Park was relegated to an outside position near a Pepsi stand and merely inquired which of the exhibits visitors had appreciated most.

The dome and the exhibition hall, mated by their convex and concave shapes, acted as the primary joint around which the exhibition articulated. A trip to the exhibition hall showed how the ideas of the dome resulted in consumer goods to which Americans had access. The two-story glass and aluminum display allowed Russians to examine these goods from all angles. If the visitor wanted more substantial items, the car pavilions behind the exhibition hall placed automobiles on turntables for close inspection. Other examples from Ford, Chrysler, and Chevrolet were positioned "normally" in this part of the exhibition space: "passenger cars beside the model home, station wagons beside the camping grounds, and trucks and jeeps near the farming equipment."[41]

Directing the easy flow of the exhibition space was the ideology of postwar American abundance. This was an exhibition that concentrated on goods of a specific sort. The Russians had brought the products of heavy industry to New York, the might that had produced both sputnik and gigantic intercontinental ballistic missiles. The Americans countered with kitchen conveniences and power tools. Inside the exhibition hall were items that easily could come to hand in a trip down any main street. The kitchen in the model home contained the labor-saving devices that were becoming standard equipment for the middle-class home. Small farm machinery was shown, implying a contrast to collectivist modes of agriculture. That this was a culture of leisure and convenience was made explicit through the camping display that gave Russians a vision of Americans at their ease.

All Americans were represented here by their goods, but middle-class preferences were given the ideological weight. This was a display oriented toward the suburbs. Cities were represented not through their inhabitants but through their architecture: skyscrapers and even a recording of "traffic noises in Times Square"[42] proclaimed that this was not where typical Americans lived. Home was on the quickly developing periphery, in structures like the forty-four-by-twenty-six-foot tract home dissected for careful study at the rear of the exhibition. This carefully prepared area was "landscaped to appear as much as possible as it would in a typical American community."[43] The intention was to give "Mr. and Mrs. Soviet Citizen and children a chance to see how Mr. and Mrs. America and their children live in the United States."[44]

The Americans represented here belonged to families that were both the location for consumption and the foundation for the American way of life portrayed in Moscow. The fashion show, for example, presented only eight professional models among the forty people who walked out onto the platform. Represented among the remaining thirty-two were three families, of which the Davises were one: "a needle trade union worker and his wife and children; a city family; and a suburban or country family."[45] No anorexic high-fashion models were selected. The auditions had asked applicants to sing, dance, and extemporize replies to shouted questions. The product of this pageant was well-fed, cheery, wholesome—typically American in the way of an Atlantic City pageant. These individuals could be identified according to a familiar family taxonomy: an elderly matron, a mother or a father, or a teenager— the same cluster of relatives as the group of manikins blown up in the Nevada desert. From this family base the show elaborated a melting-pot theory of American design: "A montage of fashion suggests that many nationalities in America give an international influence to numerous designs."[46] In an otherwise asymmetrical ground plan for the exhibition, it is clear that the fashion show was paired with *The Family of Man*. The two pavilions debated each other across the central axis of ideas and goods: changing fashion against enduring sentiment, three-dimensional superficiality against the depth of a photographic surface.

Two men arrived for the opening of the American exhibition in Moscow in July 1959. Richard Nixon, the vice-president of the United States, came to compete with Nikita Khrushchev. He was prepared to do battle over Berlin, ICBMs, and nuclear-testing treaties. He expected to spar over the recent proclamation of Captive Nations Week, a time of congressionally recommended prayer for those Eastern European nations enslaved by the Soviet Union. Sports images abound in his description of the encounter in *Six Crises*: for him this was the big leagues or the heavyweight fight of the decade. Having been pumped full of "Communist strategy and tactics" by his handlers, he announced that "I ha[d] never been better prepared for a meeting in which I was to participate."[47]

Edward Steichen, with Carl Sandberg in tow, appeared in Moscow for the opening of *The Family of Man*, courtesy of the State Department. For him this was the culmination of the four-year tour of the exhibition, "the high spot of the project."[48] He roamed through the collection of photographs, taking his own snapshots of the visitors in a congenial, private kind of surveillance. While in Moscow he met with photographers, two of them contributors to *The Family of Man* through the SovFoto collection that Wayne Miller had consulted in 1954. Painters also conversed with the noted American artist who had, in fact, renounced that form nearly fifty years before. To both constituencies he gave the advice to avoid abstraction, "a blind alley" to a man who had placed such an investment in the ability of clear images to tell overarching stories among world cultures.[49]

Nixon knew that he would meet up with a formidable adversary. Khrushchev was portrayed to him as cold and unpredictable. Even more disconcerting, his host was notoriously uncouth; when excited, his earthiness could turn to vitriol through "a tirade of four-letter words which made his interpreter blush."[50] The vice-president trained for restraint and resiliency. He had anticipated the context he would be entering: at the Russian exhibition in New York there had been "heavy overtones of Soviet military might."[51] In Moscow the United States would counter with consumer goods, to show the difference in standards of living. There was a strategic context that the American needed to establish.

> My visit would also afford an opportunity for high-level talks with Khrushchev in which I could make clear the United States' position on world issues and, at the same time, obtain for President Eisenhower and our policy makers some firsthand information as to Khrushchev's attitudes and views on the points of difference between the United States and the USSR.[52]

Khrushchev did not disappoint. He was confrontational and rude, accommodating and disarmingly frank. A morning meeting that was supposed to be merely a stage-setting courtesy call at the Kremlin had developed into a real confrontation in which Nixon had felt ambushed. The tour through the exhibition was stressful. Even before the famous Kitchen Debate, Nixon and the premier had clashed several times. While passing the supermarket installation Nixon mentioned that his father had been a grocer. Khrushchev retorted that grocers preyed on the working class.[53] After leaving Sokolniki Park Nixon was subjected to a thoroughly choreographed tour of Moscow and then incarcerated in Khrushchev's dacha for a five-hour discussion of military policies. Overall, the experience was an ordeal: "To keep them from winning and to win ourselves, we must have more stamina and more determination than they have."[54]

By the time Nixon appeared on the platform for the opening of the exhibition, to follow the sports metaphor of his account, he had already broken into the full sweat of the contest. Edward Steichen, seated with him, serenely held his camera in hand so that he could take pictures of the Russian media that were photographing him.[55] He, too, had prepared for this experience through the construction of *The Family of Man*. He, too, had summoned in his experts and had collected an entourage for the arduous preparation of this statement in pictures. This effort had long since concluded, and, since 1955, Steichen had measured the echoes of his proclamation around the world. By the time he arrived in Moscow he had a good idea of what he would see in the interaction between pictures and viewer.

> I have watched the reaction of the various peoples and found that, regard-
> less of the place, the response was always the same. I finally came to the
> conclusion that the deep interest in this show was based on a kind of
> audience participation. The people in the audience looked at the pictures,
> and the people in the pictures looked back at them. They recognized each
> other.[56]

Both of these American participants collected information, but the contrast in intent reveals how differently the two viewed Moscow. Nixon was himself an in- strument of surveillance. In the context of late-1950s suspicion, he had been sent to see how Khrushchev reacted to the articulation of American foreign policy. Like RAMAC, Nixon had been programmed with responses—in *Six Crises* he bragged that the premier did not ask him one question on which he had not been briefed—but the interactivity of both conversation and discovery was more than any machine could handle. The vice-president was conscious of his role as gatherer of sensitive information and articulator of the official United States position. He was cautious about eavesdropping. When he met with Ambassador Thompson, the two spoke in a small interior room at Spaso House next to the second-floor bedroom, where vig- ilant American intelligence officers maintained an area secure from electronic sur- veillance. Steichen conducted his own photographic reconnaissance of the audience and looked through the prying cameras that faced him. As he moved through the ex- hibition he did not, however, suffer the annoyance of the premier poking at him. He saw what he was prepared to see in the faces of Russian visitors.

> I stood in one spot for about twenty minutes and photographed the peo-
> ple as they looked at the section devoted to parents and babies. I decided
> that, if I were to say the snapshots had been made in Wisconsin or Iowa
> or New England, the statement would be accepted without question.[57]

Both the Captain and the vice-president recognized the gulf between the Rus- sian government and its people. Steichen acknowledged the political repression of 1950s Russia. When he arrived back in the West, in neutral Sweden, he felt that he was breathing freely again. However, he saw in Russian people the same humaneness and range of emotional response that he projected onto the rest of the world. A strong appeal to these people through photographs, he fervently believed, would make atomic war impossible. Nixon saw in campaigning among the Russian people a strategy to carry victory away from his encounter with the first secretary: "The Russian people want to live in peace, they are friendly to Americans, appreciative of U.S. aid during World War II, and they are starved for knowledge about the non-Communist world."[58]

Before the trip to Russia, Nixon had visited John Foster Dulles at Walter Reed Hospital, where the secretary of state was spending the final days of his unsuccessful fight with cancer. Dulles had "believed that I might be able to use the forum of the exhibition opening to expose at least some segment of the Russian people to the reasonableness and justice of the American position on world issues."[59] The wisdom of this counsel appeared to Nixon in epiphanies throughout the trip: in the working-class vigor of an early-morning produce market, in the warmth of individual Russians who wanted to touch him, and in the enthusiasm of a crowd in Leningrad that had to be restrained by the police. He liked the Russian people, who were "warm, friendly, gracious,"[60] but he inserted them into a black-and-white view of the world thoroughly entrenched in cold war ideology: us and them, government against people, victory versus defeat.

The American exhibition in Moscow reinforced such a view of American-Soviet interaction. By the time Nixon began to argue with Khrushchev about kitchen appliances, leaning over the rail of the model home's passageway, these consumer items had prepared the arena. The Kitchen Debate deserves its fame as a distillation of what both the stage and the actors intended the play to be. "I'm trying to show them what America is like—to give them some understanding and appreciation—and I've been fighting to keep the 'cold war' out of this thing," Harold C. McClellan had told the New York Times just before the exhibition's opening.[61] However, the cold war was built into the structure of the installation. The presence of the media made the day, in Harrison Salisbury's words, "more like an event dreamed up by a Hollywood scriptwriter than a confrontation of two of the world's leading statesmen."[62] Indeed, the dramatic treatment was written well before the two leaders began their ad-libbing.

With the political campaign for the presidency only a few months away, Richard Nixon knew that he would be judged as a potential world leader through his performance in Moscow. Those illustrious reporters who followed him through the crowds in Moscow, including James Reston and Harrison Salisbury of the New York Times, noticed that "Mr. Nixon has more reporters and photographers following him than at any time in his political career."[63] Nixon worked the crowds as though he were already in a political campaign. In this regard, Khrushchev was his equal. The American waved to onlookers; his Russian adversary embraced bare-chested workers who were still finishing the exhibition site in preparation for the opening to the public on the following day, July 26th. All the while, as Reston commented, "camera men and reporters dominated the scene, shouting and grappling with one another as if their targets were two leading presidential candidates entering a national convention hall."[64]

Nixon was clearly in his element here. He had struggled with the problems of translation up to that point, learning a few Russian proverbs to reach the people and otherwise relying on the phrase "peace and freedom," which he repeated at every opportunity. This had created a good effect—"even his Russian accent, applied to a McGuffey Reader homily of peace, was just good enough to be understood and bad enough to be both amusing and disarming," Reston reported[65]—but had put him at a disadvantage in this foreign context. Sokolniki Park was his home court, and he was determined to score some points. He decided that the kitchen would be the site of the contest, a strategy that not only gave him an arsenal of conveniences but also furnished a variety of easily recognized, evocative props for the media to film and photograph.

The effectiveness of the media in amplifying the American message already had been rehearsed in Sokolniki, through the preview of the Circarama projection. American and Soviet workers had frantically prepared the site, and only at the last minute, the day before the opening, could the 360-degree show be projected onto the inside of its small dome. The effect, according to Salisbury, was dramatic: "The Russians stood with eyes that could only be described as bulging. Their jaws dropped—as, to be honest, did those of the Americans who were watching the spectacular realism of the film."[66] The point was not just to present an argument persuasively to the Moscow audience. Words and gestures had to project beyond the exhibition, through a medium that manipulated as it promised to record realistically. Throughout the discussion of the day was woven attention over media presentation, with Khrushchev expressing concern that he be translated accurately, and Nixon eager to gain access to the Russian audience through a television address.

Nixon carried with him on his morning tour, for which he was technically the host, the text of the address opening the exhibition. In this short speech he made the same appeal to impartial fact that was such a persuasive element of the installation's argument with "the other side." Like the manufacturer of the suburban home, he was concerned that the Russians understand that a home was an essential part of American family life.

> There are 44,000,000 families in the United States. Twenty-five million of these families live in houses or apartments that have as much or more floor space than the one you see in this exhibit. Thirty-one million families own their own homes and the land on which they are built. America's 44,000,000 families own a total of 56,000,000 cars, 50,000,000 television sets and 143,000,000 radio sets. And they buy an average of nine dresses and suits and fourteen pairs of shoes per family per year.

These statistics enlisted the family in the cause of prosperity, an ideological concept in this economic battle. Nixon asserted that "the United States, the world's largest capitalist country, has from the standpoint of distribution of wealth, come closest to the ideal of prosperity for all in a classless society."[67]

The Kitchen Debate must be placed into the context of containment—both the official United States policy regarding the Soviet Union and, as Elaine Tyler May has pointed out, the cultural strategy of the gendered use of domestic space.[68] One should also be aware of the context surrounding the kitchen of the model home, where the two combatants paused for about an hour on the morning of July 25. The media had made actors of the two: the exhibition had provided the basic script, and the home had supplied the requisite blocking. Nixon began by showing the sorts of conveniences built into many of the new houses being constructed in California, and thus the curtain rose.

My purpose here is not to rehearse the debate, because before it was voiced by individuals the contest had been joined through the circumstances of the exhibition. The casting of the main actors made the discussion compelling, but the conversation grew from the site. The debate gained its audience and its notoriety through the intervention of the media, which gave the drama its life. Even at the time this was interpreted as a media event more than as a debate. Reporters asked Nixon the next day, had Mr. Khrushchev been rude? No, the vice-president replied through a spokesperson. During a six-hour meeting later that day Premier Khrushchev playfully inquired whether their debates had offended him. Nixon, a sportsman to the end, characterized the contest as "hard-hitting, direct, frank but not belligerent," a euphemism for an unpredictable joust with a very rude opponent, the author of *Six Crises* later revealed. The American people were queried, had Nixon acquitted himself well against the best competition around? The *New York Times* found that public opinion around the country was almost grudgingly favorable. A sixteen-minute film of the encounter was played on all three networks the day after the confrontation in Moscow, in violation of a bilateral agreement that would have delayed broadcast so that the footage could have been reviewed, edited, and simultaneously presented to American and Russian audiences. This was compelling news, which meant that it was also good drama.[69]

The Kitchen Debate took place at the hearth of the family home; however, this was the overtly ideological sphere of the cold war years, not the refuge of the human continuum that Steichen had depicted. As Nixon's argument moved from the labor-saving devices of the domestic front to the international scene, we can see how far removed *The Family of Man* was from the drama of the newly instituted cultural exchange. Nixon focused on competition, asking, why not compete with goods rather than with missiles? He continued:

> To me you are strong and we are strong. In some ways, you are stronger
> than we are. In others, we are stronger. We are both strong not only from
> the standpoint of weapons but from the standpoint of will and spirit.
> Neither should use that strength to put the other in a position where he
> in effect has an ultimatum. In this day and age that misses the point. With
> modern weapons it does not make any difference if war comes. We both
> have had it.[70]

Khrushchev replied with a statement reminiscent of Steichen's argument in *The Family of Man*: "If all Americans agree with you, then who don't we agree [with]? This [peaceful coexistence] is what we want."[71]

The anthropological appeal of *The Family of Man*, that all people are fundamentally the same, had been replaced by an economic assertion to which there was no acceptable rejoinder other than capitulation. The photographic exhibition had constructed a statement about common origins; the American exhibition in Moscow fought over the future. In this economic struggle, capitalism, aided by technology, would inevitably have the upper hand. The influence of people over events was subordinated to the contest between large, irreconcilable systems. In its final editorial about the Nixon visit, the *New York Times* accurately characterized the competitors.

> What is taking place in Sokolniki Park is nothing less than the confrontation
> of two civilizations, of two ways of life. One is our own, a society where
> the consumer is king, where the great bulk of the productive mechanism
> is devoted to satisfying people's wants, be they necessities or whims. The
> other is the regimented Soviet society in which for over four decades leaders such as Stalin and Khrushchev have decided what should be produced
> on the basis of an ideology which glorified the machine tool and the steel
> mill while viewing the washing machine and the dishwasher—to say nothing of the home "permanent" kit or the hi-fi set—as of scant consequence.

In such a situation, the object was not cooperation or understanding but subversion. Why, Russians were coached by their American hosts to ask, "are so few of these 'gadgets' available in the land of 'triumphant socialism'?"[72]

The Moscow exhibition contained many cultural sites where carefully selected symbols of American life instructed Russian visitors on the merits of the capitalistic system and, on the other hand, defied the organizers of the exhibition with their own, frequently contradictory, histories. *The Family of Man* was only one such site. Other locations, such as the suburban home and automobile displays, the dome, and the many areas featuring plastic products, helped create complexity and contradiction within a seemingly straightforward cultural text.

The suburban home, the most symbolic of all the structures, the center of a presumably serene middle-class life, had, in fact, brought to Moscow a history of struggle and debate. The suburban house in Sokolniki Park was dubbed "the splitnik" by its manufacturers, echoing and mocking sputnik. American builders, whom George Nelson referred to as "merchant builders,"[73] were often, like the eponymous William Levitt, also developers who knew the potency of the single-family home as an object of desire. They had been trying to harness the power of middle-class longing for over a decade. The *Life* Housing Round Table of 1948, knew what a demanding ideal they had to construct.

> [The house] is a civic or social product; and for those who live in it it has
> a spiritual significance. These elementary facts must constantly be borne in
> mind if our efforts to house ourselves better are not to meet with disaster.[74]

Prefabrication would not be a solution; these builders had anticipated this in 1948. Even though the Lustron house could be forged and bonded in a factory procedure, resulting in a steel and porcelain structure of about 650 square feet, the real hope lay with efforts like William Levitt's to bring assembly-line techniques out onto the site. The demand of the late 1940s had to be satisfied, builders knew, because the web of city, county, and state regulations could easily be replaced by the intervention of the federal government. While there was money to be made in the construction business, the power of the structure being marketed could overwhelm the seller: "the Devil is the product itself: the Devil is the house."[75]

The federal government helped developers deal with this devil through the mortgage programs and tax incentives of the late 1940s, a sunny exorcism that enriched the likes of Levitt and filled truck gardens and disused lots with large, planned commuter communities. Both families formed after the war and older families prevented by the war from establishing households had rushed to suburban developments during the ten years previous to the Moscow exhibition. The roof of this typically one-story or split-level ranch-style house lengthened or broadened as the middle-class family laid claim to as much private space as earning power and mortgage requirements would allow. Market research had told builders that three bedrooms and two bathrooms were most desired. While the Federal Housing Administration discovered by survey during the 1950s that homeowners were generally happy with their purchases,[76] the craving for more space was not satisfied. The unfulfilled longing of the late 1940s had been reduced to a homeowner's desire for more space, something that could be satisfied with more capital; until that larger downpayment could be made, at least those filling out their forms were sitting in their own living rooms. Even though the size of the average suburban home had nearly doubled within a decade, families wanted still larger houses.

For the present, though, they had to be content with what developers could turn out in a hurry. By 1957 the increasingly generous policies of the federal government had produced 4.5 million homes financed by federal loans, at least 30 percent of all homes built during the decade.[77] The demand for these homes, amplified by the availability of both land and capital, resulted in a change in the way subdivisions sprang to life. In previous decades of more modest, privately financed growth, a developer would allow building on only a portion of available land at a time, often relinquishing actual construction to a subcontractor. Now several hundred virtually identical houses could be assembled at once, with the promise that all would be occupied quickly.[78] Thus was created the well-publicized assembly-line technique of William Levitt's towns.

> The construction process itself was divided into twenty-seven distinct
> steps—beginning with laying the foundation and ending with a clean
> sweep of the new home. Crews were trained to do one job—one day the
> white-paint men, then the red-paint men, then the tile layers. Every possi-
> ble part, and especially the most difficult ones, were preassembled in cen-
> tral shops, whereas most builders did it on site. Thus, the Levitts reduced
> the skilled component to 20 to 40 percent.[79]

For George Nelson a family home like the splitnik would have been as forward-looking a structure as the geodesic dome that was the signature of the Moscow exhibition. This house would be transformed into an easily manufactured, widely replicable space that would alter fundamentally the way the majority of Americans lived. Space, he reasoned, would become the prime commodity, as families, surrounded by their accumulated goods, turned inward. Nelson posited that as consumers became more affluent they would discover prefabricated housing, as "gracious living" gave way to a generalized celebration of prosperity.[80] With affluence would come acquisition of labor-saving devices and the equipment of leisure, both of which would require added storage. With increased time free from work would come the specialized interests of family members: the hi-fi would have to be separated from both the television and the father's study. Nelson concluded that a house assembled in a factory rather than in mass on-site maneuvers by platoons of workers, as in the Levitt model, would provide both the low cost per square foot and the multiplicity of separate rooms that would be required by the American middle class. This vision was, for him, to be encouraged into reality as a sign of prosperous, egalitarian times.

> To see the real meaning of the industry-made house, we must somehow shed ourselves of the fear that we as people have to become standardized when we accept standardized tools, toys or shelters. The creaking platitude "clothes make the man" no longer holds when everyone can be well-dressed.[81]

Technology had brought both the anxiety of the bomb and the prosperity that would allow the middle class to overcome modern perils. Like many others, Nelson underestimated the conservative aesthetic of American homeowners. They knew what a house was supposed to look like.

Standardization vexed critics like Lewis Mumford and Ada Louise Huxtable, who worried about the little boxes springing up in fields all over Long Island. However, people actually living in these developments were relatively content, a sign of how effectively middle-class desires had been satisfied in the decade before the exhibition. Not only that, but the sociologist Herbert Gans, among others, discovered that the monotony of mass-produced housing was diminished through the customizing of interiors. Homeowners would have been intimidated by Premier Khrushchev's proclamation that "we build for our grandchildren"—many people considered the tract house to be only a first purchase from which one could trade up as earning power increased.

This home was located farther away from cities, to be reached by private car instead of public transportation.[82] Suburbanization decreased the density of metropolitan areas, a phenomenon at odds with the postwar redevelopment of most European cities but a relief to Civil Defense planners anticipating an atomic attack on population centers. Architectural similarity characterized suburban homes—the ranch-style invaded from the American West and held stylistic sway for the decade—so picking out a house for Moscow was easy: roughly the same building could have been found in newly graded fields near New York City, Houston, or Los Angeles. As Mr. Nixon pointed out, the mass production of single-family dwellings had made home ownership a middle-class commonplace, so the older association of a suburban house with wealth was now broken. So far, these distinguishing characteristics of post–World War II suburban development, as delineated by Kenneth Jackson, would seem to support precisely the intention of the fashioners of the splitnik. However, even the home was a contested site in postwar America.

Because of the nature of development and because of the shaping hand of the federal government, suburbs also tended to be far more homogeneous than prewar settlements. If Harold McClellan had wanted to show an integrated America, the contemporary suburb, protected by zoning requirements, mortgage eligibility regulations, and restrictive covenants, was not the place to turn. It was ironic that the splitnik, although presented as the seat of innovation within American consumer culture, was actually a fortress built against social change. The suburb was already white; the force of the emerging urban-focused civil rights movement was making this enclave more reactionary. In an argument about the future, the kitchen of a suburban home was a strange choice.

The mass production of the home—increasingly the province of the engineer and not the architect—lessened regional variation. A home in a cold climate like Minnesota had the same picture window that had made better sense in the California prototype. The exhibition had constructed a regional reading of American culture in several other venues: the Circarama's tourist collection of notable sites, the large map in the dome, the regional art inserted into the controversial display. The exhibition focused on individual choice but then constructed a monolithic culture of consumption directing these choices. A nation of bungalows, Cape Cods, and modern colonials was being represented by the tract house, sometimes disguised with a stylistic veneer, but always supported by a mass-produced element of uniformity.

More significant, suburban homes directed more of the attention of their inhabitants inward, to the functioning of the nuclear family. As Clifford Clark points out: "Almost without thinking, middle-class suburbanites took the protected-home vision of the nineteenth-century reformers and turned it into their central preoccupation."[83] When family concerns became paramount within homogeneous suburbs, civic consciousness declined. The Americanness of the platform from which Mr. Nixon chose to speak had increasingly little to do with conventional patriotism and more to do with what Elaine May has called "privatized abundance"[84]—the ability to contribute to a national economy that promised adequate financial return.

The splitnik was not the only easily fabricated building at the exhibition; a well-traveled geodesic dome, a familiar symbol of post-World War II American technological sophistication, was at the center of Sokolniki Park. This was far from the first time that such a dome had represented American interests. Indeed, by this time the dome had become so familiar a part of American international presentations that its use in Brussels in 1957 was considered unimaginative. In 1956 the Department of Commerce had placed a dome in an International Trade Fair in Kabul.[85] The large structure, one hundred feet in diameter, was flown in on one DC-4 airplane and was assembled in short order under the supervision of a single American engineer. It was said to remind Afghani workers of a *yurt*. The theater of the assembly process, the oddness of the shape, the unfamiliar texture of aluminum frame and nylon skin made the dome a great success. "The geodesics, it was argued, dramatized American ingenuity, vision, and technological dynamism; as structures to house American trade exhibits they would be tangible symbols of progress."[86] Domes were therefore deployed throughout the rest of the decade at fairs and expositions, in Poland, India, Burma, and Thailand, for example.

From the beginning of the decade, the dome represented "technology in building."[87] The even distribution of load, the portability of both materials and completed buildings, and the aerodynamic qualities of the structure presented great advantages, since mobility meant coexistence with the extremes of world climates. Through its unusual geometry, the design of this invention projected the viewer into the non-linear world of the future. Because of its circular footprint, the geodesic dome efficiently commanded space: "One of the things to come has come—this design represents the highest practical point so far in the skeletal enclosure of space."[88] As Harold McClellan had stated, "The idea has been for the first building, the dome, to establish credibility for what we have to say. We want to give irrefutable evidence in the first building people enter that what we are saying is the truth."[89]

In their manufacture and use, domes would reveal themselves as American structures. The process of dome-making was patented by R. Buckminster Fuller in 1951. Through the several corporations Fuller created, and with the help of Kaiser Aluminum, this structure remained a part of Fuller's enterprise throughout the decade. The first major dome commission came from the Ford Corporation, for which Fuller fashioned a lightweight geodesic cap for their headquarters in Michigan in honor of the fiftieth anniversary of the family-run firm. Because domes offered both cheap, clear-span enclosures and the image of futuristic technology, other commissions followed—for a concert hall in Honolulu, a train repair area in Baton Rouge. By the end of the decade, Fuller had become "the conservative industrialists' ideal of the pioneer scientist."[90] This was a comfortable form of corporate modernism, more congenial and adaptable than the regimental skyscrapers then being constructed by international style architects in major American cities.

Fuller had also proven his usefulness to the Defense Department. During the 1950s the air force stationed many "radomes" along the distant early warning (DEW) radar line at the northern border of the continent. Domes became a vital part of the early-warning system against Russian attack and a symbol of the cold war. Geodesic structures were ideal for the Arctic climate: not only could they withstand hurricane-force winds but they could be assembled in less than one day and moved to new sites easily.

Mobility therefore was transformed into deployment. A vantage point was linked to undetected surveillance. A dome in the north, *Life* magazine had pointed out, would be the first reassurance that humane American technology would prevail over Russian bombs. Replicability had already become inextricably connected with the extension of American consumer goods to the world market; now territory, space itself, could be claimed by the square foot.

This was not the intent of the designer of the dome. For Fuller, the dome offered the solution to the housing problem of a posturban world:

> a rational system for enclosing living space, mass-producible, readily erected from standardized parts, maximally economical of materials (hence of weight), and moreover something you could take apart and move, or even move intact, slung from a helicopter.[91]

By 1959, though, geodesic structures had been appropriated by the military and industry but not by the individual home owner. What he (and she) most emphatically wanted was the suburban tract home that stood behind the dome in Sokolniki Park. Between the two lay the difference between ideas and taste: as a representative of the engine of American consumer capitalism a dome would do, but it was not a home.

> No dome homes without mass production; no mass production without mass consumption, no mass consumption without mass demand, on the existence of which any company that financed the tool-up would be taking a truly enormous gamble.[92]

Fuller, like his colleague George Nelson, had run up against the last stronghold of craftsmanship and tradition—both of these simulated and exchangeable according to fashion, but potent nonetheless.

One Sokolniki Park site that attracted attention was the display of the manufacture of plastic. One could see a plastic bowl being molded here and, if one were lucky, actually take home such an artifact as a souvenir. This location merely highlighted through production what was woven throughout the implied consumption of the exhibition's economy: that plastic was an essential feature of the American way of life. It was, therefore, important to show this unnatural product being made, in order to emphasize both the magical and the profoundly ordinary properties it contained.

Certain forms of plastics—bakelite, for example—had already been employed in industrial uses for almost one hundred years. During the prewar years, more advanced products such as nylon and vinyl had brought plastics into consumer culture. Americans had been surrounded by architectural design elements and plastic gadgets before the outbreak of war. In fact, according to Jeffrey Meikle, plastic had the aura of magical properties, which were constantly extolled by enthusiastic journalists[93] and industry spokespeople: "Promoters of industrial chemistry in the United States envisioned a cornucopia of inexpensive synthetic products leading to an unprecedented democratization of life's material goods."[94]

During the war plastics became a vital part of national defense, both taking the place of scarce or rationed natural materials and serving as new elements of war-inspired designs. Glasslike acrylics, the first plastics to be derived from petroleum, became molded sections of airplanes and enthralled the public willing to see in nose cones and canopies "postwar automobiles of teardrop shape" and in the planes themselves the promise of "'the family car of the air' or 'the Ford of the skyways.'"[95] Much of the plastic available to individuals during the war was put to more mundane use. The average GI came into contact with many plastic items; those remaining at home had to make do with synthetic substitutes for materials previously harvested or mined.[96] The Museum of Modern Art featured many plastic items in its 1940 exhibition *Useful Objects under $10.00*, legitimating the practical aesthetics of this medium."[97]

After the war consumers wanted genuine items such as leather rather than passable substitutes like vinyl. Meikle comments that "young Americans of the postwar generation grew up in houses littered with obvious plastic simulations."[98] The utopian aura of plastic dissipated, and synthetics were either valued for their practical ability to imitate or rejected for the superficiality they seemed to represent.[99] One might wait for leather luggage rather than purchase a cheaper plastic set immediately. Plastic might still suit the shopper, however, and during the 1950s tableware of melamine was both fashionable and more expensive than ceramics.[100] Walking through the exhibition hall in Moscow would have brought to hand an array of molded, often streamlined, plastic products, mixed in with items fashioned from more traditional materials.

In Moscow, for the first time plastic was used for its structural and not just its decorative qualities. The fiberglass pillars supporting *The Family of Man* and two other pavilions in the outside area represented a traditional, basically industrial use of plastic in a new and flamboyantly obvious design. Whereas in previous decades a plastic distributor cap might have helped the design of a motor the driver seldom saw, here pillars and roof encased the visitor in synthetic fibers. Before the war Henry Ford had experimented with a car hood made out of plastic and vegetable fibers. This composite material, an early form of fiberglass, would, he hoped, allow much of the raw stuff for an automobile to be grown rather than mined.[101] This car hood, however, looked like any other, more conventional hood. The magical properties that allowed his sledgehammer to bounce off with no apparent effect were hidden in the molecular structure of the material. Remarkable properties allowed plastic to appear mundane, reducing the marketability of its uniqueness. The utopian spirit behind this demonstration of hocus-pocus was quickly submerged in wartime production, and by 1959 only a General Motors product, the Corvette, had explored the structural properties of fiberglass in automobile design. In postwar Moscow, one could see an entire pavilion supported by columns that proclaimed themselves to be plastic. The visitor could imagine that a building, not an automobile, had grown.

The 1955 Museum of Modern Art *Family of Man* installation had used plastic for visual effect—a lucite panel had broken down the opacity of the first wall, giving the visitor the initial view of the entire depth of the exhibition, like an overture to an opera. Here in Moscow, plastic was used as a structural element of a piece of architecture. George Nelson, the inventor of this plastic parasol system and a colleague of Buckminster Fuller's, asserted:

> As far as we know, this is the first time that a reinforced plastic has been
> used without the assist of other materials to make a piece of architecture.
> It suggests an entire family of outdoor shelters such as bus stop sheds and

kiosks. Moreover, experimentation with unusual forms is possible without large production runs because of the intrinsic qualities of plastic; its full potentialities will develop when it is treated as a unique rather than a substitute material. [102]

His goal was to contain space within a prefabricated structure that could adapt to any use. In its massing *The Family of Man* pavilion resembled the tapered pillars of Frank Lloyd Wright's Johnson Wax headquarters in Racine, Wisconsin, but now plastic had replaced structural concrete. The forthright use of structural supports as elements of design also summoned up the work of international style architects, chief among them Le Corbusier, so there was little new about the structure itself. Wright had used illuminated glass brick to mask the solidity of the walls and the lack of windows in the Racine headquarters. [103] In Moscow the ceiling filtered natural sunlight into the enclosure, and the walls virtually evaporated, highlighting the limitless expandability of plastic parasols bolted together. In the materials and the modular assembly of the space lay the experiment.

This innovation had to be tested in a hurry in the United States. The sixteen-foot parasols of plastic and fiberglass reinforcement were hooked together in a five-unit cluster, tested against the sixty-miles-per-hour prop wash of several B-26 aircraft on a Long Island airstrip, and then sent to the Soviet Union. [104] The parasols created a dramatic space for *The Family of Man*, one which, in its way, was the equal of the Museum of Modern Art installation in its ability to play with perspective and the peripheral vision of the visitor. The petals of the parasols allowed pictures to be displayed as curved panoramas. Having seen the facets of the inside of the dome, visitors would have been accustomed to the new, non-Cartesian grid underlying the display.

The material encasing the collection, however, gives us an idea of how much had changed since the January 1955 opening of the exhibition in New York. Buckminster Fuller's design for the geodesic dome had originated in his experimentation with a new projection for a world map that would not distort polar areas. The ribs of the dome actually described a grid oriented to the great circle of the building's perimeter. This was the trajectory of the exhibition's space-age geometry. Steichen had used such an elevated geometry before. For the 1945 exhibition *Power in the Pacific* Herbert Bayer had created a globe that could be entered, so that the earth's skin turned inward toward the viewer. Surrounded by land forms, one could own the earth with a powerful perspective that literally turned the world inside out.

Steichen placed the viewer firmly on the ground for *The Family of Man*—no ramps or unnatural perspectives. The people in the photographs should be met face to face. Both in New York and Moscow the exhibition was designed to envelop the viewer in a community rather than to invite the command of an all-encompassing gaze. *The Family of Man* was suited to the adjustable aluminum frames that had measured the spaces for a variety of exhibitions abroad. Height and depth could easily be accommodated, but the photographs could not achieve the three-dimensional fullness of volume in the efficient way inscribed by the great circle of Fuller's dome. Perhaps the parasols were intended to echo the rib-and-skin texture of the dome. The forms were certainly a design innovation, made all the more impressive by the exigencies of a frantic, eight-month work schedule.[105] Fundamentally, the plastic enclosure for the photographs emphasized how uneasily an exhibition constructed at the beginning of the decade coexisted with sites crafted for the world of the decade's end.

Both dome and pavilion proclaimed ideology through design reinforced by construction materials. The message of the American exhibition was delivered inside, sometimes through overwhelming media displays. Instead of surrounding audiences with images of human similarity, the aluminum dome offered "glimpses of the U.S.A." on seven twenty-by-thirty-foot screens inset in the interior panels of the enclosure. Sixteen times per day the spectators, who stood to watch the film, looked up as the 35mm projectors overwhelmed them with images of the United States. "The number of images to be seen had to be too many to comprehend individually, but not so many that the information would be confusing or hard to follow."[106] This was the familiar message of unified diversity, the democracy of information, and the subordination of individual voice to a common culture.

The assembly of this production by the office of Charles Eames resembled *The Family of Man* project. More than 2,200 still and moving images were included in this thirteen-minute demonstration of "the complexity and diversity of American life."[107] Once again the Time/Life and Magnum archives were culled and individual photographers were solicited. The film appealed directly to the purpose of the Moscow exhibition, "to illustrate such aspects of daily life as where Americans live, work, and play, how they get around, what they eat, and how they dress."[108] The object of this fragmented vision was actually monolithic, as the production's conclusion asserted. Here images of parting—"goodnights, symbols of love and friendship"—were punctuated with the single image of a bouquet of forget-me-nots.[109] If this was a glimpse, it was also a greeting card that opened to a sentimental message. The power of the display derived from postwar technology, the full persuasion of color cinematography, and the amplification of a space that digested the viewer.

The photographic exhibition's rectilinear form invited a traditional mapping of interior spaces. By the time of Sokolniki Park, a home for the show could literally be extruded to cocoon the photographs—or any object, for that matter—in a customized shelter. Or the final dislocation could occur, as the planar relationships among these two-dimensional objects were destroyed, subordinating message to an idiosyncratic structure. The future was indeed in plastics.

Roland Barthes described this new material quite accurately in *Mythologies*, the same collection containing his dismissal of *The Family of Man* to the antihistorical realm of myth. Plastic could beguile and satisfy, serve and remain whimsical. The shape of matter was no longer determined by the forge, the press, or the blacksmith. The mold would suffice. The curve or the doodle replaced the grid, and the language of building materials now included both the set type of the girder and the calligraphy of the plastic strut. Plastic, for Barthes, was "less a thing than the trace of a movement."[110]

The Family of Man proclaimed its materials, but Henry Ford already had seen another valuable property of synthetics—they could mirror natural substances. In Barthes words, plastic could "become buckets as well as jewels."[111] This indeterminacy, or indiscriminateness, was unique to plastic, "the first magical substance which consents to be prosaic."[112] No longer was there a hierarchy of substances, for plastic could become them all. American corporations had found the ideal substance to represent their global aims; technology now portended that "the whole world *can* be plasticized."[113]

The American exhibition in Moscow was a success. There were long lines throughout the six-week period during which 2.7 million people filed through; an estimated 130,000 crowded the grounds on September 4th, closing day. If the desire for entrance were a criterion, McClellan and his staff could have wished for nothing greater than the crush that was observed.

> The Soviet public evidenced a tremendous interest in the Exhibition. There was a chronic ticket shortage, and long lines formed as early as one o'clock in the morning to snap up the quota of tickets released by the Soviet authorities for the day. Easily twice as many tickets could have been sold had the exhibition site been able to accommodate the masses of Soviet citizens who wanted to see the American display. There was a good bit of black marketing of tickets, as well as counterfeiting of both tickets and passes. A fair amount of gate crashing and fence-climbing was also observed, so that actual daily attendance consistently exceeded ticket sales by a noticeable margin.[114]

The Soviet authorities had countered this popularity with displays of their own. During the time of the exhibition, hard-to-get Russian consumer goods were arrayed in Moscow parks. Visitors exiting the American exhibition were encouraged to visit the nearby Russian equivalents. A Russian version of the Circarama was unveiled. Polish and Czechoslovakian trade exhibitions arranged for Moscow at about the same time were heavily attended, due to the interest generated by the American exhibition.[115]

Not only were crowds of Russians pushing their way into Sokolniki Park, but they were interpreting correctly what they were intended to see. McClellan and his staff had hit their mark. The Russian crowds had been subjected to a combination of public opinion surveying and surveillance from the start. Questions asked of the RAMAC computer were tabulated, and the American guides reported conversations they had had while conducting tours of the grounds. American tourists in Russia were also asked to report inquiries about the United States that came their way. The results of all these sources of information were consistent: Russians envied the material success of Americans. They were less impressed with American culture and were indifferent to the influence of religion in America. But with the conditions of American life they were fascinated.

The guides had been told to expect hostile questions. There were some, perhaps attributable to the presence of agitators, but, for the most part, overtly ideological debate was left to the likes of Nixon and Khrushchev.

Few Soviet visitors seemed to be directly concerned with evaluating capitalism vs. socialism. . . . They may have wondered whether American capitalism is as evil and unjust as their own propaganda paints it, and may have regarded the proof of the pudding as being primarily in the question of how the common man in America actually lives.[116]

The official Soviet reaction to the exhibition had been a complaint that there was little attention given to American heavy industry, the sector of the American economy that manufactured American intercontinental might. Ordinary visitors were more concerned with precisely the sort of technology the exhibition displayed—consumer conveniences.[117]

The negative questions were the same ones Americans confronted in Western Europe or Japan: the Negro question and unemployment topped the list.[118] However, none of these ranked among the most popular. The top six categories read like the organizing principles of the grounds at Sokolniki: technology and science, living conditions, music, education, American awareness of the USSR, and American freedoms.[119] Russians, like Western Europeans, were most curious about American affluence.

The evaluation of the drawing power of individual exhibits in Sokolniki Park concluded that "Circarama, the automobiles, 'The Family of Man' photographic exhibit, the fashion show and color television proved to be especially popular."[120] Among these, only the photographic collection failed to whet the appetite of the visitors for goods. Earlier in the decade, the sentiment that The Family of Man constructed to draw nations together had been important, both to Steichen and to the USIA that had toured it throughout the world. Whether the world was like us or whether we were portrayed as what the world wanted to become, connections were being made and similarities were being drawn among people. Now goods were made to do the recruiting for the American side. A family of people was replaced by the things they could be expected to purchase and warehouse. Sentiment was replaced by a specific longing—a longing intended to pain, to agitate the austerely controlled viewer into action. With The Family of Man the United States had portrayed itself as humane, understanding, cultured. With the American National Exhibition in Moscow, the United States declared itself to be the winner of a battle of abundance.

EDWARD STEICHEN, ROBERT FRANK, AND AMERICAN MODERNISM

A MONTH AFTER THE OPENING OF THE MOSCOW EXHIBITION, THEOPHILUS Neokonkwo, a young Nigerian, tore down several pictures from *The Family of Man* exhibit. He justified his attack on the most popular part of the Moscow exhibition by declaring that:

> The collection portrayed white Americans and other Europeans in digni-
> fied cultural states—wealthy, healthy and wise, and Americans and West
> Indian Negroes, Africans and Asiatics as comparatively social inferiors—
> sick, raggerty [sic], destitute, and physically maladjusted. African men
> and women were portrayed either half clothed or naked. I could not stand
> the sight. It was insulting, undignified and tendentious.[1]

On almost the same day, responding to Soviet objections, the exhibition organizers removed a picture from the show, a George Silk shot of a Chinese child, supplicating with rice bowl in hand.[2] Steichen himself had, to no avail, defended the picture as a universal symbol of hunger and deprivation. No explanation was given by the American press for this removal, for, perhaps, none was needed, given the inferences that could be drawn between the self-serving intentions of two Communist countries. The *Times* obligingly published the offending picture, encouraging an ideological reading of a photograph that was taken in 1946, well before Mao's rise to national power.

George Silk's work merited a box on page three of the *New York Times*. Neither the *Times* nor the *Washington Post* mentioned Mr. Neokonkwo, who had offered an eloquent defense of his own removal plan. This journalistic silence speaks eloquently of Third World emergence and the domestic preoccupations of mass circulation dailies. Any suspicion that the Nigerian student might have been encouraged by Soviet handlers to express his outrage against so popular an exhibition for a propaganda advantage is beside the point. By 1959 *The Family of Man* had become a reified text, a static series of objects to be shaped or edited according to contemporary circumstances. It could not speak to the new order of Third World nationalisms. It did not engage the increasingly technologized armaments of the cold war. It was mute before the increasingly fractious domestic politics of class and race. Even at the Museum of Modern Art, its home base, the vocabulary used to describe it and the artistic practices it represented became emblems of transformative experiences, a different enterprise.

Todd Gitlin has remarked that the seeds of the turmoil of the 1960s were sown in the preceding decade.[3] *The Family of Man* was a victim of this process. Despite all the promotion, the drama of Steichen's work in the loft, the enthusiasm of the crowds at the Museum of Modern Art, the wide distribution of the collection throughout the world, and the assembly and display of these exhibitions—a series of activities lasting the entire decade—the photographs frequently are treated as though they are, and always have been, an anthology of middle-class tastes. Increasingly, the ability of photographs to speak to viewers has been called into question as the comforting definition of a unitary culture surrounding the interaction between viewer and text fractured into the uneasy dynamic of particularized communities constructing their own worlds of meaning. Finally, critics have challenged the ability of photographers to control the meanings of the framed worlds they had created. These critiques, based on class, reader response to text, or aesthetics, made *The Family of Man* into a static or virtually laconic display for many critics. This final chapter draws out relationships—homologies—that demarcate the barrier separating this great exhibit's message from present-day audiences.

During the late 1950s *The Family of Man* passed from the wall to the coffee table, from the debate over the world's future to the timeless realm of sentiment. The vocabulary of Steichen's text had been formed in a period of earnest belief in the power of the image to change viewers' minds through affecting their emotions. It spoke to an audience faced with a quicker and more devastating version of the global conflict of the 1940s. Through atomic weapons the duration of war was compressed, and destruction was amplified by the wild exponentiality of nuclear fission. Steichen assumed a conflict with a beginning and a terrifying end—an event of uncharacteristic brevity but of traditional identity, a war. He did not foresee the seemingly endless posturing and threat of the cold war, a world conflict fought with words, ideas, and things in a never-ending surge. His exhibition could not sustain the weight of institutions, technology, consumer desire, world tourism, or, for that matter, changing world circumstances. Flattened under such a complex mass, the images lost a dimension of meaning. Ironically, the Moscow exhibition, Steichen's triumph, was also a sign of the photographs' decline. *The Family of Man* became a soothing counterpart to high-fidelity sound; one offered a haven for the eyes, the other bathed the ear with a full range of euphonious music. At the end of his career, Steichen did not see how his text had betrayed him by becoming multivocal. *The Family of Man* continued to live in the ways that individual photographs were liberated to speak for themselves.

In effect, Steichen had constructed a mosaic out of what was really a kaleidoscope of changing meanings of individual images in motion. Increasingly, Steichen's collection was used as a counterpoint for rebellious comments, beginning with Mr. Neokonkwo and continuing through post-Vietnam photographic criticism. The product of Steichen's form of modernism was consumed by a different, newer strain. A visual shorthand of this expansive difference lies in the contrast between *The Family of Man* photography and the work of one of its contributors, Robert Frank. Frank's collection of 1950s photographs, *The Americans*, was never popular, except with scholars, artists, and the cognoscenti. It offered a highly idiosyncratic view of American life through a self-consciously skewed frame. Frank reasserted through each picture that it was unmistakably his vision that had materialized from emulsion to print, but he did not reassure his viewer with a definite narrative. His message was that photographs were framed by ambiguity. As unsettling as these photographs are, they have retained more of the vitality of their production than The Family of Man. Through looking at Steichen's work in relation to an emergent vision, represented by Frank's collection, we may come to some understanding of why one vision is so unsettling and yet current, and why one is so reassuring and yet dated.

Robert Frank, the Swiss immigrant, observed American life as an outsider, while Steichen displayed images that opened up the outside world to American empathy. The two men knew each other well. Steichen had taken Frank along as a translator on his 1952 European tour to promote the idea of The Family of Man. Frank's photographs were shown several times at the museum, most notably as a part of Young European Photographers and later in a two-man show with Harry Callahan. Steichen had proposed this as a part of his Diogenes with a Lamp series, but Frank had balked at the ostentatious title (which was dropped to keep the show intact). Mary Frank had visited Steichen and Miller in the Seventh Avenue loft; several of Robert Frank's photographs were displayed in The Family of Man; and Robert and Mary Frank had been invited to the exhibition preview. Most of the Frank photographs displayed the soft focus and disorienting frame characteristic of the body of his work and stood out amid the hundreds of hard-edge images in the show. Steichen knew talent when he saw it, much in the same way that an earlier arbiter of culture, William Dean Howells, could appreciate the artistry of younger writers whose fiction was very different from his own.

Steichen also wrote Frank a recommendation for a Guggenheim Fellowship so he could, as his application stated, tour the country photographing contemporary American conditions. While Steichen was enjoying the success of his exhibition at the Museum of Modern Art, Frank hit the road in a dilapidated Ford, promising "observation and record of what one naturalized American finds to see in the United States that signifies the kind of civilization born here and spreading elsewhere." The list of subjects for this visual survey that would later be edited into The Americans reads like a contemporary catalogue worthy of Whitman:

> a town at night, a parking lot, a supermarket, a highway, the man who
> owns three cars and the man who owns none, the farmer and his chil-
> dren, a new house and a warped clapboard house, the dictation of taste,
> the dream of grandeur, advertising, neon lights, the faces of the leaders
> and the faces of the followers, gas tanks and postoffices and backyards.

All of these photographs were to be taken with a miniature camera—the 35mm, single-lens reflex camera that war photographers had found so useful for shooting on the move. Indeed, Frank's foray through the American scene strikes an ironic parallel to the junkets of American photographers in the economy of world tourism. Life photographers lived in comfort while portraying appealing ways of life in exotic places; with spartan foundation support, Frank austerely pictured Americans at home and the view was far from comforting.

Finally, Frank's application dealt with the question of production. "The use of my project," he asserted, "would be sociological, historical and aesthetic." This cultural view would be annotated and classified "on the spot, as I proceed." At least at the beginning of the project, then, Frank saw himself as an anthropologist, moving through unfamiliar territory. He might also have been a historian, for his intention was to create a collection "such as the one in the Library of Congress." This most remarkable set of photographs, the tens of thousands of Farm Security Administration shots that his friend Walker Evans, among others, had assembled, had become historical documents, representations of the depression era. Also, from the beginning, he might have sensed the likelihood that his images would not be well received. He mentioned two possible publication outlets for the photographs: "1) M. Delpire of 'NEUF,' Paris, for book form. 2) Mr. Kubler of 'DU' for an entire issue of his magazine."[4] If his collection would be an aesthetic or historical resource domestically, the initial audience would be foreign.

Ironically, it was Frank who viewed the Farm Security Administration photographs from an institutional distance, in terms of the collection's comprehensiveness. Steichen, the master organizer, found their power to be in the individual prints. Steichen was both artist and bureaucrat. Having achieved his credentials earlier in the century, he could command authorship of his collection through the power to organize a logistically complex operation under the aegis of the Museum of Modern Art. Frank was both artist and tourist. The photographs of The Americans were profoundly disturbing to many viewers and equally exciting to photographers too young to have slogged through war with a large-format camera. They took miniature cameras for granted; the mobility that the wartime generation saw as a matter of practicality, if not survival, Frank saw as a way of quickly approaching sites throughout the country. The Americans was a product of both an aesthetic view and two years of experience traveling through a country still, in many of its particularities and regional differences, unexplored territory for him.

One December day in 1955 Frank, the photographic tourist on the road to New Orleans, was arrested by the Arkansas State Police. According to the arresting officer, Frank was "shabbily dressed, needed a shave and a haircut, also a bath." He also had with him cameras and a large, locked trunk. The police report continued:

> This officer investigated this subject due to the man's appearance, the
> fact that he was a foreigner and had in his possession cameras and felt
> that the subject should be checked out as we are continually being ad-
> vised to watch out for any persons illegally in this country in the employ
> of some unfriendly power and the possibility of Communist affiliations.[5]

He was detained in jail overnight and subjected to a series of interrogations. Suspecting that Frank was Jewish, the police found someone to speak Hebrew to him, which he did not understand. Great curiosity continued throughout the day about the locked trunk and the exposed rolls of film the photographer had kept with his equipment. The film, the police threatened, would be developed locally. The contents of the trunk (more film) would be confiscated. Frank was faced with American nativism and with the commandeering of his livelihood. Art, he informed them, could not be developed at the local drugstore.

Frank wrote immediately to Walker Evans, detailing the humiliation of the cross-examination. The experience had been both profoundly disturbing and absurd. One moment he fought against losing months worth of his work. The next he had to explain seemingly insignificant items that he had with him in the car. There was, he wrote to Evans, a bottle of Hennessey, conspicuously two-thirds empty but, more ominously, a foreign drink. He had had to translate a full page of the Swiss army handbook. His cufflinks were stored in an English licorice box (a foreign box) and the names of his two children, Pablo and Andrea, were also foreign-sounding. Among the negatives discovered were shots from the River Rouge Ford plant near Detroit. One of the patrol officers, a good tourist, had been to Detroit and knew that picture taking was prohibited in such plants. Investigators found a road map with a suggested route from Memphis to New Orleans highlighted by the American Automobile Association in green, onto which Frank had traced his actual itinerary in red—as Evans had suggested he do, he wanted his correspondent to know. When he used Edward Steichen and the Guggenheim Fellowship as character references, his interrogators left the room and returned with a question: "Are you a Commie?"[6]

One of Frank's most famous photographs—the cover of the American edition of his collection—was taken in New Orleans shortly thereafter. This view into a city streetcar shows a perfectly segmented society: a white man in the first window, followed by a white woman and white children. African Americans are still in back; Rosa Parks only in that month had challenged the color line between black and white. The Montgomery bus boycott had just begun. On the right, a black woman has turned to look back along the scene just passed, her glasses reflecting the light of the street, obscuring her eyes. Nearer the center of the frame a black man faces toward the photographer, with an enigmatic expression that might be caused by pain or exhaustion. Frank confronted viewers with the namelessness of this gaze; he did not romanticize this aesthetically sophisticated photograph by implying connections among the individuals within his view. He saw some of the particularities of American culture, each isolated in its own frame of reference, and did not allow his viewer to maintain the illusion that entering these compartments carried no cost, or, indeed, that each frame could be transgressed by the viewer. His own confinement had, perhaps, sharpened his perception.

Steichen's view of America centered on emotions that transcended class. In *Family of Man* pictures one can find individuals who are poor, but the exhibition was dominated by a rhetoric of amelioration: things would get better if people celebrated each other, pulled together, and succeeded in not blowing each other up. Frank's view of America was based on an ambiguous reading of specific occasions in day-to-day life. Here faces, often isolated at the margins of the frame, stood out from the mass. The task of the photograph was to differentiate and not to explain. Steichen's work was centripetal. He created an exhibition that drew people to the family portraits and surrounded viewers with a compendium of presumably familiar qualities, gestures, and family occasions. Frank's work was centrifugal. He did not presume to know what his subjects were thinking and his frame did not encourage viewers to create bonds among the subjects within the picture. His pictures undercut a unitary reading of American culture, the celebration of middle-class life, and, finally, the belief that photographs could tell a story about this assumed reality.

Frank's distance from his subjects had long been a part of his personal and visual style. In a 1946 photograph taken by Louis Faurer, Frank, newly arrived in the United States, stands on the periphery of a New York crowd, looking in the same direction as all other eyes are focused and yet separated from them. Later, in a photograph not included in The Americans, Frank circles another such crowd, so that he is between this collection of upturned eyes and the object of their fascination—the Wanamaker department store fire near New York's Astor Square. Frank selected an oblique angle that put the camera face-to-face with the smiling portrait of a man painted on a building across the square. The act of viewing—the implied voyeurism, the fascination with the remarkable and the bizarre, the assumed communion between the experience of the viewer and the surface of a representation—unites the elements of this photograph.

Frank photographed from the margins in, so that insiders were viewed from the perspective of the outsider. Thus, his observation of the 1956 Democratic National Convention presents a jumble of beefy backs and jowly faces. A shot of a Yale graduation frames the ambiguous, enervated gesture of the only figure, perhaps a parent or an alumnus, facing the camera. The ceremony itself occurs beyond the world of the frame. A group on a boat in New York harbor can be associated with the religious observance of Yom Kippur only through the yarmulke visible, characteristically, on the back of one of the heads turned away from the camera. Workers at the Ford assembly line—a product of the foray that the Arkansas police found so suspicious—are preoccupied with their jobs. The industrial workplace is a jumble of forms, a scene of such activity that motion has blurred some figures. No one has time to pose.

Frank more tangibly removed the viewer from the scene within the frame of the photograph. The Americans contains several photographs in which flags were used as scrims or barriers. A gigantic stars and stripes hovers over a Fourth of July celebration in Jay, New York, and viewers must pass under it to enter the scene, an impossibility in this two-dimensional medium. Two viewers of a parade in Hoboken, New Jersey, are decapitated by a flag that establishes a patriotic purpose for the occasion, while, at the same time, denying the onlookers their individuality. But Frank did not need the veil of patriotism to point out the limitations of recorded vision. In Butte, Montana, he used a curtain to frame a lifeless, industrial landscape. In South Carolina, he photographed a barbershop through a screen door. The door and the glass pane behind offer their own epiphanies. The glass reflects a house, a tree, a portion of front yard—the small-town context of the shop. The interior of the shop can be discerned through the shadow of the photographer. The ability of the viewer to see, Frank reminds his audience, is controlled by the person with the camera.

Frank makes us conscious of the camera, or, more generally, of the mediated experience of viewing. His photographs call attention to their own making by presenting skewed or blurred representations of scenes. He allowed two Native Americans from the Fort Hall reservation in southeastern Idaho to drive his car, and then managed to capture the two by jamming his camera next to the head of the passenger. To make a picture in Los Angeles he drew his camera back to look down from a second-story window onto the street, where a pedestrian marched from left to right in the direction of a neon arrow. From this strange perspective, the view is as two-dimensional as the emulsion that allows it to materialize. Frank eliminated the illusion of depth without attacking the more basic trust in the representational power of the picture. There is only a top and a bottom, a left and a right, reinforced by the obliging arrow.

In several of the pictures in *The Americans* Frank comments on the appropriation that photography represents, the invasion of the experience of others by the photographer, with his future audience egging him on. Two images stand out. In one a motorcycle gang fills the frame. Frank views this gathering from the outside—once again shooting over the shoulder of an individual into a scene. This time the camera has been discovered, and one of Frank's subjects returns the threat of being shot in the back by a photographer with an ambiguous, ominous look. The lens has interrupted the three bikers at their lunch. The beginning of a clenched fist could merely hold the end of a sandwich; a hostile expression might just be a mouthful of food. In the other, a photograph shot in San Francisco, an African American couple appears at the bottom of the frame. We view the couple in the act of discovering the photographer, who has obligingly captured both the man's hostility and, by implication, the shooter's discomfiture (and sense of mission). Perhaps Frank drew close enough to balance the couple with a dark tree at the center of the frame. To step even closer would have excluded the couple from the picture but would have increased his intrusion. To step back would have drawn them farther into the frame by maintaining a discreet distance. Frank forces his onlookers to consider the paradox of appropriating while remaining detached.

Frank loaded his photographs with the accoutrements, the lines of power, and the effluent of the middle class. He was out, after all, to capture "the kind of civilization born here and spreading elsewhere." The shoes of the businessman are finely polished, but in Frank's frame this task is performed in a restroom, to an audience of urinals. A black nanny holds a small white child who already has mastered the seigniorial gaze of command. Frank captures a traveler at his meal, surrounded by American abundance, but we view the aftermath of this feeding session—half-eaten portions, greasy plates, and the stuffed but not satisfied patron. A woman in party dress wears a most unfestive expression. Even the cowboy, the popular icon of self-reliance and individualism, is pictured out of his element, in New York and Detroit, as a loiterer—just another character to be avoided on the sidewalk. Few people smile and no one is allowed the luxury of being able to purchase fulfillment through ownership of things.

Both the practice of the photographer and the demands of reading the photograph separated Frank's world from Steichen's. During the 1920s Edward Steichen had composed advertising photographs for the J. Walter Thompson agency, depicting with a modernist aesthetic the power of American products. He was drawn to the humanism of the Farm Security Administration photographs but had in his portfolio stylized shots of cigarettes on a glass table and multiple exposures of such dissimilar subjects as the George Washington Bridge and Carl Sandburg. His was an engaged modernism, one that assumed easy communication with an audience, regardless of whether the image represented an individual vision or the interests of a corporation. This view ran counter to the oppositional modernism of the 1950s, but Steichen's aesthetic should not be minimized because of this double negative.

We do not have to leave New York City to see the construction of the two forms of modernism that Frank and Steichen exemplify. The loft in which Steichen selected *The Family of Man* photographs had been rented on the cheap because the building was slated for demolition. The transformation of the area surrounding the Museum of Modern Art had just begun. During the decade the gleaming, modernist towers of Sixth Avenue appeared, one by one, defining in glass and girders the link between modernist aesthetics and postwar corporations. The consciousness of materials, the awareness of the technological possibilities of their manipulation, the signature of the artist's hand in the shape of his work, and the emphasis on function define a monumental modernism that lines the renamed Avenue of the Americas to this day. This also describes Steichen's fashioning of *The Family of Man*. His work was underwritten with a large sum from a major source that blurred the distinction between family and corporation. He explored the technological possibilities of his medium, even transgressing the boundaries of the museum itself. The authorship of the text lay in the shape of the space and the control of the materials.

This form of modernism was easily appropriated. An international aesthetic— Mies's architecture or Bayer's design theories—was adapted to American corporate use. The renaming of Sixth Avenue as the Avenue of the Americas asserted a connection between this New York site and modernist—read American—enclaves throughout the hemisphere. The concern for Latin America that Nelson Rockefeller found as his government duty during World War II had blossomed into a formal organization after the rise of Fidel Castro in Cuba—the Organization of American States. At the same time, monolithic, corporate modernism was transforming both New York and America's image throughout the world. As Ron Robin has convincingly shown, American embassies constructed during the 1950s exhibited the placelessness of international style architecture, supplemented later by details intended to relate concrete and glass to domestic architectural traditions. "The buildings were intended to demonstrate American control and knowledge of stagnant foreign forms, while simultaneously demonstrating the power of the United States through innovative fusion of old and new, local and imported." The shallowness of this sensitivity could be seen in a roof line that was to signify either Arabic forms in Iraq or Asian techniques in Japan, or in the new national flags hoisted on Sixth Avenue.[7] Beyond the loft in which he carefully built his view of human sameness, Steichen risked surrendering control over his construction.

Steichen located his work within the Museum of Modern Art, and his exhibition demonstrated the breadth of modernist practice. His photographs defied the elitist assumptions about the audience for art by inviting into the gallery the same crowds that walked down Sixth Avenue. In her study of the Book-of-the-Month Club, Joan Shelley Rubin reminds us that an organization could have coexisting and contradictory senses of the function of reading and criticism among the audience it served. Indeed, a purveyor of books could consider itself both an agent of education and a potentially profitable business. Members of the book club's selection committee, for example, could encompass both nineteenth- and twentieth-century views of self and culture and yet exert control over a profit-making enterprise that brought serious reading to the masses. All of these forces could be held in equilibrium unconsciously by an organization that, on the face of it, merely kept its readership au courant. This was, she summarizes, the " 'middleness' of middlebrow culture."[8] Steichen did not intend to make his exhibition middlebrow, but he did want an audience. He achieved an artful clarity that made his own middlebrow version of modernism transparent.

Robert Frank's collection is more recognizably modernist and, through its idiosyncratic resistance to popularity, less subject to appropriation. The vision of the artist was the focus of his work, the confrontation of enigmatic and disturbing subjects the task of the artist. The seemingly careless qualities of the work disguised mastery over technique and proclaimed the artist's distrust of the instrument at his command. The regimentation of Sixth Avenue was not the beat of this photographer. In search of ambiguity, his eye more naturally wandered farther to the west, to the night world of Times Square. Here Frank captured three individuals in front of the railing of a subway entrance. Their gestures are self-conscious masks, their postures ambiguous. Even the gender identity of the three cannot be taken for granted. The street could not be managed and the eye resisted control. We see, Frank points out, more than we can interpret.

Yet, when Frank's work was displayed in book form, it became measured, sequential, traditional. Each photograph of *The Americans* was displayed on the right-hand page, with only a brief caption breaking the whiteness on the left. As Tod Papageorge has pointed out, Frank emulated Walker Evans's *American Photographs* in this layout and replicated the traditional, sequential display of photographs in museums: a series of steps down the wall, long since choreographed for viewers by exhibitions of paintings.[9] Frank showed one photograph at a time to break down the narrative implicit in juxtaposing one image to another. Steichen broke down the aura of the work of art to create an overall effect. In showing his wariness of the capabilities of his medium, Frank reinforced what Walter Benjamin called the aura of the work of art, defying the age of mechanical reproduction.

Ironically, Steichen and Frank saw their photographic work overcome by film. In Moscow both Walt Disney and Ray Eames were more effective in presenting audiences with an all encompassing view. *Glimpses of the U.S.A.* and Circarama accomplished their tasks by fracturing the screen, producing multiple images that were more powerful than Carl Sandburg's convex and concave mirrors that had inspired Steichen in the shaping of *The Family of Man*. Narrative possibilities had increased geometrically. Steichen's exhibition was left in the black-and-white world of cut-and-paste layout exercises. The color world of the film editor offered the interweaving of themes, the narrative syncopation, the stentorian orchestration that Steichen had found through The Family of Man project.

Frank, on the other hand, grew to distrust the ability of any photograph, no matter how self-consciously incomplete, to frame reality. He therefore turned to the 16mm camera and to the collaborative venture of creating a film. Pull My Daisy was released in 1959, the same year as the American National Exhibition in Moscow. In its visual style, its self-proclaimed reliance on improvisation, and its self-consciously oppositional stance with regard to the cultural mainstream, it defined a new location for the artist at the end of the decade.

Let a single image lead from the road to the East Village of Pull My Daisy: a 1956 photograph, shot at Hoover Dam during Frank's expedition but not included in The Americans. As one commentator on the 1950s has noted, the question underlying The Americans was: are there still stories to tell?[10] In this photograph these stories were wrapped in the enigmas of symbols that were available according to the commanding whim of any person who could enter the frame and select. Here symbols, tourist photographs, are cradled in a wire rack, awaiting purchase: the Grand Canyon, a site of natural grandeur; the utilitarian monumentality of Hoover Dam itself, with the hydroelectric potential of Lake Mead restrained behind it; and the universal sign of random, uncontrolled energy, an atomic bomb explosion. These souvenirs excerpted the history of the area, from its gradual formation to the instant of a nuclear reaction, from the creation of a scenic space in geologic time to the technological appropriation of unoccupied terrain for instantaneous, elemental reorganization. They contextualized a landscape only dimly visible beyond the concrete of the kiosk pad and parking lot. This was an uncertain world that could, perhaps, be pushed by the inattentive hand within the frame but not by the viewer from outside. Even if the photographer could have complete control over the image, the photograph seems to say, the world thus created would be contingent on what the photographer could not control—the onlooker standing beside the picture taker—and inevitably would mask some of the action frozen in the moment of capture. The invisible, potential power of the agents within the frame to change the meaning of what was being viewed was quite a different force from the hand that pushed the ring-around-the-rosie carousel in Steichen's exhibition and was told to "Clasp hands and know the thoughts of men in other lands."[11]

Pull My Daisy was shot in the loft studio of the painter Alfred Leslie. The twenty-nine-minute film drew from more than thirty hours of footage shot by Frank.[12] This was a low budget, $15,000 operation that drew on a circle of friends—chief among them Allen Ginsberg, Gregory Corso, Peter Orlovsky, and Larry Rivers—for the acting. Jack Kerouac provided the script, which built from the third act of an unpublished play entitled The Beat Generation. Kerouac, a celebrity after the publication of On the Road, had to compete with his own, newfound commercial value. The film itself had to be renamed because a major Hollywood studio had already copyrighted the play's title. The actors, beat-era luminaries in other art forms but here self-conscious amateurs, had a script but began improvising soon after shooting began. Kerouac, therefore, was confronted with a piece that had been reshaped by the performers, visualized by the cinematographer, and reassembled by the editing process. One evening at a friend's studio, headphones on, listening to jazz riffs, he ad-libbed a narrative line, what one commentator proclaimed "the most honest and honestly funny piece of beatthink within my experience."[13]

Kerouac combatted what Mary McCarthy called the "ventriloquism" of artistic form, in which the author disappeared into his or her characters.[14] Kerouac did not allow the cast to speak for him (even though they had booted him off the set because he disrupted the shooting). It is his voice we hear. In fact, we hear only one of three versions. According to one of Kerouac's biographers, he made a second narration in a Chinese accent and a third in French.[15] The spontaneity of the film and the seeming carelessness of the narration belied levels of control: of Frank, the cinematographer, over the frame; of Kerouac, the narrator, over the voice of each character; of the encroaching mainstream over the name of the film. Even Allen Ginsberg's whimsically defiant, double-entendre title, sung at the beginning of the film, was purged of some of its raunchiness.

As is the case with so many of the literary productions of this period, the work sought what Thomas Schaub had called "traction"[16]—an idea of personhood that would give meaning to a socially adversarial stance. Norman Mailer, another denizen of the counterculture of lower Manhattan, accomplished this by inventing his own celebrity. Frank, Ginsberg, and Kerouac moved to the margins to show the location of discontent. In *Pull My Daisy* the camera entered the world of an urban railroad worker, living in a claustrophobic apartment in Manhattan's Lower East Side, who happens to have poets for friends. Milo has a blue-collar job; his wife tries to keep the place neat; a clergyman, the bishop, pays a pastoral visit; little Pablo (played by Frank's son) goes off to school. The world of the frame has been knocked askew. The center of attention is the aggressive assertion of difference: the "rejectamenta" of official culture.[17] Milo works, but it is clear by the end of the film that the poets, dressed in workerly slovenliness in contrast to his neat railroad uniform, are doing the real work, which looks a lot like play. The score mixes classical-sounding music with jazz. The bishop arrives and proves to be unholy; his sanctimoniousness serves as a counterpoint to the search for transcendence in the room. Personality must be expressed, in Schaub's words, to give voice to "the communal impulses underlying the experience of alienation."[18] Surrounding this apartment is America, a presence that is not so much being addressed as confronted.

There are voices behind these 1950s images, a contested dialogue leading out from these representations and the aesthetics they portray to the culture. It is important to hear the ways in which Steichen participated in the 1950s debate over the relationship between individual and society, between artist and culture. The emergent, countercultural voices, represented here by Robert Frank and Norman Mailer, have predominated so thoroughly that it has become harder to hear the more measured pronouncements of an older generation that used the vocabulary of the engaged humanism of earlier decades. Steichen and Sandburg were such kindred spirits. But let us begin with the testament of America's most celebrated author at the beginning of the decade.

In early 1950 William Faulkner stepped forward to accept the Nobel Prize for literature from the king of Sweden. Faulkner, who had been reluctant to travel to Stockholm, mumbled his speech so softly that almost no one in the room heard it, but his words were widely reported. He uttered sentiments that reverberated through the early fifties.

> Our tragedy today is a general and universal physical fear so long sustained by now that we can even bear it. There are no longer problems of the spirit. This is only the question: When will I be blown up?

For Faulkner, this existential question had distracted artists from their true task, the exploration of the human condition. To rediscover human emotions was to give life to art.

> [The artist] must teach himself that the basest of all things is to be afraid; and, teaching himself that, forget it forever, leaving no room in his workshop for anything but the old verities and truths of the heart, the old universal truths lacking which any story is ephemeral and doomed—love and honor and pity and pride and compassion and sacrifice.

Here Faulkner reconstructed a new reading of the transcendence of art, but he did not disengage from society. The purpose of the artist was an Emersonian one—to give language, to articulate meaning, to promote the understanding that would allow a culture to prevail.

> I decline to accept the end of man. It is easy enough to say that man is immortal simply because he will endure: that when the last ding-dong of doom has clanged and faded from the last worthless rock hanging tideless in the last red and dying evening, that even then there will still be one more sound: that of his puny inexhaustible voice, still talking. I refuse to accept this. I believe that man will not merely endure: he will prevail. He is immortal, not because he alone among creatures has an inexhaustible voice, but because he has a soul, a spirit capable of compassion and sacrifice and endurance. The poet's, the writer's, duty is to write about these things. It is his privilege to help man endure by lifting his heart, by reminding him of the courage and honor and hope and pride and compassion and pity and sacrifice which have been the glory of his past. The poet's voice need not merely be the record of man, it can be one of the props, the pillars to help him endure and prevail.[19]

There is no evidence to suggest that Edward Steichen had read Faulkner's statement as he began his *Family of Man* project. However, his career was devoted to adding the photographer to Faulkner's list of artists whose "duty is to write about these things," to chronicle the transcendence of the human race. Steichen's call for exhibition photographs showed this intent clearly.

We are concerned with photographs which express the universal through the individual and the particular, that demonstrate the importance of the art of photography in explaining man to man across the world, his dreams and aspirations, mirroring the flaming creative forces of love and truth and the corrosive evil inherent in the lie. . . . It is essential to keep in mind the universal elements and aspects of human relationships and the experiences common to all mankind rather than situations that represent conditions exclusively related or peculiar to a race, an event, a time, or a place.[20]

Elements of the completed exhibition also hinted at how thoroughly Steichen projected his own values into the collection, for he embedded photographs of his own family, beginning with his mother and extending to Wayne and Joan Miller. During the making of The Family of Man, Wayne had become more of an adopted son than an assistant and the Millers had become his surrogate family.[21] Steichen's sensibility was similar to Faulkner's and was related to the prewar eye of the FSA photographers. In a world of quotidian concerns and gloomy wrongs, the family was the foundation, and fundamental change could best be made through awakening emotions here, at the roots, at home.

In 1957 Norman Mailer, freshly separated from the Village Voice and cleansed of his dependency on Seconal and Benzedrene, sat down to write what he really thought about integration. What began as a bet with a publisher friend—that the mass media would censor his blunt proclamations—turned into "The White Negro," a celebration of the other America, the urban, hip, non-middle-class, minority America. This voice was located in Robert Frank's patchwork American terrain—Greenwich Village, the Times Square zone of nocturnal adventure, the rural South, and even the hinterlands of Indian reservations. Mailer began:

Probably, we will never be able to determine the psychic havoc of the concentration camps and the atom bomb upon the unconscious mind of almost everyone alive in these years. For the first time in civilized history, perhaps for the first time in all of history, we have been forced to live with suppressed knowledge that the smallest facets of our personality or the most minor projection of our ideas, or indeed the absence of ideas and the absence of personality could mean equally well that we might still be doomed to die as a cipher in some vast statistical operation in which our teeth would be counted, and our hair would be saved, but our death itself would be unknown, unhonored, and unremarked, a death which could not follow with dignity as a possible consequence to serious actions we had chosen, but rather a death by deus ex machina in a gas chamber or a radioactive city . . .[22]

Mailer outlined the choice that, at least for his adventuring persona, was not a choice at all. Faced with the postwar world, one could either endure "a slow death by conformity with every creative and rebellious instinct stifled" or one could "divorce oneself from society" and "set out on that uncharted journey into the rebellious imperatives of the self." In this "wild West of American night life" a solitary figure was already at home: the Negro hipster. African Americans already had been marginalized; they, according to Mailer, had not subjected themselves to the chains of middle-class restraint and were enriched by their passions; they knew how to live with death on these streets and, nonetheless, to express themselves through exemplary art forms, such as jazz. Now white hipsters, the new explorers, joined them in voluntary exile.

> So there was a new breed of adventurers, urban adventurers who drifted out at night looking for action with a black man's code to fit their facts. The hipster had absorbed the existentialist synopses of the Negro, and for practical purposes could be considered a white Negro. [23]

The founding statement for "The White Negro," the response to the dare, had focused on the white envy of "the sexual potency of the Negro." These four surly paragraphs, published in a monthly newspaper, brought responses from many people, including William Faulkner. The southerner wrote:

> I have heard this idea expressed several times during the last twenty years, though not before by a man.

> The others were ladies, northern or middle western ladies, usually around 40 or 45 years of age. I don't know what a psychiatrist would find in this.

Mailer responded by dismissing the Nobel Prize winner.

> Like many novelists who have created an extraordinary body of work, Mr. Faulkner is a timid man who has led a sheltered life. So I would not be surprised if he has had his best and most intense conversation with sensitive middle-aged ladies. [24]

The difference between the ad hominem accusation and the non-answer is significant. Faulkner deftly questioned both the originality of Mailer's pronouncement and the author's manhood. Mailer responded with his own name-calling. Faulkner was effeminate because he was "timid" and "sheltered." More than that, he was "sensitive," and in Mailer's view, this belief in sentiment consigned the southerner to the protected life of the middle-aged woman. A real man would explore the dangerous landscape of American culture, confronting what he met without the acceptance, the weakness, of sentiment. "The wild West of American nightlife" was a long way from Oxford, Mississippi, or Stockholm. It was no place for sissies.

"The White Negro" had armed itself, after this attack, with unexcerptible, if not impenetrable, sentences and a powerful combination of urban hipness and cool existentialist thought. Part of Mailer's performance would have been as offensive to Robert Frank as Mailer's dare was to Faulkner. Frank would not have allowed such an identification with African Americans, whose experiences transcended Mailer's stereotypes. Many of the women pictured in Frank's work show the burden of not having been sheltered. Unlike Mailer, Frank stood at a distance that prohibited false identification with his subjects, observing non-middle-class people, and then calling attention to the act of observation. However, both Mailer and Frank set out to explore the America that did not appear in *Life* magazine, to look at the imprint of American consumerism and at the ethnic and class subversions of this sameness.

Faulkner and Mailer are two representative voices of the 1950s. The first was formed before World War II, in the experience of the depression and the New Deal. Faulkner saw "the people" instead of the masses and trusted to the immense, compensatory power of human emotion to combat new and frightening technologies. This was the spirit of *The Family of Man*. As we have already seen, this voice was easily appropriated or silenced, as the logic of the cold war spun away from its time of origin. Mailer's voice, too, originated in World War II, in a younger generation that had confronted the bomb and the concentration camp in their twenties and thirties. This voice did not speak to everyone. It abandoned the work-a-day middle class to a life of conformity and encouraged a hearty remnant to arm itself—to armor the self—for a trip through a world, signified by the postwar city, that no longer made sense. To express the self, to irritate, to see anew the realities of America became prime goals. Mailer's voice and Frank's vision would become a part of the counterculture of the 1960s.

The difference between Frank and Steichen could be viewed through the depiction of the family. Frank offered a contrary vision of the family—idiosyncratic, particularized, class-specific. The universalizing, centripetal life of all families that Steichen saw was continually subverted in *Pull My Daisy*. The main desire was to get out, to engage the adventure of the streets, as Milo and his buddies did, leaving the little missus with the detritus of an evening's beat entertainment. But the film assigned roles as much as Steichen had done: the father is the breadwinner, even if he is oppressed and, finally, irresponsible; the mother is the moral anchor, even if, in the view of the film, she is constantly trying to pull the buoyant poets down with her; and the child—when he is allowed on camera—shows his innocent creativity. The family might have acted out its role differently, but the cast of characters remained the same. *Pull My Daisy* attacked directly the American world described by the Moscow exhibition; here was another vision of "how America lives, works, learns, produces, consumes, and plays." The most radical challenge to the traditional family—the homosexuality and bisexuality of the cast—was suppressed, so that a structure that Steichen would have recognized still dominated. Steichen and Frank might have offered strikingly different visions, but they focused on the same culture.

Steichen had been careful to ground *The Family of Man* in the soil; Ansel Adams's *Mount Williamson* had been one of the most striking, even unavoidable, photographs of the collection. By the 1960s the American terrain had undergone the upheaval of massive social shifts. There was now a different topography. During the time in which *Pull My Daisy* was being produced, *Newsweek* published a feature story on New York City. "Metropolis in a Mess" focused literally on the "Negro streets" that Allen Ginsberg had evoked in his great poem of the period, *Howl*, and that Mailer had so eagerly sought to explore. *Newsweek* operated more in the tradition of Hemingway than the beat poets. The article began, "When summer comes to Harlem, it comes hot and oppressive, like the scavenger breath of a jackal."[25] This was a New York of burgeoning slums, an evacuating white middle class, and increasing crime, particularly among juveniles. "More and more New York is becoming a city of the well-to-do, who are too few in numbers to be an important political factor, and the very poor."[26]

Post–World War II New York had changed under the force of suburbanization. During the 1950s the metropolis ceased to be a city of manufacturing and became more than ever a service center for home offices of large corporations. By the end of the decade, 135 of the top five hundred companies in the United States were headquartered in Manhattan. During the 1950s, an average of 2 million square feet of office space was being created each year. In this decade, 800,000 whites left the city for the suburbs and were replaced by an almost equal number of African Americans and Puerto Ricans. Meanwhile, 320,000 people were evicted from the South Bronx so that an expressway could be constructed.[27] This was a period of large-scale development, consolidation of capital, and the claiming of turf within New York City. Edward Steichen lived in the emerging corporate order of Sixth Avenue and its commuter corridor to the suburbs. The wistful evocation of agricultural life and celebration of manual labor of The Family of Man belied the suburban, consumer-oriented sensibility of both its creator and its audience. Robert Frank remained in the center of resistance to change—the indigestible lump of tenements, ethnic and racial minorities, voluntary exiles, and working-class Americans on the Lower East Side.

By the turn of the decade, Steichen's work had become static, important for what it revealed about a former era but mute in the face of contemporary issues. Robert Frank's work hinted at the aesthetic distance between the aged photographer and the young practitioners surrounding him. The world beyond the realm of art, the larger populace that Steichen so consciously appealed to, had also turned to other matters. On the domestic scene, issues of race and class inequity fractured whatever sentimental unity Steichen had constructed for "the people." Internationally, technological advances in weaponry and increasingly rigidified rhetorical platforms constructed by the two superpowers made The Family of Man's faith in humankind's ability to be shocked by a single mushroom cloud seem naive. The fractures that would make our world so different from Steichen's were already apparent. Three representative texts of the period, John Kenneth Galbraith's The Affluent Society, Michael Harrington's The Other America, and the Rockefeller Panel Report on international security, point to differences that were manifested in the Kennedy administration's reaction to the increasingly shrill world of the 1960s.

The Affluent Society chronicled the development of post–World War II leisure and the naturalizing of the world of the middle class, a social environment in which the conventional wisdom dictated etiquette. Here, in the author's droll phrase, the bland led the bland.[28] In a chapter that was written while The Family of Man drew crowds to the Museum of Modern Art, Galbraith pointed out that goods that had been considered luxuries to parents were now regarded as necessities to their children. The productive capacity of industry had expanded, but the appetites of consumers had kept pace.[29] In fact, by the end of his study, Galbraith was ready to assert the emergence of a New Class, a well-educated cohort of professionals who were not alienated from their work, who, indeed, had removed work from its industrial location to the office, the study, and the courtroom. These people were not out for wealth but for satisfaction and social stature.[30] Far from supporting the agriculturally based view of the folk posited by The Family of Man, Galbraith described a consumer economy and looked forward to the establishment of a managerial culture.

Galbraith saw clearly that this transformation affected national security. Through an analysis of the national economy during World War II, he pointed out that true civic sacrifice had been an illusion. Americans had offered up some goods to the war effort, to be sure, but the real story of the war had been the blossoming of the productive capacity of the nation's industries. The war had demanded more, but more could be drawn from the work place. Americans had never been in the situation of its adversaries who were bombed ever closer to the poverty line and nonetheless responded to calls for more war-related output. Increase in gross national product (GNP) during the cold war period, then, did not signal improvements in national security because it was not at all clear from recent experience that Americans would give up what they had come to think of as necessities of life—the habits of ten years of consumption—in a time of national emergency. In this view the array of American goods at the exposition in Moscow could, paradoxically, be considered a reservoir of internal resistance rather than an arsenal of national strength. Galbraith echoed David Potter's analysis of the burdens of a people of plenty. Both believed that international displays of abundance would alienate the less fortunate from the United States; the problem of global poverty in an economic system dominated by American consumers had to be solved, Galbraith believed.

Indeed, Galbraith could point to contemporary events to dislodge the complacent assumption that GNP growth engendered an increase in national security. The Soviet Union had managed to develop the sputnik without increasing the overall wealth of its citizens. The ability of a government to focus on technological development was more important than overall social improvement. A tightly controlled system was, it seemed, in a better position to wage such campaigns.[31] Here Galbraith responded directly to the report of an influential panel of experts convened by Henry Kissinger with support of the Rockefeller Brothers Fund to study national security. This panel reported that national security should be America's first priority, that "the security of the United States transcends normal budgetary considerations and that the national economy can afford the necessary measures."[32]

Galbraith spoke a language that Steichen would have understood. His New Class offered the possibility of rationality and restraint; the common sense innate to human beings everywhere was concentrated in one class, but it was still there. However, the technological capabilities and appetites of consumption could now scarcely be restrained. Galbraith saw the same nuclear flash that had so preoccupied Steichen, but space and time had changed since the threatening but strategically undirected test explosions of the early 1950s. No longer would the United States be required to convert to a war economy as it had done in World War II. A limited war would not require this, and a nuclear one would not allow enough time. According to the Rockefeller Panel Report, this new circumstance meant that massive stockpiles must be accumulated to anticipate a war that traveled at the speed of intercontinental ballistic missiles. Galbraith put his faith in the power of this New Class to make rational decisions to prevent war—a half-way point between Steichen's simple appeal to human decency and the abandonment of rationality through the policy of mutually assured destruction.[33]

A look at *The Other America* shows how quickly domestic events were moving away from Steichen, who was eighty-one years old at the end of the 1950s. Michael Harrington's book, which was to have legendary influence on the democratic administrations of the 1960s, was fired with the passion of experience. The author's point of view was neither the detached vantage point of the universalist nor the puzzled frame of the self-proclaimed foreigner but the engaged perspective of the social activist. Steichen and Frank had formed their texts through an eclectic tourism. True, their albums had been collected at considerable cost—Steichen's three years of effort and Frank's sometimes horrific travel experiences demonstrated this—but these fragments were assembled through an enfranchisement of the photographer on the road. Whether formally commissioned or informally conscripted, the curiosity of the eye kept the photographer moving, the shutter clicking.

Harrington's tourist was, by now, a familiar figure, an impediment to social change who glided by what should be seen on the way to work or a well-earned vacation: "The ordinary tourist never left the main highway, and today he rides interstate turnpikes."[34] Fresh pavement and the technologically paced experience of driving exposed the remote topography of Appalachia and its inhabitants to the eye of the weekend visitor seeking the exotic: "Seeing in them a romantic image of mountain life as independent, self-reliant, and athletic, a tourist could pass through these valleys and observe only quaintness." But Harrington reminded his readers of the ability of aesthetics to mask incalculable social wrong: "suddenly the mountain vista will reveal slashed, scarred hills and dirty little towns living under the shadow of decaying mining buildings. . . . They suffer terribly at the hands of beauty."[35] Both rural and urban poverty could be ignored because the home base of the tourist was the segregated suburb. Harlem and the Bowery, the city that they came to represent, became as foreign to the commuter as the faraway hills: "the very development of the American city has removed poverty from the living, emotional experience of millions upon millions of middle-class Americans."[36]

Steichen obliterated a class reading of society through his assumptions about the common emotional life of human beings; Frank shrouded class in the folds of the dark cloak of the Other. Class was, for Harrington, the compelling lens through which American culture had to be viewed. The realities surrounding the writer demanded this interpretation. To become a tourist under these conditions meant to see the sameness of American culture in a new and depressing way. A trip to California revealed the flip side of the Chamber of Commerce postcard.

> South from Stockton, along the Riviera coast near Santa Barbara, I remember seeing a most incredible contrast: the lush line of beach, coastal mountains, and rich homes, and, passing by, a truck-load of stolid-faced Mexican-Americans coming back from work.[37]

Chicago and St. Louis became like New York, and all three resembled the Bowery, where Harrington worked during 1951 and 1952. The terrain was the same and so were the people. There was "a language of the poor, a psychology of the poor, a world view of the poor."[38] Technological advances helped create the Other Half, and poverty, in turn, reshaped its victims through constructing "a personality of poverty."[39] What had heretofore been a "social product"—the inevitable tailings of economic processes—had been transformed into a "personal fate."[40] If you were born poor, Harrington proclaimed, your fate was sealed. Little more needed to be known about qualities of character, personal aspirations, or depth of beliefs, than this fundamental accounting.

This culture of poverty was shaded by racism and stooped by the weight of discrimination against the aged; it was pervasive and enduring. It demanded engagement and would not allow for distance or the lack of attention that grand statements had come to represent. Like Steichen, Harrington placed hope in the emotions of his readers, but this was the instrumental fire of social commitment in the face of an alternative as abhorrent as the brief, consuming flash of fundamental annihilation that Steichen envisioned.

> After one reads the facts either there are anger and shame, or there are
> not. And, as usual, the fate of the poor hangs upon the decision of the
> better-off. If this anger and shame are not forthcoming, someone can
> write a book about the other America a generation from now and it will
> be the same, or worse.[41]

Writing from the perspective of thirty years' distance, this foreboding prediction seems to have come true. Any gaze through the American landscape, from the cities of the northeast to South Central Los Angeles will support what statistics reiterate in excruciating and distressingly mind-numbing detail.

Harrington's view of poverty contested what John Kenneth Galbraith had said only a few years earlier: that aside from some particularly hard cases of poverty, those who could not or would not remove themselves from squalor, and some resistant areas of deprivation—the Harvard economist referred to Appalachia—the country had succeeded in creating a middle-class society. Galbraith, too, was concerned with the naturalization of poverty. Now that most people were not poor, he reasoned, it would be increasingly difficult to help the needy through the instruments of government. In his view, however, this class represented about 10 percent of Americans, not the burgeoning 33 percent that Harrington had identified. Harrington would not let his readers forget the poor; Galbraith spent more time discussing the short-term needs of the unemployed as they paused in their progress from one career to another. The people, as Steichen viewed them, could survive any hardship. Poverty, in Harrington's analysis, was a social problem that revealed the class fractures of American life.

The Family of Man has retained its stature as a great production but has been reified as a collection on the other side of relevance; it has become, in effect, a benchmark against which aesthetic advances have been measured. This effort to place *The Family of Man* within the history of photographic aesthetics has stripped the collection of its complexity and even misrepresented its intent. In the introduction to his influential 1978 exhibition of contemporary photography, *Mirrors and Windows*, John Szarkowski, Steichen's successor at the Museum of Modern Art, declared that "the general movement of American photography during the past quarter century has been from public to private concerns." The 127 photographs on display were divided according to the interlocking themes of self-expression and exploration, roughly the permeable boundary between the romantic and the realistic sensibilities. Several forces, he maintained, caused this turning away from the world that photographers had been so eager to explore. The power of the photography magazines had declined; even those on assignment for *Life* shot their own work in spare moments. More significant, increasingly complex events of the day could no longer be explained through photographic essays. A magazine such as *Life* "thought it could deal with anything," but, in retrospect, the simpler events of the past were easier to capture in these features. Advances in photographic technology had put cameras into the hands of amateurs who produced their own snapshots, depicting a private world of family get-togethers and tourist tableaux. This proliferation of images was mirrored on the professional level, as academic departments of photography churned out masters of that fine art.[42]

Of Szarkowski's three most significant photographic events of the 1950s—the exhibiting of *The Family of Man*, the publication of Robert Frank's *The Americans*, and the founding of *Aperture* magazine—only Steichen's achievement was "a popular success." For Szarkowski, the exhibition represented the end of the predominance of a photojournalistic tradition, "in which the personal intentions of the photographer are subservient to a larger, overriding concept." Crowds might have made the collection an important facet of popular culture, but "in spite of its artistic quality and enormous success, it had little perceptible affect on the subsequent directions of American photography."[43] The older, public role of the photographer, ascribed to figures like Steichen who believed that "it was the photographer's function to act as a trustworthy interpreter of the events and issues he was privileged to witness," was supplanted by the individual peculiarities of vision.[44]

Robert Frank represented this new vision and was, for Szarkowski, one of the exemplary photographers of the 1950s. Frank avoided "hortatory postures" and did not take it upon himself to suggest "a comprehensive or authoritative view of the world, or a program for its improvement."[45] Similarly, the photographer was not seduced by his own image; that is, he resisted producing glossy, facile, beautiful photographs. He had learned to distrust the soothing ability of his medium to portray itself—even to its practitioners—as unproblematic. The photographs of *The Americans* received scathing criticism from both professional and amateur photographers, not so much for the subject matter within the frame as for the self-consciously idiosyncratic lens constructing the image. "The subject of Frank's later pictures seemed tentative, ambivalent, relative, centrifugal; the photographer's viewpoint and the disposition of the frame seemed consistently precarious and careless . . ."[46]

To describe the impression that Frank's photographs made on many viewers, Szarkowski used a peculiar word—"pharisaical." His definition appeared in an appositive phrase: "lacking in sensitivity to, or affection for, the medium."[47] Frank may have seen his photographs as desacralizing what had been considered a public communion; however, the logic of Szarkowski's criticism was significantly muddled. The Pharisees were, after all, hypocritical practitioners of a religion that they had rationalized into a self-serving web of particular observances and prohibitions. Frank never has been viewed, then or now, as a photographer espousing an orthodoxy. His location was not within the temple but out on the street, amid new epiphanies. The orthodoxy within the temple ostracized Frank—exiled him to the desert of American bohemia. Those outside the comforting circle of 1950s conformity considered him a truth-teller, a prophet, or, to extend Szarkowski's analogy, even a Jeremiah. The location of the photographer was doubly vague in Szarkowski's scheme because the cultural terrain was subordinated to the instrument surveying it. Szarkowski saw Frank's images as a "searing personal view of this country during the Eisenhower years."[48] Sketching that view was Szarkowski's concern, not reflecting on the manufacture of these images during that singular period.

This individualized view of photographic practice since World War II has prevailed. On one side of Szarkowski's divide of the 1950s stood Steichen in the company of other photojournalists, the magazines to which they contributed, and the public to whom they presumed to speak. To preside over this world Szarkowski chose the figure of Eisenhower, who represented the legions of middle-class Americans he led out of World War II into the suburban world of his decade. On the other side stood the pioneers of modern photography, Robert Frank and Minor White. This new tradition, explored in *Mirrors and Windows*, was articulated in *Aperture* magazine and reinforced by the dislocating experiences of the 1960s. Szarkowski's view, as useful as it is, shows the limits of a criticism that relies solely on images. Passing off the site of photographic production as "the Eisenhower years" does not eliminate the necessary economy between photographer and subject. Such statements prepare the way for the aetheticization of the upheavals of the 1960s.

Susan Sontag has more recently described the chasm separating us from the world that Edward Steichen addressed. The lineage that quickly returned *The Family of Man* to the affirming, compendious voice of Whitman through the generation of Steichen and Sandburg had been truncated after the Second World War. No longer was it possible to revel in the beauty of the mundane world or to marvel at the luster of the well-crafted photograph. Sontag asserted that Walker Evans, in his views of the simpler, depression-era Alabama world of *Let Us Now Praise Famous Men*, was the last to do this successfully. Surrounded by the unfamiliar life of the sharecropper, everything was equally important to Evans, but "this was a leveling up, not down."[49] After the war the Whitmanian tradition split in two. One strand was the sentimental humanism of Steichen, "the last sigh of the Whitmanesque erotic embrace of the nation, but universalized and stripped of all demands."[50] The other, more tortured thread was represented by Diane Arbus, who relentlessly catalogued grotesques. The message was simple. "In photographing dwarfs, you don't get majesty and beauty. You get dwarfs."[51]

This "private vision" was supported by a public audience for whom viewing photographs was "a self-willed test of hardness."[52] Sontag proclaimed that modern viewers have become inured to the pain, the horror, of both the physical and psychological dislocations of life. She held up Arbus's photographs as a "good instance of a leading tendency of high art in capitalist cultures: to suppress, or at least reduce, moral and sensory queasiness. Much of modern art is devoted to lowering the threshold of what is terrible."[53] Photographs no longer spoke to the culture; the image became an illusion. Arbus's view gave contemporary viewers "the anti-humanist message which people of good will in the 1970s are eager to be troubled by,"[54] but made these spectators into voyeurs. Viewers were now only superficially passive, because the "pseudo-familiarity with the horrible"[55] sucked them into an insidious complicity that began with empathy and was enticed by curiosity. Four Arbus photographs were placed in the exploration section of John Szarkowski's exhibition; in Sontag's analysis, published in the same year as *Mirrors and Windows*, Arbus's work represented the malign inarticulateness, the sullenness of the photographer's voice in contemporary culture.

In both these influential views, Steichen was consigned to the congenial irrelevance of superannuation. Sontag's *On Photography* described a world of images that would not offer the comfort of coherence. Steichen had infused his work with a "pious uplift" that was out "to show that individuals are born, work, laugh, and die everywhere in the same way." *The Family of Man* revealed once again to its later critics that people in the 1950s wished "to be consoled and distracted by a sentimental humanism." Finally, and most ominously, Steichen's anthology denied "the determining weight of history." The viewer was no longer a voyeur but was encouraged to revel in the universality of the self. For Sontag, Steichen and Arbus both "render history and politics irrelevant. One does so by universalizing the human condition, into joy; the other by atomizing it, into horror."[56]

As in Szarkowski's scheme, Sontag's analysis created a convenient stereotype of *The Family of Man*. A sophisticated reader of cultural productions, here Sontag limited herself to the book of images that has survived. She did not examine the manufacture of this text—how it was constructed, how it came to its voice, and how it was heard in mid-1950s America. Steichen's message gained its articulateness through the exhibition. The formation of this humanistic testimony was shaped by specific circumstances during "the Eisenhower years," the criteria for the display of photographs, and a particular reverberation of life experiences and historical interpretations. All of these tones contributed to Steichen's celebration of the importance of sentiment and great, humanizing emotions enacted by seemingly ordinary, virtually interchangeable people.

The voices that add their testimony to Steichen's in this chapter are of an older generation that had come to maturity long before the Second World War. They spoke expansively to a popular audience and, with the confidence of a creative self that was able to weave continuity amid the chaos of events, used the past as prologue to the present. We do not have to retreat to Whitman's era to find a representative figure: Carl Sandburg, Steichen's brother-in-law and confidant during the exhibition's assembly, who had recently completed his own monumental performance, his biography of Abraham Lincoln. Steichen and Sandburg held the phrase "the family of man" in common. Both appreciated the emotional import of the four words of. Abraham Lincoln's that had become, for Susan Sontag, banal.

Sandburg was more than a troubadour with guitar in hand—a populist persona he liked to claim for himself through his many appearances during the 1930s; he also had proclaimed himself as the biographer of the Great Emancipator. Steichen helped him select photographs for the massive, four-volume *Abraham Lincoln: The War Years*, which appeared to both critical acclaim and popular success in 1939. It was in the first of these tomes that "the family of man" reference appears. Let us resituate this phrase. Lincoln was in transit between Springfield and Washington for his inauguration, making whistle-stops along the way. Because he was still only president-elect, he said little in his many speeches, while admitting that a momentous decision awaited him after March 4th. On the night of February 12, 1861, he addressed a group of German American workers in Cincinnati. One of the two versions of his brief remarks carried the reference that is presumed to have given voice to Steichen's exhibit.

> In regard to Germans and foreigners, I esteem foreigners no better than
> other people, nor any worse. They are all of the great family of men, and
> if there is one shackle upon any of them, it would be far better to lift the
> load from them than to pile additional loads upon them.[57]

To paraphrase a later, more celebrated Lincoln oration, the turn of phrase of the soon-to-be sixteenth president of the United State was little noted nor long remembered.

The phrase is embedded in the construction of Sandburg's Lincoln, a Rooseveltian figure among the many manifestations of the Civil War president that appeared at the end of the 1930s.[58] *The War Years* opened with Lincoln's trip to the nation's capital, as the federal union was breaking apart. The humble man from Illinois was confronted by the unrestrained passions of the beginning of the Civil War, an elaborate sample of which Sandburg presents to the reader as a pastiche of 1861 unreason. Caught between peace and war, between election and inauguration as chief magistrate, Sandburg's Lincoln is suspended before a decision that will contradict his faith in the people but will preserve the union according to his higher duty as president. Indeed, the true import of the short speech on his birthday in 1861 may have been its location, just across the river from the ambiguous yet familiar terrain of Kentucky. Lincoln the humanist, burdened by the accumulated weight of history, had to face the dark realities of a landscape that was no longer home. Sandburg's volumes written during the midst of the depression must have seemed quite up-to-date to the current occupant of the White House, an admirer of Sandburg's and, more recently, an appropriator of the Lincolnian tradition.[59] For Roosevelt, viewing from afar the disintegration of Europe and anticipating aid to the Allies, the first chapter of Sandburg's epic work must have sounded prophetic: "America—Whither?"

Sandburg positioned the familiar figure of Lincoln, the "mystery in smoke and flags" that had begun to consume his attention, at the center of *The People, Yes*. This speaker of aphorisms and practitioner of pragmatic action ("My policy is to have no policy") represents the people, and, according to Sandburg, is created by them.[60] Sandburg's later Lincoln showed this relationship to the people through the more than 1 million-word biography. "As Lincoln rose steadily to the responsibility," wrote Alfred Jones summarizing Sandburg's point of view, he "drew strength from the people who had forced it upon him. At the same time, in their consciousness, he became an extension of their own character and purposes."[61] Among the Lincoln sayings refashioned into verse by Sandburg is the following: "The strongest bond of human sympathy, outside of the family relation, should be one uniting all working people, of all nations and tongues and kindreds."[62] This precis of Lincoln's Cincinnati speech was the essence of the "family of man" spirit that resulted in Steichen's exhibition: the primacy of the family, the bond of human sympathy, and the power of this emotion to transcend nationalistic acrimony and linguistic boundaries.

This mixture of the hortatory and the colloquial, the national and the universal, we have seen over and over again through the careers of *The Family of Man* and its maker. Edward Steichen was indeed Whitmanesque, but for him sentiment served the purpose of drawing people together, of sensitizing them to the "genuine and historically embedded differences, injustices, and conflicts,"[63] as other, more overtly socially conscious photographers had undertaken. In the 1960s this sensibility had been silenced by a long catalogue of injustices that were excerpted into an anthology of disturbing images that pictures could no longer explain. Steichen's collection was formed in a specific historic moment and showed, in its own career, the determining weight of history. *The Family of Man* was flattened by the cold war of the late 1950s. Its sentimental approach did intend to console but not to distract its audience; to the hardness of circumstances it could offer little resistance.

Edward Steichen retired from the Museum of Modern Art in 1962. His last exhibition before his departure was *The Bitter Years*, a review of the Farm Security Administration's accomplishment of the 1930s. His justification, related in *A Life in Photography*, echoed Galbraith and revealed the persistence of his view of humankind portrayed in *The Family of Man*. In this last display, Steichen encouraged viewers to look through the economic fluctuations in prosperity during the preceding several years to a time of true hardship in the Great Depression. The flood of goods and capital during the 1950s had made luxuries commonplace and had obscured the record of achievement during the privations of two decades before.

> In 1962 the time seemed ripe for a reminder of those "bitter years" and for bringing them into the consciousness of a new generation that had problems of its own but was largely unaware of the endurance and fortitude that had made the emergence from the Great Depression one of America's victorious hours.[64]

Always the anthologizer, Steichen also hoped to foster the creation of "a permanent photographic organization" that would document "all phases and activities of the

United States and its people." The distinction between the civic entity and its human population maintained the photographer's patriotism and his allegiance to a broader humanism. The image of "the bitter years" might serve to revitalize a patriotic vigor gone soft through a decade of un-self-conscious indulgence. The human qualities that Steichen saw so clearly through these photographs were still the best antidote against the "race suicide" of the ever-present atomic bomb.

The discipline of the photographer now, as always, was to produce images that would allow his viewers to see the world clearly. At the beginning of the century Steichen had schooled himself in photography through meticulous studies of a cup and saucer, an arrangement of pears and apples. Now, in his retirement, he turned to the medium of film, examining in detail a shadblow tree behind his Connecticut home. Eighty-four at the time of the writing of his autobiography, he felt compelled to leave young photographers with some advice. Three perils faced the creative life of an artist. He or she could succumb to the demands of the state: "totalitarian, political, or national ideologies that seek to direct or channel the arts are pernicious." The demands of the marketplace, the desire to be in vogue, could distract any photographer. Finally, however, the greatest enemy came from within and had to be controlled through the self-discipline of artistic commitment.

> So often, what may have begun as fresh thinking and discovery is turned
> into a routine and reduced to mere habit. Habits in thinking or technique
> are always stultifying in the long run. They are also contagious, and when
> a certain set of habits becomes general, a whole art period can condemn
> itself to the loss of freedom. It is probably this stultifying process, more
> than anything else, that transforms the avant-garde of one generation into
> academicians in the eyes of the next.[65]

Ever the optimist, he saw in the exuberance of the contemporary art scene insurance against conformity.

This was Steichen the autobiographer, responding to the same call that had made Benjamin Franklin put pen to paper—the desire to relate a life well lived and to see younger generations heed sage advice. Like Thoreau, he turned to nature to liberate himself from routine, to serve as a connecting metaphor, and, one suspects, to prepare himself for the concluding act in his life cycle. Steichen lived long enough to shape a myth of himself as photographer, bureaucrat, statesman, and visual poet. While acknowledging the mythic quality of his persona, we should honor the ineluctable urge to put a life into perspective, to make sense of it all, to construct the seamless narrative that gives fulfillment and, finally, resignation.

Steichen functioned well in a visual world in which each image related to the next through the same jigsaw puzzle of meaning that confronted verbal expression when thought had to be articulated into words and sentences. He could not have been prepared for a world in which the meaning of the photograph had to remain contingent on its surroundings and the eyes through which it was viewed. He certainly could not have anticipated that his own motives, his earnest connection to his visual text, would be dislodged from the meaning he had seemingly shaped so clearly. Where he trusted images to move people to action, contemporary commentators have seen another aspect of a discredited liberal ideology. He believed that his photographic anthology allowed him to speak to great numbers of people. These efforts at finding a capacious middle ground have been dismissed as bourgeois.[66] We need what Allan Sekula has called "a grounded sociology of the image,"[67] but in the case of The Family of Man we also require a broader, historical dimension, for this text reveals a double dislodgment, the first provided by Steichen in his Seventh Avenue loft and the second by the forced tour that brought these images around the world, through the decades, and to our living rooms.

Throughout this book I have made the case that The Family of Man was more complex than the collection appears to us now. It took shape during one of the great common experiences of the twentieth century—World War II—and was composed in the early 1950s with a syntax that would, Steichen assumed, be read and understood by a wide audience. Given these assurances, its rhetoric was proclamatory and its vocabulary assumed the full, articulate use of a common visual dictionary. Perhaps this topical use of timeless themes was destined to fall under the weight of its own contradictions. In any case, as we have seen, by the end of the 1950s the collection had settled into the cultural niche it occupies today: a compendium of beautiful but unchallenging photographs to be paged through as a relief from a world of harsher realities. The collection is not considered by scholars to be vital; it merely retains its celebrity as the one photographic collection that many Americans can name.

Edward Steichen opened the exhibition's world tour in August 1955 at the Corcoran Gallery in Washington, D.C. The photographs could be mounted on frames which would adapt to almost any space. Photo: National Archives.

Photographs of the traveling exhibition established new contexts, beginning at the Corcoran. The daughter of the ambassador from the Republic of China looks at a photograph of herself on the wall while examining the same picture in The Family of Man book. Photo: National Archives.

National connections were easily made between viewers and an exhibition depicting sixty-eight different countries. In Amsterdam, Queen Juliana of the Netherlands views a representation of two of her subjects. Photo: National Archives.

Some viewers were struck by finding themselves among the representations of the world's peoples, creating set pieces that were a publicist's dream. Here Yugoslav villagers point to familiar faces in a picture taken in their home town of Sisak.
Photo: National Archives.

The photographs were large enough to envelop their audience, as in Paris, where viewers were inserted into a European street scene. Photo: National Archives.

The American Exhibition in Moscow (1959) thrust The Family of Man (to the right of the geodesic dome) into a war of consumer goods the epicenter of which was the fan-shaped building behind the dome. Photo: National Archives.

More than 2.7 million visitors crowded into the Solkoniki Park site during the six weeks of the exhibition's opening.
Photo: National Archives.

Richard Nixon came to open the American contribution to the first binational exchange between the United States and the Soviet Union and to engage the leader of the Soviet Union, Nikita Khrushchev, in debate. Photo: National Archives.

Edward Steichen, with his brother-in-law Carl Sandburg, came to the opening as well and found a community of Soviet photographers, which allowed for a congenial use of a familiar medium. Photo: Elliott Erwitt, courtesy Magnum Photos.

Many of the exhibits were encased in structures entirely made of plastic. The experimental units of fiberglass were hurriedly tested for stability in the wind by blasting a test module with the prop wash from several airplanes on a Long Island airstrip. Photo: National Archives.

Inside the dome, a Charles Eames multiscreen presentation, projected overhead onto seven screens, introduced visitors to American abundance. Photo: National Archives.

Richard Nixon and Nikita Khrushchev played to the medium of television, then experimenting with color cameras and videotape which made the replay of their exchanges both more lifelike and immediate. Photo: National Archives.

The Kitchen Debate, the culmination of the exchanges between the two leaders, required a more symbolic stage. Among the appliances of the model home, William Safire, in the foreground, prepares to take the photograph that has come to represent this Cold War episode. Photo: Elliott Erwitt, courtesy Magnum Photos.

Space age fins and all, this shiny convertible achieved its purpose in creating a dreamy look of longing in its Russian passenger. Photo courtesy of UPI/Bettmann.

The proliferation of consumer goods—as infinitely replicable as the plastic bowls handed out as souvenirs—
was irresistible, even to the Soviet premier. Photo: National Archives.

The Family of Man drew large crowds and was identified by viewers as among the best features of the exhibition.
Photo: National Archives.

The fiberglass structure housed The Family of Man in a space that in its aesthetics and its materials proclaimed a space age vastly different from the world that Steichen had addressed in 1955. Photo: National Archives.

Steichen documented one of the most important moments in the life of his exhibition by contextualizing these representatives of The Other Side into his world family. Photo: Elliott Erwitt, courtesy Magnum Photos.

Steichen, the master photographer. Photo: Wayne F. Miller, courtesy Magnum Photos.

NOTES

Introduction

1. James Nelson, ed., *Wisdom: Conversations with the Elder Wise Men of Our Day,* (New York, 1958), 10.

2. Ibid., 41.

3. Ibid.

4. Ibid., 42.

5. Ibid.

6. Ibid., 41.

7. Ibid., 39.

8. Ibid., 42.

9. Ibid., 42–43.

10. Russell Lynes, *The Good Old Modern: An Intimate Portrait of the Museum of Modern Art* (New York, 1973), 325–26.

11. Paul Hill and Thomas Cooper, *Dialogue with Photography* (New York, 1979), 357–58.

12. David Potter, *People of Plenty: Economic Abundance and the American Character* (Chicago, 1954), 84.

13. Ibid., 142–65.

14. Ibid., 141.

14. Ibid.

15. Ibid., 112.

16. Ibid., 115.

17. Ibid., 33.

18. Ibid., 36–37, 42.

19. "A Life Round Table on The Pursuit of Happiness," *Life*, 12 July 1948, 97.

20. Henry Steele Commager, *The American Mind: An Interpretation of American Thought and Character Since the 1880's* (New Haven, 1950), 411.

21. "Pursuit of Happiness," 108–10.

22. Potter, *People of Plenty*, 181.

23. Ibid., 183.

24. Ibid., 185.

25. Quoted in *New York Times*, 1 April 1973, II, 18.

26. James Guimond, *American Photography and the American Dream* (Chapel Hill, 1991), 161.

27. Ibid., 152.

28. Andrew Ross, *No Respect: Intellectuals and Popular Culture* (New York, 1989), 55.

29. Elaine Tyler May, *Homeward Bound: American Families in the Cold War Era* (New York, 1988), and Stephanie Coontz, *The Way We Never Were: American Families and the Nostalgia Trap* (New York, 1992).

30. Guimond, *American Photography*, 171–73.

31. Eric Sandeen, "The Family of Man at the Museum of Modern Art: The Power of the Image in '50s America," *Prospects* 11, 1987, 367–91.

32. The photographs were reinstalled in 1994. They were previewed in Toulouse, France and Tokyo. According to Wayne Miller, several museums have already requested the exhibit, so there may well be a second coming of *The Family of Man*. At present, it seems, the photographs have retained some power. Miller was talking to one of the organizers of the Toulouse preview, who quietly directed his attention to a woman who was standing amid the family portraits. She was weeping.

chapter one
Constructing a World of Photography

1. Margaret Bourke-White, *The Taste of War*, Jonathan Silverman, ed. (London, 1985), 49.

2. Vicki Goldberg, *Margaret Bourke-White: A Biography* (New York, 1987), 245–46.

3. "Moscow Fights off the Nazi Bombers and Prepares for a Long War," *Life*, 1 September 1941, 15.

4. Goldberg, *Bourke-White*, 260.

5. See Richard Whelan, *Robert Capa: A Biography* (New York, 1985).

6. Susan Moeller, *Shooting War: Photography and the American Experience of Combat* (New York, 1989), 181–84.

7. Carl Mydans, *Carl Mydans, Photojournalist* (New York, 1985), 22–23.

8. Ibid., 24.

9. Ibid., 31.

10. Hill and Cooper, *Dialogue with Photography*, 260.

11. William S. Johnson, ed., *W. Eugene Smith: Master of the Photographic Essay* (New York, 1981), 14.

12. See Paul Fussell, *Wartime: Understanding and Behavior in the Second World War* (New York, 1989), for a good description of the new horrors of killing.

13. Loudon Wainwright, *The Great American Magazine: An Inside History of Life* (New York, 1986), 151.

14. John G. Morris, "This We Remember: The Pictures that Make Vietnam Unforgettable," *Harper's*, September 1972, 74.

15. Moeller, *Shooting War*, 210–11.

16. Christopher Phillips, *Steichen at War* (New York, 1981), 19.

17. Edward Steichen, *A Life in Photography* (New York, 1984 [1963]), Chapter 12.

18. Wayne Miller, interview by author, 21 April 1991.

19. Ibid.

20. Phillips, *Steichen at War*, 38–39.

21. Ibid., 43.

22. Ibid., 29.

23. Ibid., 33.

24. Steichen, *A Life*, Chapter 12; Susan Moeller comments that in mid-war, images begin to focus on individuals rather than groups but that, overall, "in the microcosm could be found the macrocosm" (Moeller, *Shooting War*, 211).

25. See Allan Sekula, *Photography Against the Grain: Essays and Photo Works, 1973–1983* (Halifax, 1984).

26. Steichen, *A Life*, Chapter 12.

27. Beaumont Newhall, *The History of Photography* (New York, 1982), 263.

28. Naomi Rosenblum, *A World History of Photography* (New York, 1984), 473–77.

29. David Nye, *Image Worlds: Corporate Identities at General Electric, 1890–1930* (Cambridge, 1985).

30. See James Curtis, *Mind's Eye, Mind's Truth: FSA Photography Reconsidered* (Philadelphia, 1989), and James Guimond, *American Photography and the American Dream* (Chapel Hill, 1991), for the most recent additions to an already large body of criticism.

31. Maren Stange, *Symbols of Ideal Life: Social Documentary Photography in America, 1890–1950* (New York, 1989).

32. Quoted in Newhall, *History of Photography*, 260.

33. *National Geographic*, a magazine that had capitalized on the hitherto vicarious wanderlust of American readers for decades, experienced a similar growth. The Society grew from 1.1 million members at the beginning of the war to 1.6 members in 1947. By the mid-1950s, almost 2.2 million people subscribed to the magazine. See Howard Abramson, *National Geographic: Behind America's Lens on the World* (New York, 1987), 181–87.

34. Abramson, *National Geographic*, 181.

35. Gilbert Grosvenor, "Maps for Victory: National Geographic Society's Charts Used in War on Land, Sea, and in the Air." *National Geographic* 81, May 1942, 667.

36. Ibid., 689.

37. C. D. B. Bryan, *The National Geographic Society: 100 Years of Adventure and Discovery* (New York, 1987), 252.

38. Ibid., 254.

39. James L. Baughman, *Henry R. Luce and the Rise of the American News Media* (Boston, 1987), 170.

40. Quoted in Wilson Hicks, *Words and Pictures: An Introduction to Photojournalism* (New York, 1952), 118.

41. Phillips, *Steichen at War*, 51.

42. Dmitri Kessel, *On Assignment: Dmitri Kessel, Life Photographer* (New York, 1985), 43.

43. Ibid., 35.

44. Hicks, *Words and Pictures*, 106.

45. Ibid., 85.

46. Ibid., 137.

47. Ibid., 119.

48. Quoted in ibid., 98.

49. Wainwright, *Great American Magazine*, 179–80.

50. Miller, interview, 21 April 1991. Miller would later become president of Magnum.

51. Hill and Cooper, *Dialogue with Photography*, 259.

52. Johnson, *W. Eugene Smith*, 41.

53. Hill and Cooper, *Dialogue with Photography*, 58.

54. Ibid., 67.

55. Whelan, *Capa*, 252.

56. Ibid., 271.

57. Ibid., 252.

58. Robert Doisneau, quoted in Hill and Cooper, *Dialogue with Photography*, 95.

59. Hill and Cooper, *Dialogue with Photography*, 59.

60. "People Are People the World Over," *Ladies' Home Journal*, May 1948, 42–43.

61. "Woman's World Revolves Around the Kitchen," *Ladies' Home Journal*, May 1948, 44–45.

62. "People Are People," 43.

63. "This Is the World at Home," *Ladies' Home Journal*, December 1948, 44.

64. "This Is the Way the World Farms," *Ladies' Home Journal*, July 1948, 36–37.

65. "This Is How the World Gets Around," *Ladies' Home Journal*, February 1949, 44.

66. "This Is How the World Eats," *Ladies' Home Journal*, November 1948, 73.

67. "This Is the Way the World Shops," *Ladies' Home Journal*, March 1949, 75.

68. "This Is How the World Eats," 73.

69. See Christopher Lasch, *The True and Only Heaven: Progress and Its Critics* (New York, 1991).

70. "This Is the Way the World Studies," *Ladies' Home Journal*, October 1948, 68.

71. "This Is the World at Home," 45.

72. "This Is the Way the World Studies," 69.

73. "This Is How the World Gets Around," 45.

74. See Whelan, *Capa*, 254, for example.

75. George F. Kennan [X, pseud.], "The Sources of Soviet Conduct, *Life*, 28 July 1947, 53.

76. Ibid., 54.

77. Ibid., 56.

78. John Lewis Gaddis, *Strategies of Containment: A Critical Appraisal of Postwar American National Security Policy* (New York, 1982), 56.

79. Edmund Wilson, *Europe Without Baedeker: Sketches Among the Ruins of Italy, Greece and England* (New York, 1966 [1947]), 217.

80. David W. Ellwood, *Rebuilding Europe: Western Europe, America and Postwar Reconstruction* (London, 1992).

81. Gaddis, *Strategies*, 40.

82. Kennan, "Sources," 63.

83. Potter, *People of Plenty*, the map appears on page 82.

84. "A Life Round Table on The Pursuit of Happiness," *Life*, 12 July 1948, 113. The three other Round Tables that appeared over the next year were: "A Life Round Table on Modern Art," *Life*, 11 October 1948, 56–79; "A Life Round Table on Housing," *Life*, 31 January 1949, 73–86; "A Round Table on the Movies," *Life*, 27 June 1949, 90–110.

85. Henry Nash Smith, *Virgin Land: The American West as Symbol and Myth* (Cambridge, 1950), xi.

86. See Philip Gleason, "World War II and the Development of American Studies," *American Quarterly* 36 (Bibliography), 1984, 343–58.

87. Margaret Mead, "National Character and the Science of Anthropology," in Seymour Martin Lipset and Leo Lowenthal, eds., *Culture and Social Character: The Work of David Riesman Reviewed* (New York, 1961), 16.

88. Andrew Ross, *No Respect*, 59.

89. Ibid., 60.

90. Jon Halliday and Bruce Cumings, *Korea: The Unknown War* (New York, 1988), 78.

91. Phillip Knightly, *The First Casualty: From the Crimea to Vietnam, The War Correspondent as Hero, Propagandist, and Myth Maker* (New York, 1975), 341.

92. Quoted in Moeller, *Shooting War*, 278.

93. Among the most recent accounts of the war are Halliday and Cumings, *Korea*, and Richard Whelan, *Drawing the Line: The Korean War, 1950–1953* (Boston, 1990). Especially interesting are the memoirs of correspondents and photographers, particularly Carl Mydans, Reginald Thompson, and Marguerite Higgins.

94. "How the Truce Came to Korea," *Life*, 10 August 1953, 18.

95. Ibid., 23–27.

96. Quoted in Moeller, *Shooting War*, 252.

97. Knightley, *First Casualty*, 342. See also Halliday and Cumings, *Korea*, Chapter 2.

98. Moeller, *Shooting War*, 280.

99. See Frances FitzGerald, *America Revised: History Schoolbooks in the Twentieth Century* (Boston, 1979), for one account of Korea's substitu-

tion for Vietnam in schoolbooks of the 1960s
and 1970s.

100. Moeller, *Shooting War*, 312.

101. Ibid., 294.

102. Knightly, *First Casualty*, 346–47.

103. "The Blessing of God," *Life*, 25 December 1950, 20.

104. David Douglas Duncan, "There Was a Christmas," *Life*, 25 December 1950, 13.

105. Ibid., 10.

106. Moeller, *Shooting War*, 304.

107. Carl Mydans, *More than Meets the Eye* (New York, 1959), 3–4, quoted in Moeller, *Shooting War*, 297.

108. "Other U.N. Troops: They Also Serve," *Life*, 26 February 1951, 104–7.

109. Steichen, *A Life*, Chapter 13.

110. David Douglas Duncan, *This Is War!: A Photo Narrative in Three Parts* (New York, 1967 [1951]), n.p.

111. Ibid.

112. Ibid.

113. Letters to the editors, *Life*, 15 January 1951, 10.

1. Minor White, "Museum of Modern Art Exhibition," *Aperture* 9, 1961, 41.

2. Miller, interview by the author, 19 June 1993.

3. Miller, interview by the author, November 1984.

4. Miller, interview, 21 April 1991.

5. Miller, interview, 19 June 1993.

6. Miller, interview, November 1984.

7. News Release, "Museum of Modern Art Plans International Photography Exhibition," 31 January 1954, Steichen archives, MoMA.

8. Miller, interview, November 1984.

9. Steichen, *A Life*, Chapter 13.

10. Miller remembers that Steichen attributed the phrase to both Sandburg's writings and the common vocabulary established through decades of conversations between the two brothers-in-law.

11. Penelope Niven McJunkin, "Steichen and Sandburg," *Horizon*, August 1979, 50.

12. Ibid.

13. Carl Sandburg, *The People, Yes* (New York, 1936) 3.

14. Sandburg, *The People, Yes*, 55.

15. Quoted in Sandburg, *Home Front Memo* (New York, 1943), 306.

16. Sandburg, *Home Front Memo*, 309.

17. Miller, interview, November 1984.

18. Ibid.

19. Miller, interview, 19 June 1993.

20. Miller, interview, November 1984.

21. Edward Steichen, *The Family of Man* (New York, 1955), introduction, n.p. Steichen's tally (two million) does not take into account Wayne Miller's search through the *Life* files.

22. Steichen, *The Family of Man*, introduction, n.p.

23. Ibid.

24. Miller, interview, November 1984.

25. Miller interview, 21 April 1991.

26. Miller, interview, November 1984.

27. Miller, interview, 19 June 1993.

28. Steichen, *A Life*, Chapter 13.

29. Edward Steichen, "The FSA Photographers," in Beaumont Newhall, *Photography, Essays and Images: Illustrated Readings in the History of Photography* (New York, 1980), 268.

30. Jacob Dischin, in "The Controversial Family of Man," *Aperture* 3, 1955, 9.

31. Barbara Morgan, in "The Controversial Family of Man," 25.

32. Aline Saarinen, in ibid., 10.

33. Ibid., 11.

34. Dorothy Norman, in ibid., 15.

35. Ibid., 16.

36. Ibid.

37. Ibid.

38. Phoebe Lou Adams, "Through a Lens Darkly," *Atlantic* 195, April 1955, 69.

39. Ibid., 70.

40. Ibid., 72.

41. Morgan, in "The Controversial Family of Man," *Aperture* 3, 25.

42. Adams, "Lens Darkly," 72.

43. *Family of Man* (film), United States Information Agency, National Archives.

44. Morgan, in "The Controversial Family of Man," *Aperture* 3, 27.

45. Roland Barthes, "The Great Family of Man" in *Mythologies*, Annette Lavers, trans. (New York, 1972), 100. This essay was written to review the opening of *The Family of Man* in Paris in 1956.

46. Barthes, *Mythologies*, 101.

47. "The American Family in Trouble," *Life*, 26 July 1949, 83–99.

48. "*Life* goes to an Oldsters' Outing," *Life*, 22 September 1947, 154–55.

49. Nat Farbman, "The Bushmen: An Ancient Race Struggles in the South African Desert," *Life*, 3 February 1947, 95.

50. These associations are, paradoxically, one of the exhibition's enduring strengths. In 1989 I lectured on *The Family of Man* in Turkey. Many of the members of my audience remembered the significance of one picture taken in that country. This photo, a part of the civic responsibility section, showed an elderly woman voting. It was significant to my audience because this was the first election in which women were allowed the franchise.

51. *Family of Man* (film).

52. Edward Steichen, "The Family of Man," *Picturescope* 3, July 1955, 7.

53. Wayne Miller, "Steichen, My Friend," in *Steichen/109* (Milwaukee, 1988), n.p.

54. Peter B. Hales, "The Atomic Sublime." *American Studies* 32, Spring 1991, 5–31.

55. Jacques Barzun, *The House of Intellect* (New York, 1959), 28–29.

56. Ibid., 30.

57. See "Parnassus, Coast to Coast," *Time*, 11 June 1956.

58. Barzun, *House*, 30.

59. Quoted in Christopher Phillips, "The Judgment Seat of Photography," *October* 22, Fall 1982, 48.

60. John Szarkowski, *Mirrors and Windows: American Photography since 1960* (New York, 1978), 17.

61. "A *Life* Round Table on Modern Art," *Life*, 10/11/48, 64.

62. Ibid., 70.

63. Alan Sekula, "The Traffic in Photographs," *Art Journal* 41, Spring 1981, 20.

64. Gwen Finkel Chanzit, *Herbert Bayer and Modernist Design in America* (Ann Arbor, 1987), 3–84.

65. Chanzit, *Bayer*, 112.

66. Arthur Cohen, *Herbert Bayer: The Complete Work* (Cambridge, 1984), 314; Chanzit, *Bayer*, 112.

67. Chanzit, *Bayer*, 115.

68. The reference here is to Benjamin's seminal essay, "The Work of Art in the Age of Mechanical Reproduction," in *Illuminations*, Hannah Arendt, editor (New Yor, 1968).

69. Miller, interview, 19 June 1993.

70. Jonathan Green, *American Photography: A Critical History, 1945 to the Present* (New York, 1984).

71. "U.S. Growth," *Life* 36, 4 January 1954. For all subsequent references to this issue, the page number(s) will appear (in parentheses), in the text.

72. In addition to Elaine May's elaborate exploration of containment, *Homeward Bound* (New York, 1988), Dolores Hayden's work, especially *Redesigning the American Dream* (New York, 1984), eloquently places this postwar phenomenon in a durable, and enduring, American domestic sphere. Parenthetically, it is interesting to note how the "American kitchen" introduced to Europeans after World War II was taken in this new location as a symbol of emancipation.

73. Peter Rowe's fine *Making a Middle Landscape* (Cambridge, 1991), exemplifies the burgeoning literature devoted to postwar American suburbia.

74. *Life* could not foresee the day, after the bicentennial, when the United States would follow the course of Great Britain from creditor to debtor.

75. "A-Bomb vs. House," *Life*, 30 March 1954, 21.

76. Ibid., 24.

77. Ibid., 22.

78. Ibid., 24.

79. Ibid.

80. Ibid.

81. Peter B. Hales, "The Atomic Sublime," *American Studies* 32, Spring 1991, 5–31.

82. I surveyed volumes 20 through 38 of the magazine using *Life's* index categories.

83. "Explosion of a Myth," *Life*, 8 June 1953, 32–33; and "Atomic Explosion Stopped at Millionths of a Second," 9 November 1953, 33.

84. "5-4-3-2-1 and the Hydrogen Age Is Upon Us," *Life*, 12 April 1954, 25.

85. Ibid., 28.

86. "First Casualties of the H-Bomb," *Life*, 29 March 1954, 17.

87. Ibid., 20.

88. Ibid., 30.

89. "5-4-3-2-1," 38.

90. "High-Brow, Low-Brow, Middle-Brow," *Life*, 11 April 1949, 99–102.

91. Lynes, "Highbrow, Lowbrow, Middle-brow," *Harper's* 198, February 1949, 27.

92. Bradford Collins, "*Life* Magazine and the Abstract Expressionists, 1948–51: A Historiographic Study of a Late Bohemian Enterprise," *Art Bulletin* 78, June 1991, 285–86.

93. Ibid., 291.

94. Jonathan Green, an authority on the snapshot, comes to the conclusion that "there are no snapshots" in *The Family of Man*, (*American Photography*, 39). This out-of-hand dismissal reveals an aesthetic view of the exhibition quite foreign to Steichen's intent.

95. Dwight Macdonald, "Masscult and Midcult II," in *Partisan Review* 27, Spring 1960, 600.

96. Ibid., 616.

97. Leslie A. Fiedler, "The Middle Against Both Ends," *Encounter* 5, August 1955, 16–23.

98. Containment strategies overlapped in ways unknown to most readers in the 1950s. *Encounter* magazine, for example, was covertly supported by the Central Intelligence Agency. See Thomas W. Braden, "I'm Glad the CIA is 'Immoral,'" *Saturday Evening Post* 240, May 20, 1967, 12.

99. Joan Shelley Rubin, *The Making of Middle Brow Culture* (Chapel Hill, N.C., 1992), xv.

100. Lynes, "Highbrow," 28.

101. Ross, *No Respect*, 55–61.

102. Collins, "*Life* Magazine," 293–98.

103. Russell Lynes, *The Tastemakers* (New York, 1954), 326–27.

104. "Common Bonds of Man," *Life*, 14 February 1955, 132–43.

105. Ibid., 29.

106. The only picture of the bomb room can be found in the selection of installation shots included in the deluxe edition of *The Family of Man*, which was not widely distributed and has been out of print since the 1950s.

107. Miller, interview, 19 June 1993.

108. Susan Sontag, *On Photography* (New York, 1973), 22–23.

109. Green, *American Photography*, 40ff.

110. Alan Sekula, "The Traffic in Photographs," *Art Journal* 41, Spring 1981, 21ff.

chapter three
The Family of Man on the Move

1. Porter McCray, director of circulating exhibitions, to Wayne Miller, 18 January 1957, collection of Wayne Miller.

2. "'Family of Man' Exhibits: Program Costs," USIA memo, 28 July 1955, MoMA archives.

3. McCray to Miller.

4. Ibid.

5. "Family of Man Attendance Figures," 1 May 1960, MoMA archives.

6. "Family of Man: The Netherlands," undated memo, MoMA archives.

7. "The Family of Man," USIA to all posts, 10/20/55, USIA archives.

8. Internal MoMA memo to Edward Steichen et al., 13 May 1957, MoMA archives.

9. Frank Ninkovich, *The Diplomacy of Ideas: U.S. Foreign Policy and Cultural Relations* (Cambridge, 1981), 157.

10. Robert Elder, *The Information Machine* (Syracuse, 1968), 36.

11. Leo Bogart, *Premises for Propaganda: The United States Information Agency's Assumptions in the Cold War* (New York, 1976), xiv.

12. Ninkovich, *Diplomacy*, 153.

13. Reported in *New York Times*, 13 February 1953, 6.

14. Reported in *New York Times*, 14 February 1953, 1.

15. Reported in *New York Times*, 4 March 1953, 1.

16. Questions during two presidential news conferences (February 25 and March 5) offered Eisenhower the possibility of sharpening his stance regarding McCarthy. Eisenhower demurred. See *Public Papers of the Presidents of the United States: Dwight D. Eisenhower, 1953* (Washington, 1960), 62, 88.

17. David M. Oshinsky, *A Conspiracy So Immense:*

The World of Joe McCarthy (New York, 1983), 276.

18. Reported in *New York Times*, 5 March 1953, 1.

19. Reported in *New York Times*, 22 February 1953, IV, 3.

20. Editorial, *New York Times*, 15 February 1953, 16.

21. Editorial, *New York Times*, 24 February, 1953, 24.

22. Editorial, *New York Times*, 27 February 1953, 20.

23. Jack Gould, *New York Times*, 6 March 1953, 14.

24. Reported in *New York Times*, 7 March 1953, 10.

25. Reported in *New York Times*, 8 March 1953, IV, 7.

26. Reported in *New York Times*, 27 February 1953, 12.

27. Elder, *Information Machine*, 39.

28. Martin Merson, *The Private Life of a Public Servant* (New York, 1955), 63.

29. Ibid., 64–66.

30. Ibid., 70.

31. Ibid., 76.

32. Ibid., 19.

33. Ibid., 38.

34. Ibid., 78.

35. Ibid., 22–24.

36. Ibid., 105.

37. Ibid., 97.

38. Ibid., 25.

39. Ibid., 29.

40. Ibid., 103.

41. Bogart, *Premises for Propaganda*.

42. Ibid., 13.

43. Ibid., 33.

44. Ibid., 16.

45. Ibid., 64.

46. Ibid., 71.

47. Ibid., 74.

48. American Assembly, *The Representation of the United States Abroad* (New York, 1956), 69.

49. Wilson Dizard, *The Strategy of Truth: The Story of the U. S. Information Service* (Washington, D.C., 1961), 6.

50. Oren Stephens, *Facts to a Candid World: America's Overseas Information Program* (Stanford, 1955), 87.

51. American Assembly, *Representation*, 102.

52. Ninkovich, *Diplomacy*, 115–20.

53. Emily Rosenberg, *Spreading the American Dream: American Economic and Cultural Expansion, 1890–1945* (New York, 1982), 210.

54. Ibid., 211.

55. Frank Ninkovich, "The Currents of Cultural Diplomacy: Art and the State Department, 1938–1947," *Diplomatic History* 1, 1977, 234–35ff.

56. Ibid., 140.

57. Ibid., 168.

58. Rosenberg, *Spreading the American Dream*, 219.

59. Ninkovich, *Currents*, 169.

60. Ibid., 170.

61. Ibid., 174.

62. Ibid., 175–76.

63. Ibid., 177.

64. Ibid., 179.

65. *Public Papers, Eisenhower*, 351.

66. Ibid., 352.

67. Ibid., 353.

68. "Mission of USIA Defined," Department of State Bulletin 29, 30 November 1953, 756.

69. Theodore Streibert to Bedell Smith, 1 March 1954, in *Foreign Relations of the United States, 1952–1954*, vol. 2, part 2 (Washington, 1984), 1763.

70. Ibid., 1754.

71. Ibid., 1755.

72. Ibid.

73. Ibid., 1763.

74. Ibid., 1764.

75. Ibid., 1766.

76. *Foreign Relations of the United States, 1955–1957*, vol. 9 (Washington, 1987), 506–7.

77. Streibert to all posts, 24 August 1955, *Foreign Relations, 1955–1957*, 528. Emphasis in original.

78. George V. Allen, hearing before the Appropriations Committee, House of Representatives, February 1958, 7. The strategy of portraying a similarity between the United States and emerging Third World countries beckoned. Seymour Martin Lipset's book, *The First New Nation: The United States in Historical and Comparative Perspective* (New York, 1963), is a good example of this alliance (and control), through comparative history.

79. Allen, hearing before the Appropriations Committee, House of Representatives, 7 April 1959, 10.

80. *Foreign Relations*, 1952–1954, 1782–83.

81. Allen to Appropriations Committee, February 1958, 15.

82. Streibert to all posts, *Foreign Relations*, 1952–1954, 1773.

83. Allen to Appropriations Committee, February 1958, 8.

84. Streibert, hearing before the Foreign Affairs Committee, House of Representative, February 1958, 7.

85. Streibert to all posts, 6 July 1954, *Foreign Relations*, 1952–1954, 1755.

86. Hearing before the Foreign Relations Committee, House of Representatives, March 1956, 155.

87. Allen in hearing before the Appropriations Committee, House of Representatives, February 1958, 16.

88. Hearing before the Subcommittee on State Department Organization and Foreign Operations of the Foreign Relations Committee, House of Representatives, 22 September 1958, 6.

89. Allen to Appropriations Committee, February 1958, 45.

90. Allen to Appropriations Committee, February 1958, 30.

91. Allan Sekula, "The Traffic in Photographs," *Art Journal* 41, Spring 1981, 15–25. The article was later collected in *Photography Against the Grain: Essays and Photo Works, 973–1983* (Halifax, 1984), 77–101.

92. Ninkovich, *Currents*, 233–34.

93. *Foreign Relations*, 1955–1957, 534.

94. USIS Bonn to USIA Washington, 20 November 1958. USIA archives, Washington, D.C.

95. From USIS Belgrade to USIA Washington, 11 December 1958, USIA archives.

96. *Foto*, May 1956, 158. I am indebted to Liz Latham of Laramie, Wyoming, and the staff at the Netherlands Institute for Advanced Studies in the Humanities and Social Sciences for translations of these Dutch articles.

97. "We People: What Can an Amateur Learn from This," *Focus*, 12 May 1956, 230.

98. Ibid.

99. Reported in *Foto*, May 1956, 158.

100. Ibid.

101. Ibid.

102. Reported in *Focus*, 14 April 1956, 169.

103. From USIS Beirut to USIA Washington, 8 January 1959, USIA archives.

104. Quoted in Bonn USIS to USIA Washington, from the *Sontagsblatt*, 24 August 1958.

105. USIS Bonn to USIA Washington, 20 November 1958.

106. From USIS Mexico to Department of State, Washington, 3 January 1956, USIA archives.

107. From USIS Kabul to USIA Washington, 20 September 1962, MoMA archives.

108. A cable from Egypt in spring 1961 reflected the same dynamics (USIS Cairo to USIA Washington, 19 April 1961).

chapter four
The Family of Man in Moscow

1. Ron Robin, *Enclaves of America: The Rhetoric of American Political Architecture Abroad, 1900–1965* (Princeton, 1992), 140–41.

2. McClellan in hearings before the Committee on Foreign Affairs, House of Representatives, 6 March 1956, 20.

3. McClellan to Foreign Affairs Committee, 6 March 1956, 23.

4. Hearings before the Subcommittee on Appropriations, House of Representatives, President's Special International Program, 10 March 1957, 589.

5. Appropriation Hearings, 10 March 1957, 620.

6. Ibid., 619.

7. Ibid.

8. *Official Training Book for Guides at the American National Exhibition in Moscow, 1959*, ed. Dorothy E. L. Tuttle, United States Information Agency, USIA archives, 12.

9. Felix Belair, *New York Times*, 24 January 1959, 3.

10. Reported in *New York Times*, 15 March 1959, VIII, 2.

11. Reported in *New York Times*, 15 May 1959, 31.

12. Reported in *New York Times*, 27 June 1959, 7.

13. Quoted in Lloyd Goodrich, "Paintings and Sculpture from the American National

Exhibition in Moscow," for the Whitney Museum, 1959, USIA archives, 4.

14. Ibid., 5.

15. Reported in *New York Times*, 23 March 1959, 24.

16. "A Review of the American National Exhibition in Moscow, July 25–September 4, 1959" [hereafter cited as Exhibition Review], USIA archives, 1.

17. *Excerpts of Roundtable Discussion on Plans for Moscow Exhibition Held with Newspaper Correspondents in New York City*, 8 January 1959, Office of American National Exhibition in Moscow, USIA archives.

18. Ibid., 1.

19. Ibid., 3.

20. Ibid., 4.

21. Ibid., 6.

22. Ibid., 10.

23. Ibid., 14.

24. Memo from Charles Noyes to Rockefeller Brothers Fund, 10 March 1959, [hereafter cited as McCray memo] Rockefeller Brothers Fund Collection, Rockefeller archives.

25. McCray memo.

26. Memo from EW to Dana S. Creel, 3 March 1959, Rockefeller Brothers Fund Collection, Rockefeller archives.

27. McCray memo.

28. Memo from Charles Noyes to Rockefeller Brothers Fund, 5 March 1959, Rockefeller Brothers Fund Collection, Rockefeller archives.

29. Docket memorandum to Rockefeller Brothers Fund, 23 April 1959, Rockefeller Brothers Fund Collection, Rockefeller archives.

30. See, for example, George Nelson's admiring description in his *Display* (New York, 1953).

31. G. Nelson, *Display*, 134–37.

32. Ibid., 116.

33. A chapter title in George Nelson, *Problems of Design* (New York, 1957).

34. G. Nelson, *Design*, 63.

35. Ibid., 65.

36. Ibid., 71.

37. Ibid., 74.

38. *Official Training Book*, 12.

39. Ibid., 18.

40. Ibid., 19.

41. Ibid., 138.

42. Ibid., 141.

43. Ibid., 138.

44. Ibid., 155.

45. Ibid., 168.

46. Ibid.

47. Richard Nixon, *Six Crises* (New York, 1962), 236.

48. Steichen, *A Life*, Chapter 13.

49. Ibid.

50. Nixon, *Six Crises*, 236.

51. Ibid., 237.

52. Ibid.

53. Ibid., 255.

54. Ibid., 261.

55. Steichen, *A Life*, Chapter 13.

56. Ibid.

57. Ibid.

58. Nixon, *Six Crises*, 249.

59. Ibid., 241.

60. Ibid., 278–79.

61. Reported in *New York Times*, 23 July 1959, 6.

62. Harrison Salisbury, *New York Times*, 24 July 1959, 2. Salisbury, who died in July 1993, won a Pulitzer Prize for his coverage of the Soviet Union during 1959.

63. James Reston, *New York Times*, 24 July 1959, 2.

64. Reston, *New York Times*, 25 July 1959, 3.

65. Reston, *New York Times*, 24 July 1959, 2.

66. Salisbury, *New York Times*, 24 July 1959, 2.

67. Reported in *New York Times*, 25 July 1959, 2.

68. May, *Homeward Bound*, Chapter 7.

69. Reported in *New York Times*, 26 July 1959, 1; 27 July 1959, 9; 27 July 1959, 13. Nixon's commentary on Khrushchev's combativeness accompanies his play-by-play narration of the Kitchen Debate (Nixon, *Six Crises*, 252–61).

70. Reported in *New York Times*, 25 July 1959, 3.

71. Reported in *New York Times*, 25 July 1959, 3.

72. Editorial, *New York Times*, 27 July 1959, 24.

73. Nelson, *Design*, 121.

74. "Round Table on Housing," 78.

75. Ibid., 86.

76. Clifford Clark, Jr., *The American Family Home, 1800–1960* (Chapel Hill, 1986), 239.

77. Gwendolyn Wright, *Building the Dream: A Social History of Housing in America* (Cambridge, 1981), 248.

78. Wright, *Building the Dream*, 248.

79. Kenneth Jackson, *Crabgrass Frontier: The Sub-urbanization of the United States* (New York, 1985), 234–35.

80. Nelson, *Design*, 125.

81. Ibid., 133.

82. Jackson, *Crabgrass Frontier*, 238–41.

83. Clark, *American Family Home*, 236.

84. May, *Homeward Bound*, 172.

85. Robert W. Marks, *The Dymaxion World of Buckminster Fuller* (New York, 1960), 59.

86. Ibid., 59–60.

87. "Geodesic Dome," *Architectural Forum* 95, August 1951, 145.

88. Ibid.

89. Roundtable, 2.

90. Marks, *Fuller*, 61.

91. Hugh Kenner, *Bucky: A Guided Tour of Buckminster Fuller* (New York, 1973), 233.

92. Ibid., 225.

93. Jeffrey Meikle, "Plastic, Material of a Thousand Uses," in *Imagining Tomorrow: History, Technology, and the American Future*, ed. Joseph Corn (Cambridge, Mass., 1986), 83.

94. Jeffrey Meikle, "Beyond Plastics: Post-modernity and the Culture of Synthetics," *Odense American Studies International Series* [Denmark] 5, 1993, 1.

95. Meikle, "Thousand Uses," 91.

96. Ibid., 90.

97. Sylvia Katz, *Plastics: Common Objects, Classic Designs* (New York, 1984), 12.

98. Meikle, "Beyond Plastics," 2.

99. Meikle, "Thousand Uses," 93.

100. Katz, *Plastics*, 13. During this period imitation fiesta wear competed with the real thing, which was being disarmed of its original, uranium-enriched glaze.

101. Meikle, "Thousand Uses," 89.

102. Quoted in *Official Training Book*, 138.

103. Marcus Whiffen and Frederick Koeper, *American Architecture, 1607–1976* (Cambridge, 1981), 332.

104. "Plastic Parasols for Moscow," *Architectural Record* 126, November 1959, 238.

105. Ibid.

106. John Neuhart et al., *Eames Design: The Work of the Office of Charles and Ray Eames* (New York, 1989), 239.

107. Ibid.

108. Ibid., 241.

109. Ibid., 241.

110. Barthes, *Mythologies*, 97.

111. Ibid.

112. Ibid., 98.

113. Ibid., 99.

114. Exhibition Review, 3.

115. Exhibition Review, 6.

116. "Moscow Exhibit, 1959," USIA archives, 3.

117. Ibid., iii.

118. Ibid., ii.

119. Ibid., 23.

120. Exhibition Review, 3.

chapter five
Edward Steichen, Robert Frank, and American

1. Reported in *Afro-American* (Washington, D.C.), 22 August 1959. From the Steichen archives, MoMA.

2. Reported in *New York Times*, 25 August 1959, 3.

3. Todd Gitlin, *The Sixties: Years of Hope, Days of Rage* (New York, 1987), 12.

4. Anne Wilkes Tucker, ed., *Robert Frank: From New York to Nova Scotia* (Boston, 1986), 20–21. Arnold Kubler had also been a visitor to Steichen's loft.

5. Tucker, *Frank*, 24.

6. Tucker, *Frank*, 25.

7. Ron Robin, *Enclaves of America: The Rhetoric of American Political Architecture Abroad, 1900–1965* (Princeton, 1992), 142–66.

8. Rubin, *Making of Middle Brow Culture*, 144ff.

9. Tod Papageorge, *Walker Evans and Robert Frank: an Essay on Influence* (New Haven, Conn., 1981).

10. W. T. Lhamon, *Deliberate Speed: The Origins of a Cultural Style in the American 1950s* (Washington, D.C., 1990), 125.

11. Frank's photograph is also a sign of his emerging postmodern sensibility. The critique of photographs expounded by Frederic Jamison in "Postmodernism, or the Cultural Logic of Late Capitalism" (*New Left Review* 146, July-August 1984, 53–92) comes immediately to mind.

12. Barry Miles, *Ginsberg: A Biography* (New York, 1989), 258.

13. Jerry Tallmer's introduction to Jack Kerouac, *Pull My Daisy*, (New York, 1959), 18.

14. Quoted in Thomas Schaub, *American Fiction in the Cold War* (Madison, Wis., 1991), 69–70.

15. Gerald Nicosia, *Memory Babe: A Critical Biography of Jack Kerouac* (New York, 1983), 584.

16. Schaub, *Fiction*, 73.

17. The word comes from Lhamon's discussion of 1950s culture, *Deliberate Speed*, 115.

18. Schaub, *Fiction*, 73.

19. William Faulkner, "Nobel Prize Address," in *The William Faulkner Reader: Selections from the Work of William Faulkner* (New York, 1954), 4–5.

20. "Museum of Modern Art Plans International Photography Exhibition," 31 January 1954, MoMA archives.

21. Miller, "Steichen, My Friend," n.p.

22. Norman Mailer, *Advertisements for Myself* (London, 1961), 282.

23. Ibid., 283–84.

24. Ibid., 279.

25. Reported in *Newsweek*, 27 July 1959, 29.

26. Ibid., 30.

27. Leonard Wallock, "New York City: Capital of the Twentieth Century," in *New York: Culture Capital of the World, 1945–1960* (New York, 1988), 29–40.

28. John Kenneth Galbraith, *The Affluent Society* (Boston, 1958), 5.

29. Ibid., Chapter 12.

30. Ibid., Chapter 14.

31. Ibid., 352.

32. *Rockefeller Panel Report* (Garden City, 1961), 93.

33. Galbraith framed his argument in national terms. As Elizabeth Walker Mechling and Jay Mechling point out in "Hot Pacifism and Cold War: The American Friends Service Committee's Witness for Peace in 1950s America," *Quarterly Journal of Speech* (May 1992), the AFSC's 1955 pamphlet, *Speak Truth to Power*, would soon appeal through the perspectives of the social sciences to a New Class that transcended the nation-state.

34. Michael Harrington, *The Other America: Poverty in the United States* (Baltimore, 1962), 11.

35. Ibid., 44.

36. Ibid., 12.

37. Ibid., 54.

38. Ibid., 23.

39. Ibid., 120.

40. Ibid., 17.

41. Ibid., 156.

42. Szarkowski, *Mirrors and Windows*, 11, 14.

43. Ibid., 16, 17.

44. Ibid., 11.

45. Ibid., 18.

46. Ibid., 20.

47. Ibid., 20.

48. Ibid., 17.

49. Sontag, *On Photography*, 31.

50. Ibid., 32.

51. Ibid., 29.

52. Ibid., 40.

53. Ibid., 40.

54. Ibid., 32.

55. Ibid., 41.

56. Ibid., 33.

57. Roy P. Basler, Editor, *The Collected Works of Abraham Lincoln*, vol. 1 (New Brunswick, 1953), 203.

58. See for example, Alfred Jones, *Roosevelt's Image Brokers: Poets, Playwrights, and the Use of the Lincoln Symbol* (Port Washington, 1974).

59. Ibid., 65–67.

60. Sandburg, *The People, Yes* (New York, 1936) 134, 135.

61. Jones, *Roosevelt's Image Brokers*, 56. The issue is complicated by the fact that Sandburg subjected Lincoln to the same sort of myth/symbol criticism that John William Ward employed in his study of Andrew Jackson. Later, both Sandburg and Sandburg's Lincoln were analyzed from the same point of view.

62. Sandburg, *The People, Yes*, 137.

63. Sontag, *On Photography*, 40.

64. Steichen, *A Life*, Chapter 14.

65. Ibid.

66. Allan Sekula, "The Instrumental Image: Steichen at War," in *Photography Against the Grain: Essays and Photo Works, 1973–1983* (Halifax, 1984), 34–49.

67. Allan Sekula, "On the Invention of Photographic Meaning," in *Photography Against the Grain*, 6.

BIBLIOGRAPHY

Abramson, Howard. *National Geographic: Behind America's Lens on the World*. New York: Crown Publishers, 1987.

Adams, Phoebe Lou. "Through a Lens Darkly," *Atlantic* 195 (April 1955): 69–72.

Ambrose, Stephen E. *Nixon: The Education of a Politician, 1913–1962*. New York: Simon and Schuster, 1987.

American Assembly. *The Representation of the United States Abroad*. New York: Graduate School of Business, Columbia University, 1956.

————. *The Representation of the United States Abroad*. Rev. ed. New York: Frederick A. Praeger, 1965.

Barthes, Roland. *Mythologies*. Translated by Annette Lavers. New York: Noonday Press, 1972.

Barzun, Jacques. *The House of Intellect*. New York: Harper & Row, 1959.

Basler, Roy P., ed. *The Collected Works of Abraham Lincoln*. Vol. 1. New Brunswick: Rutgers University Press, 1953.

Baughman, James L. *Henry R. Luce and the Rise of the American News Media*. Boston: Twayne Publishers, 1987.

Benedict, Burton. *The Anthropology of World's Fairs: San Francisco's Panama Pacific International Exposition of 1915*. Berkeley: Scolar Press, 1983.

Benjamin, Walter. *Illuminations*. Edited by Hannah Arendt, translated by Harry Zohn. New York: Harcourt, Brace & World, 1968.

Berkhofer, Robert F. "Clio and the Culture Concept: Some Impressions of a Changing Relationship in American Historiography," *Social Science Quarterly* 53 (June 1972): 297–320.

Bloom, Alexander. *Prodigal Sons: The New York Intellectuals and Their World*. New York: Oxford University Press, 1986.

Bogart, Leo. *Premises for Propaganda: The United States Information Agency's Operating Assumptions in the Cold War*. New York: Free Press, 1976.

Boorstin, Daniel. *The Image: A Guide to Pseudo-Events in America*. 1961. Reprint, New York: Atheneum, 1982.

Bourke-White, Margaret. *The Taste of War*. Edited by Jonathan Silverman. London: Century Publishing, 1985.

Boyer, Paul. *By the Bomb's Early Light: American Thought and Culture at the Dawn of the Atomic Age*. New York: Pantheon Books, 1985.

Braden, Thomas W. "I'm Glad the CIA is 'Immoral,'" *Saturday Evening Post* 240 (May 20, 1967): 10–14.

Braisted, Paul J., ed. *Cultural Affairs and Foreign Relations.* Washington, D.C.: Columbia Books, 1968.

Bryan, C. D. B. *The National Geographic Society: 100 Years of Adventure and Discovery.* New York: Harry N. Abrams, 1987.

Carter, Paul. *Another Part of the Fifties.* New York: Columbia University Press, 1983.

Caute, David. *The Great Fear: The Anti-Communist Purge Under Truman and Eisenhower.* New York: Simon & Schister, 1978.

Chanzit, Gwen Finkel. *Herbert Bayer and Modernist Design in America.* Ann Arbor: UMI Research Press, 1987.

Clark, Clifford, Jr. *The American Family Home, 1800–1960.* Chapel Hill: University of North Carolina Press, 1986.

Cockcroft, Eva. "Abstract Expressionism, Weapon of the Cold War," *Artforum* 12 (June 1974): 39–41.

Cohen, Arthur. *Herbert Bayer: The Complete Work.* Cambridge: MIT Press, 1984.

Collins, Bradford. "Life Magazine and the Abstract Expressionists, 1948–51: A Historiographic Study of a Late Bohemian Enterprise," *Art Bulletin* 78 (June 1991): 283–308.

Commager, Henry Steele. *The American Mind: An Interpretation of American Thought and Character Since the 1880s.* New Haven: Yale University Press, 1950.

Compton, Wilson. "Information and U.S. Foreign Policy," *Department of State Bulletin* 28 (16 February 1953): 252–56.

"The Controversial Family of Man," *Aperture* 3 (1955): 8–27.

Coontz, Stephanie. *The Way We Never Were: American Families and the Nostalgia Trap.* New York: Basic Books, 1992.

Corn, Joseph, ed. *Imagining Tomorrow: History, Technology, and the American Future.* Cambridge: MIT Press, 1986.

Curtis, James. *Mind's Eye, Mind's Truth: FSA Photography Reconsidered.* Philadelphia: Temple University Press, 1989.

Davenport, Russell. *The Dignity of Man.* New York: Harper & Brothers, 1955.

Dizard, Wilson. *The Strategy of Truth: The Story of the U.S. Information Service.* Washington, D.C.: Public Affairs Press, 1961.

Dietz, Albert. "Plastic Parasols for Moscow," *Architectural Record* 126 (November 1959): 238.

Duncan, David Douglas. *This Is War!: A Photo-Narrative in Three Parts.* 1951. Reprint, New York: Bantam Books, 1967.

Elder, Robert E. *The Information Machine: The United States Information Agency and American Foreign Policy.* Syracuse: Syracuse University Press, 1968.

Ellwood, David W. *Rebuilding Europe: Western Europe, America and Postwar Reconstruction.* London: Longman, 1992.

Etzold, Thomas H and John Lewis Gaddis, eds. *Containment: Documents of American Policy and Strategy, 1945–1950.* New York: Columbia University Press, 1978.

Faulkner, William. *The Faulkner Reader: Selections from the Works of William Faulkner.* New York: Random House, 1954.

Fiedler, Leslie A. "The Middle Against Both Ends," *Encounter* 5 (August 1955):16–23.

FitzGerald, Frances. *America Revised: History Schoolbooks in the Twentieth Century.* Boston: Little, Brown and Company, 1979.

Foreign Relations of the United States, 1952–1954. Vol. 2. Washington D.C.: Government Printing Office, 1984.

Frank, Robert. *The Americans.* 1959. Reprint, New York: Pantheon Books, 1986.

————. *The Lines of My Hand.* New York: Pantheon Books, 1989.

Fussell, Paul. *Wartime: Understanding and Behavior in the Second World War.* New York: Oxford University Press, 1989.

Gaddis, John Lewis. *Russia, the Soviet Union, and the United States: An Interpretive History.* New York: McGraw-Hill, 1978.

————. *Strategies of Containment: A Critical Appraisal of Postwar American National Security Policy.* New York: Oxford University Press, 1982.

Galbraith, John Kenneth. *The Affluent Society.* Boston: Houghton Mifflin, 1958

Gee, Helen. *Photography of the Fifties: An American Perspective.* Tucson: Center for Creative Photography, 1980.

"Geodesic Dome," *Architectural Forum* 95 (August 1951): 145.

Gitlin, Todd. *The Sixties: Years of Hope, Days of Rage.* New York: Bantam Books, 1987.

Gleason, Philip. "World War II and the Development of American Studies," *American Quarterly* 36 (Bibliography issue; 1984): 343–358.

Goldberg, Vicki. *Margaret Bourke-White: A Biography.* New York: Harper & Row, 1987.

Goodman, Paul and Percival Goodman. *Communitas: Ways of Livelihood and Means of Life.* 1947. Reprint, New York: Columbia University Press, 1991.

Goodrich, Lloyd. "Paintings and Sculpture from the American National Exhibition in Moscow," New York: Whitney Museum of Art, 1959. Copy in USIA archives.

Green, Jonathan. *American Photography: A Critical History, 1945 to the Present.* New York: Harry N. Abrams, 1984.

Greenberg, Clement. "Avant-Garde and Kitsch," in *The Partisan Reader,* edited by William Phillips and Philip Rahv, 378–92. New York: Dial Press, 1946.

Grosvenor, Gilbert. "Maps for Victory: National Geographic Society's Charts Used in War on Land, Sea, and in the Air," *National Geographic* 81 (May 1942): 667–90.

Guilbault, Serge. *How New York Stole the Idea of Modern Art: Abstract Expressionism, Freedom, and the Cold War.* Chicago: University of Chicago Press, 1983.

Guimond, James. *American Photography and the American Dream.* Chapel Hill: University of North Carolina Press, 1991.

Hales, Peter B. "The Atomic Sublime," *American Studies* 32 (Spring 1991): 5–31.

Halliday, Jon and Bruce Cumings. *Korea: The Unknown War.* New York: Pantheon Books, 1988.

Hansen, Allen C. *Public Diplomacy in the Computer Age.* New York: Frederick A. Praeger, 1989.

Harrington, Michael. *The Other America: Poverty in the United States*. Baltimore: Penguin Books, 1962.

Hartz, Louis. *The Liberal Tradition in America: An Interpretation of American Political Thought Since the Revolution*. New York: Harcourt, Brace, 1955.

Harvey, David. *The Condition of Postmodernity: An Enquiry into the Origin of Cultural Change*. Oxford: Basil Blackwell, 1989.

Hayden, Dolores. *Redesigning the American Dream: The Future of Housing, Work, and Family Life*. New York: W. W. Norton, 1984.

Henderson, John W. *The United States Information Agency*. New York: Frederick A. Praeger, 1969.

Hicks, Wilson. *Words and Pictures: An Introduction to Photojournalism*. New York: Harper & Brothers, 1952.

Higgins, Marguerite. *War in Korea: The Report of a Woman Combat Correspondent*. Garden City, N.Y.: Doubleday and Company, 1951.

Hill, Paul and Thomas Cooper. *Dialogue with Photography*. New York: Farrar, Straus, Giroux, 1979.

Hine, Thomas. *Populuxe*. New York: Alfred A. Knopf, 1986.

Inkeles, Alex and Daniel J. Levinson. "National Character: The Study of Modal Personality and Sociocultural Systems," in *Handbook of Social Psychology*. Vol. 2. Cambridge, Mass.: Addison-Wesley, 1954.

Jackson, Kenneth. *Crabgrass Frontier: The Suburbanization of the United States*. New York: Oxford University Press, 1985.

Jacoby, Russell. *The Last Intellectuals: American Culture in the Age of Academe*. New York: Basic Books, 1987

Johnson, William, ed. *W. Eugene Smith: Master of the Photographic Essay*. Millerton, N.Y.: Aperture, 1981.

Jones, Alfred. *Roosevelt's Image Brokers: Poets, Playwrights, and the Use of the Lincoln Symbol*. Port Washington, N.Y.: Kennikat Press, 1974.

Katz, Sylvia. *Plastics: Common Objects, Classic Designs*. New York: Harry N. Abrams, 1984.

Kenner, Hugh. *Bucky: A Guided Tour of Buckminster Fuller*. New York: William Morrow and Co., 1973.

Kerouac, Jack. *Pull My Daisy*. Introduction by Jerry Tallmer. New York: Grove Press, 1961.

Kessel, Dmitri. *On Assignment: Dmitri Kessel, Life Photographer*. New York: Harry N. Abrams, 1985.

Knightley, Phillip. *The First Casualty: From the Crimea to Vietnam: The War Correspondent as Hero, Propagandist, and Myth Maker*. New York: Harcourt, Brace, Jovanovich, 1975.

Kouwenhoven, John. *The Arts in Modern American Civilization*. 1948. Reprint, New York: W. W. Norton, 1967.

Lasch, Christopher. *The Agony of the American Left*. New York: Alfred A. Knopf, 1969.

———. *The New Radicalism in America, 1889–1963: The Intellectual as Social Type*. New York: Alfred A. Knopf, 1965.

———. *The True and Only Heaven: Progress and Its Critics*. New York: W. W. Norton, 1991.

Lhamon, W. T., Jr. *Deliberate Speed: The Origins of a Cultural Style in the American 1950s*. Washington, D.C.: Smithsonian Institution Press, 1990.

Lipset, Seymour Martin. *The First New Nation: The United States in Historical and Comparative Perspective.* New York: Basic Books, 1963.

Lipset, Seymour Martin and Leo Lowenthal, eds. *Culture and Social Character: The Work of David Riesman Reviewed.* New York: Free Press, 1961.

Lynes, Russell. *The Good Old Modern: An Intimate Portrait of the Museum of Modern Art.* New York: Atheneum, 1973.

————. "Highbrow, Lowbrow, Middlebrow," *Harper's* 198, February 1949, 19–28.

————. *The Tastemakers.* New York: Harper & Brothers, 1954.

Macdonald, Dwight. *Against the Grain: Essays on the Effects of Mass Culture.* New York: Random House, 1962.

————. "Masscult and Midcult," *Partisan Review* 27 (Spring 1960): 589–631.

McCormick, Thomas J. *America's Half-Century: United States Foreign Policy in the Cold War.* Baltimore: Johns Hopkins University Press, 1989.

McJunkin, Penelope Niven. "Steichen and Sandburg," *Horizon* 22 (1978): 46–53.

Mailer, Norman. *Advertisements for Myself.* London: A. Deutsch, 1961.

Marks, Robert W. *The Dymaxion World of Buckminster Fuller.* New York: Reinhold Publishing, 1960.

Mathews, Jane de Hart. "Art and Politics in the Cold War," *American Historical Review* 81 (October 1976): 762–87.

Matthews, Samuel W. "Nevada Learns to Live with the Atom," *National Geographic Magazine* 103 (June 1953): 839–50.

May, Elaine Tyler. *Homeward Bound: American Families in the Cold War Era.* New York: Basic Books, 1988.

May, Lary, ed. *Recasting America: Culture and Politics in the Age of Cold War.* Chicago: University of Chicago Press, 1989.

Mead, Margaret. *And Keep Your Powder Dry: An Anthropologist Looks at America.* New York: William Morrow, 1943.

Mechling, Elizabeth Walker and Jay Mechling. "Hot Pacifism and Cold War: The American Friends Service Committee's Witness for Peace in 1950s America," *Quarterly Journal of Speech* 78 (May 1992): 173–96.

Meikle, Jeffrey. "Beyond Plastics: Postmodernity and the Culture of Synthetics," *Odense American Studies International Series* 5 (1993) [Denmark].

Meltzer, Milton. *Dorothea Lange: A Photographer's Life.* New York: Farrar, Straus, Giroux, 1978.

Merson, Martin. *The Private Life of a Public Servant.* New York: Macmillan, 1955.

Miles, Barry. *Ginsberg: A Biography.* New York: Simon and Schuster, 1989.

Miller, Wayne. "Steichen, My Friend," in *Steichen/109.* Milwaukee: University of Wisconsin-Milwaukee Gallery of Art, 1988.

Moeller, Susan. *Shooting War: Photography and the American Experience of Combat.* New York: Basic Books, 1989.

Morris, Charles R. *Iron Destinies, Lost Opportunities: the Arms Race Between the U.S.A. and the U.S.S.R., 1945–1987.* New York: Harper & Row, 1988.

Morris, John G. "A Photographic Memoir," *Exposure* (1982): 4–33.

————. "This We Remember: The Pictures that Make Vietnam Unforgettable," *Harper's* (September 1972): 72–78.

Mydans, Carl. *Carl Mydans, Photojournalist*. New York: Harry N. Abrams, 1985.

——. *More Than Meets the Eye*. New York: Harper & Brothers, 1959.

Nelson, George. *Display*. New York: Whitney Publications, 1953.

——. *Problems of Design*. New York: Whitney Publications, 1957.

Nelson, James. *Wisdom: Conversations with the Elder Wise Men of Our Day*. New York: W. W. Norton, 1958.

Neuhart, John, Marilyn Neuhart, and Ray Eames. *Eames Design: The Work of the Office of Charles and Ray Eames*. New York: Harry N. Abrams, 1989.

Newhall, Beaumont. *The History of Photography*. Revised and enlarged, New York: Museum of Modern Art, 1982.

——. *Photography, Essays and Images: Illustrated Readings in the History of Photography*. New York: Museum of Modern Art, 1980.

Nicosia, Gerald. *Memory Babe: A Critical Biography of Jack Kerouac*. New York: Grove Press, 1983.

Ninkovich, Frank. "The Currents of Cultural Diplomacy: Art and the State Department, 1938–1947," *Diplomatic History* 1 (1977): 215–37.

——. *The Diplomacy of Ideas: U.S. Foreign Policy and Cultural Relations, 1938–1950*. Cambridge: Cambridge University Press, 1981.

Nixon, Richard. *Six Crises*. Garden City, N.Y.: Doubleday & Company, 1962.

Nye, David. *Image Worlds: Corporate Identities at General Electric, 1890–1930*. Cambridge: MIT Press, 1985.

Official Training Book for Guides at the American National Exhibition in Moscow. Edited by Dorothy E. L. Tuttle. Washington, D.C.: United States Information Agency, 1959.

Oshinsky, David M. *A Conspiracy So Immense: The World of Joe McCarthy*. New York: Free Press, 1983.

Papageorge, Tod. *Walker Evans and Robert Frank: An Essay on Influence*. New Haven: Yale University Art Gallery, 1981.

Pells, Richard. *The Liberal Mind in a Conservative Age: American Intellectuals in the 1940s and 1950s*. New York: Harper & Row, 1985.

Phillips, Christopher. "The Judgment Seat of Photography," *October* 22 (Fall 1982): 27–63.

——. *Steichen at War*. New York: Harry N. Abrams, 1981.

Potter, David. *People of Plenty: Economic Abundance and the American Character*. Chicago: University of Chicago Press, 1954.

Public Papers of the Presidents of the United States: Dwight D. Eisenhower. 1953. Washington, D.C.: Government Printing Office, 1960.

Riesman, David, with Nathan Glazer and Reuel Denney. *The Lonely Crowd: A Study of the Changing American Character*. 1950. Reprint, New Haven: Yale University Press 1961.

Robin, Ron. *Enclaves of America: The Rhetoric of American Political Architecture Abroad, 1900–1965*. Princeton: Princeton University Press, 1992.

Rockefeller Brothers Fund. *Prospect for America: The Rockefeller Panel Reports*. Garden City, N.Y.: Doubleday & Company, 1961.

Rosenberg, Emily. *Spreading the American Dream: American Economic and Cultural Expansion, 1890–1945*. New York: Hill and Wang, 1982.

Rosenblum, Naomi. *A World History of Photography*. New York: Abbeville Press, 1984.

Ross, Andrew. *No Respect: Intellectuals and Popular Culture*. New York: Routledge, 1989.

Rovere. Richard H. *Senator Joe McCarthy*. New York: Harcourt, Brace, Jovanovich, 1959.

Rowe, Peter. *Making a Middle Landscape*. Cambridge.: MIT Press, 1991.

Rubin, Joan Shelley. *The Making of Middle Brow Culture*. Chapel Hill: University of North Carolina Press, 1992.

Rydell, Robert W. *All the World's a Fair: Visions of Empire at American International Expositions, 1876–1916*. Chicago: University of Chicago Press, 1984.

Safire, William. *Before the Fall: An Inside View of the Pre-Watergate White House*. Garden City, N.Y.: Doubleday & Company, 1975.

Sandburg, Carl. "Abraham Lincoln: The Incomparable," *Vital Speeches of the Day 25* (1959): 293–94.

———. *Abraham Lincoln: The War Years*. Vol. 1. New York: Harcourt, Brace, 1939.

———. *Home Front Memo*. New York: Harcourt, Brace, 1943.

———. *The People, Yes*. New York: Harcourt, Brace, 1936.

———. *The Sandburg Range*. New York: Harcourt, Brace, 1957.

Sandburg, Helga. *A Great and Glorious Romance: The Story of Carl Sandburg and Lillian Steichen*. New York: Harcourt, Brace Jovanovich, 1978.

Sandeen, Eric. "*The Family of Man* at the Museum of Modern Art: The Power of the Image in '50s America," *Prospects 11* (1987): 367–91.

Sayre, Henry. *The Object of Performance: The American Avant-Garde since 1970*. Chicago: University of Chicago Press, 1989.

Schlesinger, Arthur, Jr. *The Vital Center: The Politics of Freedom*. 1949. Reprint, Boston: Houghton Mifflin, 1962.

Schaub, Thomas. *American Fiction in the Cold War*. Madison: University of Wisconsin Press, 1991.

Sekula, Allan. *Photography Against the Grain: Essays and Photo Works, 1973–1983*. Halifax: Press of the Nova Scotia College of Art and Design, 1984.

———. "The Traffic in Photography," *Art Journal 41* (Spring 1981): 15–25.

Shapiro, David and Cecile. "Abstract Expressionism: The Politics of Apolitical Painting," *Prospects 3* (1977): 175–214.

Smith, Henry Nash. *Virgin Land: The American West as Symbol and Myth*. Cambridge: Harvard University Press, 1950.

Sontag, Susan. *On Photography*. New York: Farrar, Straus, Giroux, 1977.

Speak Truth to Power: A Quaker Study of International Conflict. Philadelphia: American Friends Service Committee, 1955.

Stange, Maren. *Symbols of Ideal Life: Social Documentary Photography in America, 1890–1950*. New York: Cambridge University Press, 1989.

Steichen, Edward. *The Family of Man*. New York: Museum of Modern Art, 1955.

———. *A Life in Photography*. Reprint, New York: Bonanza Books, 1984.

———. ed. *Sandburg: Photographers View Carl Sandburg*. New York: Harcourt, Brace, 1966.

Steichen the Photographer. Garden City, N.Y.: Doubleday & Company, 1961.

Stephens, Oren. *Facts to a Candid World: America's Overseas Information Program*. Stanford: Stanford University Press, 1955.

Szarkowski, John. *Mirrors and Windows: American Photography since 1960.* New York: Museum of Modern Art, 1978.

Thompson, Reginald. *Cry Korea.* London: MacDonald and Co., 1951.

Tucker, Anne, ed. *Robert Frank: From New York to Nova Scotia.* Boston: Little, Brown and Company, 1986.

"U.S.A.: The Permanent Revolution," *Fortune* 43 (February 1951).

Wainwright, Loudon. *The Great American Magazine: An Inside History of Life.* New York: Alfred A. Knopf, 1986.

Wallock, Leonard, ed. *New York: Culture Capital of the World, 1945–1960.* New York: Rizzoli, 1988.

West, Cornel. "The New Cultural Politics of Difference," *October* 53 (Summer 1990): 93–109.

Whelan, Richard. *Drawing the Line: The Korean War, 1950–1953.* Boston: Little, Brown and Company, 1990.

———. *Robert Capa: A Biography.* New York: Alfred A Knopf, 1985.

Whiffen, Marcus and Frederick Koeper. *American Architecture, 1607–1976.* Cambridge: MIT Press, 1981

Whitfield. Stephen J. *The Culture of the Cold War.* Baltimore: Johns Hopkins University Press, 1991.

Whitton, John Boardman. *Propaganda and the Cold War.* Washington, D.C.: Public Affairs Press, 1963.

Wilson, Edmund. *Europe Without Baedeker: Sketches Among the Ruins of Italy, Greece and England.* 1947. Reprint, New York: Farrar, Straus, Giroux, 1966.

Wright, Gwendolyn. *Building the Dream: A Social History of Housing in America.* Cambridge: MIT Press, 1981.

Archives Consulted

Stichting Nederlands Foto-& Grafisch Centrum, Haarlem, the Netherlands.
National Archives, Washington, D.C.
Rockefeller Archives, Tarrytown, New York.
Steichen Archives. Museum of Modern Art, New York.
United States Information Agency Archives, Washington, D.C.

Journals / Newspapers / Magazines

Department of State Bulletin

Harper's

Ladies' Home Journal

Life

New York Times

Partisan Review

Saturday Evening Post

Government Documents

Hearing before a Subcommittee of the Committee on Foreign Relations, United States Senate, 82nd Congress, Second Session, and 83rd Congress, First Session. Overseas Information Programs of the United States. Washington, D.C., 1953.

Hearings before the Permanent Subcommittee of Investigations of the Committee on Government Operations, United States Senate, 83rd Congress, First Session. State Department Information Program—Voice of America. Washington, D.C., 1953.

Report of the Committee on Foreign Relations, United States Senate. Overseas Information Programs of the United States. Washington, D.C.: 1953.

Hearings before the Subcommittee of the Committee on Appropriations, House of Representatives, 85th Congress, Second Session. United States Information Agency, President's Special International Program. Washington D.C., 1958.

Hearings before the Committee of Foreign Affairs, House of Representatives, 84th Congress, Second Session. Draft Bill Proposed in Executive Communications No. 863, No. 953, and No. 1601. Amending the United States Information and Educational Exchange Act of 1948, and No. 1409, providing for cultural and athletic exchanges and participation in international fairs and festivals. Washington, D.C., 1958.

Hearings before the Subcommittee on State Department Organization and Foreign Operations of the Committee on Foreign Affairs, House of Representatives, 85th Congress, Second Session. Review of United States Information Agency Operations. Washington, D.C., 1959.

INDEX

A Life in Photography, 178
A World History of Photography, 18
Abraham Lincoln: The War Years, Sandburg, 177
abstraction, 138
abundance, 5–6, 28, 32, 146
Acheson, Dean, 102
Adams, Ansel, 47, 59, 169
Adams, Phoebe Lou, 52–53
Adler, Mortimer, 70
Advancing American Art, 110, 119
advertising, 7–8, 26
Advisory Committee on Government Organization, 100
aerial photography, 17, 20, 36
aesthetics, 59, 70–71. See also taste
affluence, 28, 145
Affluent Society, The, Galbraith, 28, 170
Allen, George V., 105, 115, 117, 118–19
America, the meanings of, 5–6. See also culture, defining American
American Dream, 43
American Mind, The, Commager, 7
American National Exhibition, Moscow, 127, 135–37, 164, illustrations of, 186, 194
American Photographs, Evans, 163
Americanism, internationalized, 98
Americans, The, Frank, 156, 160–61, 163, 164, 174
Andriesse, Emmy, 121
Anlitz der Zeit, Sander, 56
anthropology, perspectives of, 20, 24, 25, 40, 53–54, 58, 75, 111, 143, 158
Aperture, 51, 52, 174, 175
Arbus, Diane, 175, 176
art, 40, 42, 51, 61, 69–70, 128–29, 132; class and, 72; legibility of, 60; photography as, 52, 174; reproduction and, 163; role of, 166, 176; ventriloquism of, 165
artists, 179; artist as editor, 53

Atlantic, The, 52
atom, peaceful use of the, 127; atomic power, 28; the bomb, 48, 53, 58, 62, 64–68, 74, and illustration of, 93
audience, 4, 5–6, 8, 15, 18, 19, 29, 30, 36, 38, 39, 43, 45, 50–51, 56, 61, 68–69, 72, 122, 134, 139, 156, 163, 176; critics on the, 58–59; leading the, 47–48, 53; USIA and its, 98; viewing environment for the, 61

Barthes, Roland, 54–55, 151–52
Barton, Betsy, 30
Barton, Bruce, 30
Barzun, Jacques, 58–59
Bassow, Whitman, 129
Bayer, Herbert, 44, 60–61, 133–34, 150
Belair, Felix, 128
Benjamin, Walter, 61, 163
Bitter Years, The, MoMA, 178
Bogart, Leo, 107
bomb, the, 48, 53, 58, 62, 64–68, 74, and illustration of, 93
book on the exhibition, 40, 48, 73–74, 96, 176, and illustrations on the, 86, 87, 89, 90
Book-of-the-Month Club, 163
books, photographs in, 163. See also book on the exhibition
Bourke-White, Margaret, 11–12, 15, 17
Brady, Matthew, 40
Bristol, Horace, 16
Bureau of Motion Pictures, 109

Caldwell, Erskine, 11
Callahan, Harry, 157
Callman, Howard, 127
cameras, 12, 13, 16–17, 37, 66, 157, 158, 174
Capa, Robert, 12, 17, 22, 23
Carroll, Lewis, 40
Cartier-Bresson, Henri, 21, 22, 58, 73

Central Intelligence Agency, 99

Chicago Merchandise Mart, 134

Churchill, Winston, 19

Circarama, the, 141, 146, 163

Clark, Clifford, 146

class, 71–72, 172. See also taste

Cohn, Roy, 100, 105

cold war, 39, 111–12, 147

collage, 57; three dimensional, 44

Collier's, 12

Collins, Bradford, 72

Commager, Henry Steele, 7, 8

Commerce Department, 129

Committee on International Programs, 100

commonality, the assumption of, 54

containment, 26–27, 30, 63, 71, 141

Coontz, Stephanie, 9

corporations, photography used by, 18

Corso, Gregory, 164

counterculture, 165, 169

Crane, Ralph, 70

criticism, assumptions in, 53

culture, advertising and, 8; class in, 172, and
    popular, 71; defining American, 6, 29–32,
    60, 68, 70–71, 104, 107–9, 117–18, 127,
    143–46, 159, 165; plastic and, 148; ques-
    tions for, 153; the exhibition and, 53

Daniel, E. Clifton, 129, 130

Davenport, Russell, 29, 30

Davis, R. Ted, and family, 128

depth of field, 40

D'Harnoncourt, René, 42

diplomacy, American, 109

diplomacy, cultural, 95–124

Dischin, Jacob, 51

Disney, Walt, 163

Doisneau, Robert, 70

Doyle, Arthur, 16

Dulles, John Foster, 102, 106, 140

Duncan, David Douglas, 15, 33, 35–38, 57

Eames, Charles, 151

Eames, Ray, 163

Einstein, Albert, 54; illustration with, 89

Eisenhower, President, 102, 106, 112–13, 128,
    129, 175

Ellwood, David, 28

essays, photographic, 14, 18–19, 23–25,
    55–56, 174

ethnography, federal agency for, 107

Europe, Americanization of, 28, 55; gathering
    images from, 41

European Recovery Administration, 98

Europeans, 107

Evans, Walker, 59, 158, 159, 163, 175

exhibition, authorship and the, 42, 50, 55,
    61; captions and text for the, 44–48, 53,
    55, 69, 90, and lighting, 48, and musical
    accompaniment, 45; catalog for the, 119,
    121; color in the, 48, 67; costs of, 42, 95,
    131–33, 152; darkroom technology for, 49,
    59, 121; design structure of the, 43–45,
    47–49, 53–54, 60–61, 134, 149–51, 163,
    167, and context, 54–56, and illustrations
    of, 81–85, 89, 91, 92, 181, 185, 197; nam-
    ing the, 43, 177; purpose and intent of
    the, 40, 46–47, 50, 53, 56, 64, 74, 94,
    166, and selection for, 40–42, 44–45, 55,
    69–70, and illustrations of, 78, 80; recep-
    tion of the, 49, 51, 52, 60, 120, 139, in
    illustrations, 182–84, 187, 196, 198; re-
    movals from, 49, 155; reviews and crit-
    icism on the, 52, 53, 58, 70–73, 176,
    and restructuring the content, 53–55, 62,
    173–74; statistics on the, 40–43, 46, 61,
    95–96; Steichen evaluation of the, 57; van-
    dalism to the, 155; the book on the, 40, 48,
    73–74, 96, 176, and illustrtions of, 86, 87,
    89, 90

family, the, 23, 26, 45–47, 55–58, 62–63, 73,
    169

Farbman, Nat, 54, 55

Farm Security Administration, 13, 17, 18, 43,
    50, 158, 178

Fast, Howard, 102

Faulkner, William, 109, 166, 168, 169

Faurer, Louis, 160

Federal Housing Administration, 144

Federation of Modern Painters and Sculptors,
    118

Feininger, Andreas, 48, 73

Fiedler, Leslie, 71, 109

film, 163, 179; film introducing the exhibi-
    tion, 96; filmstrips, 25

flute-layer, 45

Focus, 121

Ford, Henry, 149

Foreign Affairs, 26

Fortune, 29

Foto, 120, 121

Frank, Mary, 157

Frank, Robert, 4, 41, 156–65, 168–69,
    174–75

Fromm, Erich, 7, 30

Fulbright, Senator, 106

Fuller, R. Buckminster, 147, 148, 150

Gaddis, John Lewis, 28
Galbraith, John Kenneth, 28, 170–71, 173
Gallagher, Barrett, 16
Gans, Herbert, 145
geodesic domes, 146–48, 150
Ginsberg, Allen, 164, 169
Gitlin, Todd, 156
Glimpses of the USA, 163
Goodrich, Lloyd, 129
Gould, Jack, 103
Green, Jonathan, 75
Greenberg, Clement, 30, 70
Greene, Theodore, 60
Grosvenor, Gilbert, 19
Guimond, James, 9

Hales, Peter B., 58, 66
Harper's, 3, 29, 68
Harrington, Michael, 170, 172–73
Harris, Eugene, 45
Harris, Reed, 101–105
Hemingway, Ernest, 12
Hickenlooper, Bourke, 100
Hicks, Wilson, 21, 22
history, photographing erasures of, 13; the
    determining weight of, 54–55, 176, 178
Hollywood, 109
Hook, Sydney, 30
Hoover, Herbert, 106
House Foreign Affairs Committee, 118
House Un-American Activities Committee
    (HUAC), 129
Howl, Ginsberg, 169
Huxtable, Ada Louise, 145

ideology, 5, 26, 44, 111–12, 133–35, 151
Illustrated, 12
imagery, excerption of, 55–56; multiple, 163,
    and illustrated, 191; of the exhibition, 40,
    49, 53–54, 61; the commerce of, 18
International Information Administration
    (IIA), 99, 101–106
International Trade Fairs, 126, 146

Jackson, Kenneth, 146
Jackson, William, 100
Jacobs, Fenno, 16
Jacoby, Russell, 6
Johnson, Robert, 105, 106
Jorgensen, Victor, 16
Judd, Walter, 118

Kalb, Marvin, 129
Kaplan, Raymond, 103

Kennan, George F., 26–28
Kerlee, Charles, 16
Kerouac, Jack, 164
Kessel, Dmitri, 20
King Football, Harris, 101
Kissinger, Henry, 171
Kitchen Debate, 140–42
Korea, 13–14, 32–38, 57
Khrushchev, Nikita, 135, 137–43, and illustra-
    tions with, 192, 193, 195

Ladies' Home Journal, 21, 23–25, 29, 53, and illus-
    tration of layout for, 88
Lange, Dorothea, 42, 69
Larsen, Arthur, 105
Last Intellectuals, The, Jacoby, 6
Leen, Nina, 55, 72
Leslie, Alfred, 164
Let Us Now Praise Famous Men, Evans, 175
Levitt, William, 30, 143, 144
Lexington, Steichen on the, 17, and illustration
    of, 77
libraries, removing books from, 102
Life, 3, 6–9, 11–13, 18–22, 26–27, 29, 33–36,
    49, 52, 54–56, 58, 61–68, 147; as a source
    for the exhibition, 40, 55; reviewing the
    exhibition, 72; Steichen letter to, 37
Lincoln, Abraham, 43, 177
Lionni, Leo, 73
Lonely Crowd, The, Riesman, 72
Look, 9, 18, 21, 41
Luce, Henry, 21, 29
Luxembourg, 10
Lynes, Russell, 3, 68, 71, 72

Macdonald, Dwight, 70
magazines. See separately by name
Magnum, 13, 22–23, 38
Mailer, Norman, 165, 167–69
Maloney, Tom, 16
Marshall Plan, 109
Masefield, John, 47
Mason, Jerry, 40, 42, 73, 96
"Masscult and Midcult," Macdonald, 70
May, Elaine Tyler, 9, 141, 146
McCarthy, Joseph, 100–106
McCarthy, Mary, 165
McClellan, Harold, 126, 127, 129–32, 140, 147
McCombe, Leonard, 19
McCray, Porter, 131, 132
Mead, Margaret, 31
Meikle, Jeffrey, 148, 149
Merson, Martin, 105–106
Mexico City, 122

Migrant Mother, Lange, 69

Miller, Joan, 45, 57, and illustration with, 80

Miller, Wayne, 1, 3, 8, 9, 10, 15–17, 22, 38, 40–41, 43, 45, 49, 55, 57, 72, 138, and illustration with, 79

Mirrors and Windows, Szarkowski, 174, 175

modernism, 4, 51–53, 60, 61, 133, 162

Moeller, Susan, 15, 35

Morgan, Barbara, 51, 53, 54

Morris, John, 14, 23

Moscow, Soviet Union, 4, 11, 127–28

Mount Williamson, Adams, 47, 169

Mumford, Lewis, 145

Museum of Modern Art (MoMA), 3, 15, 40, 44, 51–52, 59–60, 72, 132, 149, 174, 178

museums, the role of, 53, 60–62, 68–69, 163

Mydans, Carl, 13, 14, 27, 33, 35

Mythologies, Barthes, 151

National Geographic, 18, 19

National Security Council, 113

Nelson, George, 129, 133–34, 143, 144, 148, 149

Neokonkwo, Theophilus, 155

Netherlands, 120

New Deal, 18

New York City, 169–70

New York Times, 51, 101–105, 128, 140, 142, 143, 155

Newhall, Beaumont, 17

Newsweek, 169

Ninkovich, Frank, 99, 109, 111–12

Nixon, Richard M., 117, 135, 137–43, and illustrations with, 188, 192, 193, 195

No Respect, Ross, 32, 71

Norman, Dorothy, 44, 52, 69

Noyes, Charles, 132

nuclear age, 45. See also bomb, the

Nye, David, 18

Office of Strategic Services (OSS), 99, 116

Office of War Information (OWI), 99, 116. See also Voice of America

On Photography, Sontag, 176

On the Road, Kerouac, 164

Operation Ivy, 66

Operation Snapshot, 20

Organization of American States, 162

Orkin, Ruth, 41

Orlovsky, Peter, 164

Other America, The, Harrington, 170, 172

Page, Homer, 42, 49

Papageorge, Tod, 163

Partisan Review, 29

"People Are People the World Over," 23–25

People of Plenty, Potter, 6, 28, 63

People, Yes, The, Sandburg, 43

peripheral vision, 40, 44

personality, 6

photographers, editorial control and, 21–23, 55–56; status of the postwar, 20, 25; status of the wartime, 14–15

photographs, legibility of, 4, 10, 36, 45, 49, 50, 54, 57, 156–57, and context, 54–57; meanings of, 19, 21, 25, and revelatory power of, 2, and as invasive, 161

photography, as a democratic medium, 51, 69–70; as art, 8; history of, 173–76; meanings of, 39, 55; perspectives in, 161; principles of, 4

photojournalism, 11–22, 174

plastic, 148–52, and illustrations of, 190, 195, 197

Plato, 45

Pollock, Jackson, 68

Popular Photography, 45

populism, conservative, 8

Potter, David, 5–6, 8, 28, 63, 171

poverty, 172–73

Power in the Pacific, Bayer, 150

Power in the Pacific, MoMA, 15

Private Life of a Public Servant, The, Merson, 105

propaganda, 102

public affairs officers, 97, 110

Pull My Daisy, Frank, 164, 169

Radford, A. W., 16

radio, 110

reconstruction, 27–28

Reston, James, 140, 141

Riesman, David, 72

Rivers, Frank, 164

Road to Victory, MoMA, 15, 44

Robin, Ron, 162

Rockefeller, Blanchette, 131

Rockefeller, Nelson, 97, 100, 131, 162

Rockefeller Panel Report, 170, 171

Rodger, George, 13, 22

Roosevelt, Franklin, 19

Ross, Andrew, 9, 32, 71

Round Tables, Life, 7, 29–32, 38, 51, 60, 68, 143

Rubin, Joan Shelley, 71, 163

Rudolph, Paul, 44, 134

Ruohomaa, Kosti, 55

Russell, Bertrand, 48

Saarinen, Aline, 51
Sadkin, Herbert, 128
Salisbury, Harrison, 140, 141
Sandburg, Carl, 43, 46, 138, 163, 176–77
Sander, August, 56
Saturday Evening Post, 21
Schapiro, Meyer, 30
Schary, Dore, 30
Schaub, Thomas, 165
Schine, David, 100, 105
Schlesinger, Arthur, 112
Schorr, Daniel, 129, 130
Second World War, 11–13, 15–20, 38, 98, 175
Sekula, Allan, 75, 119, 180
Senate Foreign Relations Committee, 100
Seymour, David, 22
Shahn, Ben, 129
Shooting the Russian War, 12
Silk, George, 155
Six Crises, Nixon, 138, 139
Smith, Henry Nash, 31
Smith, W. Eugene, 13, 14, 15, 17, 22, 49, 69
Smith-Mundt Act, 99
snapshot, 70
Sontag, Susan, 75, 175, 176
Sophocles, 48
Soviet Union, 4, 26–28, 99, 171. See also Moscow, Soviet Union
SovFoto, 138
Stange, Maren, 18
State Department, 26, 99, 102, 105–6, 110, 125, 129
Steichen, Edward, biographical notes on, 1, 10, 15–17, 36–38, 43, 50–52, 57, 70, 138, 161–62, 167, 178, 179, and illustrations with, 79, 199
Steichen the Photographer, Sandburg, 43
Stieglitz, Alfred, 1, 52
Storyteller, The, Farbman, 54–56
Streibert, Theodore, 105, 107, 113–15, 117–18
streetcar, photograph of the, 159
Stryker, Roy, 17
suburbanization, 145
Swope, John, 16
Szarkowski, John, 59, 174–75

taste, 32, 51, 58–59, 68. See also class
Tastemakers, The, Lynes, 72

television, 103
Third World, 155
This Is War!, Duncan, 36
tourism, 120; tourists, 111, 172, and photographers as tourists, 12, 13, 19–20, 37
Training Book for Guides, 136
Truman administration, 27
Turner, Frederick Jackson, 5

United Nations, 25, 27, 28, 48
U.S. Camera, 16
United States Information Agency (USIA), 4, 40, 95, 125, 129, 131–32; creation and development of the, 97–100, 104, and mission, 106, 110–18, and personnel, 108; criticism on, 118; disclaimer by, 122
universalism, 27
Useful Objects under $10.00, MoMA, 149

values, brokering, 21, 24–25
Vandivert, Bill, 22
Vietnam, 14, 34
Village Voice, 167
Vincent, John Carter, 102
Vital Center, Schlesinger, 112
Voice of America, 100, 101, 104, 107, 110

Wainwright, Loudon, 14, 21
Walk to Paradise Garden, The, Smith, 49, 69
Walter, Francis E., 129
war, photographing, 1–2, 11–22, 32–38, 44, 57
War Assets Board, 110
Washburn, Abbott, 129, 131, 132
White, Minor, 3, 40, 175
Whitney Museum, 128
Wilson, Edmund, 27
Winogrand, Gary, 70
Wisdom, 1
Words and Pictures, Hicks, 21, 22
World War I, 17
World War II, 11–13, 15–20, 38, 98, 175
World's Fair, Brussels, 127
Wright, Frank Lloyd, 150

Young, Robert, 30
Young European Photographers, MoMA, 157